THE FUTURE OF PUBLICLY FUNDED FAITH SCHOOLS

The Future of Publicly Funded Faith Schools addresses and critically examines the arguments both for and against the continued maintenance of faith-based schools within a publicly funded state system. Addressing the issue systemically, first grounding the discussion in the practical world of education before raising the central philosophical issues stemming from faith-based education, it provides a balanced synthesis of the different arguments surrounding faith schools.

The book expounds upon the different threats facing faith-based schools, including their perceived potential to undermine social cohesion within a multi-cultural society, and the questioning of their right to receive public funding, and examines what these mean for their future. Examining these threats, it questions:

- What it means for a school to be 'faith-based'.
- The nature of religious education both within and without a faith-based school environment.
- The ethical, epistemological, and political issues arising from faith-based education.
- The concepts of the common good and social cohesion.
- Whether there is possible reconciliation between opposing parties.

The Future of Publicly Funded Faith Schools makes a unique contribution to the literature in this area and is crucial reading for anyone interested in what the future holds for publicly funded faith schools including academics, researchers, and postgraduate students in the fields of education, religious studies, policy, and politics of education, sociology, and philosophy.

Richard Pring is Emeritus Professor of Education, and was formerly Director of Department of Educational Studies, University of Oxford, UK.

THE FUTURE OF PUBLICLY FUNDED FAITH SCHOOLS

A Critical Perspective

Richard Pring

LONDON AND NEW YORK

First published 2018
by Routledge
2 Park Square, Milton Park, Abingdon, Oxon OX14 4RN

and by Routledge
711 Third Avenue, New York, NY 10017

Routledge is an imprint of the Taylor & Francis Group, an informa business

© 2018 Richard Pring

The right of Richard Pring to be identified as author of this work has been asserted by him in accordance with sections 77 and 78 of the Copyright, Designs and Patents Act 1988.

All rights reserved. No part of this book may be reprinted or reproduced or utilised in any form or by any electronic, mechanical, or other means, now known or hereafter invented, including photocopying and recording, or in any information storage or retrieval system, without permission in writing from the publishers.

Trademark notice: Product or corporate names may be trademarks or registered trademarks, and are used only for identification and explanation without intent to infringe.

British Library Cataloguing-in-Publication Data
A catalogue record for this book is available from the British Library

Library of Congress Cataloging-in-Publication Data
A catalog record for this book has been requested

ISBN: 978-1-138-56967-6 (hbk)
ISBN: 978-1-138-56968-3 (pbk)
ISBN: 978-0-203-70416-5 (ebk)

Typeset in Bembo
by Deanta Global Publishing Services, Chennai, India

To Isaac, Eleanor, Dominic, Isobel, Lucy, Mary, Elisabette, and Gustave.

'Civilisation hangs suspended, from generation to generation, by the gossamer strand of memory. If only one cohort of mothers and fathers fails to convey to its children what it has learnt from its parents, then the great chain of learning and wisdom snaps. If the guardians of human knowledge stumble only one time, in their fall collapses the whole edifice of knowledge and understanding'.

Jacob Neusmer, quoted by Rabbi Jonathan Sacks
in *The Politics of Hope.*

CONTENTS

Acknowledgements	ix
Introduction	1

PART I
Context   **5**

1 Contemporary political and cultural context	7
2 Historical background and the current position	21
3 Making sense of facts and figures	38
4 International perspective	48

PART II
Religious education   **61**

5 Three traditions	63
6 Response to the secular age	81
7 Religious education: An extended vision	93
8 Service to society	102

viii Contents

PART III
Key issues emerging: The need for philosophy **111**

9 Ethics: Education and its aims 113

10 Epistemology: Knowledge, truth, and reason
in religious education 129

11 Civic society: Common good and social pluralism 144

PART IV
Drawing conclusions **161**

12 For or against faith schools? Finding an answer 163

Author index *177*
Subject index *180*

ACKNOWLEDGEMENTS

Many are those whom I have conversed with in writing this book and for whose views and criticisms I am most grateful. In particular, I would like to mention:

Professor Gerald Grace, Founding Director of the Centre for Research and Development in Catholic Education, 1997 to 2015, UCL Institute of Education, and currently Visiting Professor at St. Mary's London.

Dr Sean Whittle, Research Fellow at London University Heythrop College, and a former Secondary School teacher of religious education and philosophy.

Dr Farid Panjwani, Director of the Centre for Research and Evaluation of Muslim Education at UCL Institute of Education and a member of the National Council on Religious Education.

Fr Dermot Lane, formerly President of Mater Dei Institute of Education, Dublin City University.

Dr Liam Gearon, University Lecturer in Religious Education, University of Oxford.

Mr Stephen Tierney, CEO of Blessed Edward Bamber Catholic Multi-Academy Trust, and Chair of Head Teachers' Roundtable, established in 2012.

Mr John Harris, former Head Teacher of a Leicestershire primary school, and former Primary Adviser in Norfolk, and currently Chair of the governing bodies of two primary schools.

x Acknowledgements

Mr John Prangley, formerly Head Teacher of St. Augustine's joint Catholic/Church of England secondary school, Oxford.

Mr John Fox, formerly Teacher of Religious Education and History at Cherwell Comprehensive School, Oxford.

INTRODUCTION

Public funding, which has been provided for Faith schools in England and Wales for nearly 200 years, is being questioned. Increasingly, such financial support is seen to have no place in a secular society. This book addresses the criticisms but ultimately offers a defence for the continued public maintenance of Faith schools within this society, although, in the light of the criticisms, the book concludes with the need for certain reforms.

The focus is on the provision and the demand for such schools in England and Wales, but the issues thereby raised are of international significance as illustrated in Chapter 4.

The establishment and growth of Faith schools took place within the different Christian traditions (Church of England, Non-conformist and Roman Catholic) and were, therefore, formerly referred to as 'Church Schools'). However, they now embrace a considerable number of Jewish and Islamic schools, plus a very small number of those of other religions. Hence, the shift of title from Church schools to Faith schools. Between the three monotheistic religions, there is common interest in preserving the religious foundation to schooling, and therefore their affinities are addressed throughout.

However, the right for public funding for religiously affiliated schools is increasingly coming under threat. That threat, especially in relation to Catholic schools (which constitute the vast majority of voluntary aided schools – see Chapter 2) is summarised by Sean Whittle (2015, pp.11–24) in terms of external and internal threats. The external threats are seen to be the questioning of the right of religiously affiliated schools to receive public funding from the tax payer, the perceived undermining of social cohesion by religiously selective schools in multi-cultural societies, the claimed encouragement of indoctrination, and the control by government of what is taught. The internal threats are the decline in religious practice within an

2 Introduction

increasingly secular society and the failure to articulate a philosophical justification for a faith-related religious education.

The book aims to expound upon and address these different threats, and, in so doing, to raise the central philosophical issues which too often get neglected.

There were, at the time of writing this book, nearly 7,000 state-funded Faith schools in England and Wales, and these included 35% of all state-funded primary schools. There were 658 religiously selective secondary schools in England and Wales – 339 Catholic, 209 Church of England, 60 'generically Christian', 11 Jewish, and 9 Muslim (19% of the total number of secondary schools). There are many more religiously affiliated primary schools – more comprehensive figures are given in Chapter 3. But, whatever the historical reasons for their inclusion within the state system (and these shall be given in Chapter 2), it is increasingly felt that, in a more secular society (as described in Chapter 1), religiously selective schools should not be funded by the general taxpayer. If Faith schools are to retain such funding (so it is argued), then they should be totally inclusive. Therefore, the Fair Admissions Campaign within the British Humanist Society is campaigning for all state-funded schools in England and Wales to be open equally to all children without regard to religion or belief.

This book, therefore, aims to examine critically the different claims and arguments being made for and against the retention and indeed expansion of Faith schools. Such an examination needs to be located in the current social and political context in which doubts are being raised and defence is being pursued, and that context is given in Chapter 1. But in the more global world of comparisons and competitions between systems, the international scene, as shown in Chapter 4, is clearly important. How far are different solutions to religious educational provision to be located in different historical settings? History (as accounted for in Chapter 2) leaves legacies which should not be ignored. It warns against too hasty an implant on English and Welsh soil of the solutions found in post-revolutionary France, say, or in post-colonial America.

Therefore, Chapter 5 outlines the 'traditions' (both religious and secular) which have shaped, and currently continue to shape, the system we have inherited, including the purpose and nature of religious education in schools. Having examined such backgrounds or traditions, we will be in a better position to understand in Chapters 6, 7, and 8 the distinctive nature and contribution of religious education.

Then, in Chapters 9, 10, and 11 we can reflect systematically on the philosophical questions which underpin the arguments and decisions – concerning, for instance, the aims of education, the rational basis for religious beliefs and the accusation of indoctrination, the contribution to the 'common good', the primacy of parental choice in what and where learning should take place, and the obligation (if at all) of the state to support a diversity of religious and secular schools.

Only then are we able to address critically, in Chapter 12, the arguments for and against support for preserving and expanding Faith schools within the state system, perhaps calling for concessions on both sides as differences of argument are weighed up and compromises sought.

Note

Although England and Wales are treated as a single entity for the purposes of this book, since parliamentary devolution in 1998, Wales has developed its own programme of educational policies – including the support for Local Education Authority responsibility for schools. But the establishment of the National Assembly for Wales, with responsibility for health and education, has not affected the issues concerning Faith schools with which this book is concerned.

PART I

Context

1

CONTEMPORARY POLITICAL AND CULTURAL CONTEXT

Introduction

The system of education in England and Wales is rooted in religious foundations. 'Church schools' were never an add-on to an essentially secular system. Rather were they in many respects the foundation of the system from its beginning in the 19th century, when, in 1833, the first government grant of £20,000 was given to the existing elementary schools run by the National Schools Society of the Church of England and by the British and Foreign Schools Society of the Dissenters. Not until the Forster Act of 1870 were there established local School Boards (eventually as many as 2,650) with the powers to raise local rates to ensure elementary education for all, whether in the Church Schools or in the new Board Schools. But even in these Board Schools, there was to be religious teaching, albeit of a non-denominational kind.

By 1900, there were over 2,500 school board elementary schools, compared with the 14,000 managing bodies of denominational elementary schools, mainly Church of England, but also Non-conformist and now Catholic, all of which were in receipt of government funding.

Therefore, whatever denominational differences there were, it was assumed that England was basically Christian and that the school system should reflect that religious character of education. This continued to be the case with the development of secondary schools following the Balfour Act of 1902 when local education authorities (LEAs) replaced the school boards. What were referred to (and continued to be referred to) as 'voluntary schools' were supported by the rates but with concessions to some control by the LEAs. Such an arrangement was reinforced by the 1944 Education Act, which introduced secondary education for all. Hence, there developed from primary through to secondary a national system of community and voluntary schools, locally maintained, with different admissions arrangements to take account of the religious affiliations of the voluntary schools.

8 Context

The voluntary aided schools (mainly Catholic with some Jewish) as opposed to the voluntary controlled schools (mainly Church of England) were for the most part under the trusteeship of religious bodies. But they paid for the privilege of greater control over their own admissions and staffing by having to pay a substantial proportion of the costs of building and of maintaining their schools.

Moreover, even in the community non-denominational schools, religious education and daily assemblies of a mainly Christian nature were required of every school.

It is this religious background to education in England and Wales – both the public support of schools that have a specific religious allegiance and the assumption of a basically religious ethos within even the non-denominational schools – which is now being severely challenged.

This introductory chapter will

- set out the social changes that have taken place in Britain which affect the assumptions that have shaped the history of education, and in particular the defence of religious affiliation or Christian ethos permeating the school system;
- specify how those social changes entered into the political challenges to the system of differentiated schooling which has evolved over a period of nearly 200 years;
- focus on what is central to the controversies over faith schools, namely, different admission arrangements which schools of different kinds need to agree with, to publicise and to adhere to;
- summarise what seem to be the key issues, in anticipation of further analysis and possible ways forward.

As stated in the Introduction, the focus in Part I is on England and Wales. But that provides a 'concrete case', which brings out the issues (particularly philosophical) that are of universal significance and which will be examined more thoroughly in Parts II and III.

Social changes

Four relevant social changes need to be picked out, namely, 'the secularisation of society', 'the multi-cultural nature of society', 'the changing moral climate', and 'concern over extremism'.

Secularisation of society

The decline within a generation in the numbers of people who would describe themselves as religious has been considerable. The Commission on Religion and Belief in Public Life (Butler-Sloss Report, 2015) found that almost half the UK population now describes itself as 'non-religious'.

The Archbishop of Canterbury, Colin Welby (as reported in *The Guardian*, 13.1.16) warned of an anti-Christian culture, as numbers of those attending church each week

Contemporary political and cultural context **9**

slides below one million (less than 2% of the population) with Sunday attendances falling to 760,000. That is a decline of 12% in the last decade and now less than half the levels of the 1960s. This decline is noticeable in other religious practices; there were but 130,000 baptisms in 2014 (down 12% since 2004), 50,000 marriages (down 19%), 146,000 church funerals (down 29%). In the 2011 UK census, 59% defined themselves as Christian, down from 72% in 2001. One in four said they had no religion, up from 15% in 2001. All this, according to the Archbishop, results from, or reflects, the growing secularisation of society (for instance, in sexual morality).

A recent report continues in the same vein. According to analysis of the data from the annual British Social Attitudes Survey (2016) and the biennial European Social Survey (2016), the avowedly non-religious (the 'nones') constitute 48.6% of the British population (Anglicans, 17.1%, Catholics 8.7%, other Christian 17.2%, non-Christians 8.4%). Between 1983 and 2015, those who identified themselves as Christian fell from 55% to 43% whilst members of non-Christian religions quadrupled. More than six in ten 'nones' were brought up as Christian, mainly Catholic or Anglican (Bullivant, 2017).

The 2017 Social Attitudes Survey claimed that more than half the population would describe themselves now as not religious. Of adults under 24, 3% describe themselves as Anglican, and fewer than 5% as Catholic. Almost three-quarters of those aged 18–24 say they have no religion – a considerable rise since 2015. In the 25–34 age group, 5% identify themselves as Anglican and 9% as Catholic (a percentage swollen no doubt by immigrant workers) with only about 40% claiming to be Christian. These figures show a considerable decline over the last 30 years. Of those with religious affiliation who would describe themselves as religious, an increasing number would not be Christian. Our society is seen to be increasingly secular and multi-cultural.

But the decline in Christian practice also must be seen in the light of the greater religious diversity and the ageing profile of the worshipers. It leads to the question asked by Linda Woodhead and Andrew Brown (2016): 'Can [the Church of England] any longer be the established Church?' In asking 'how the Church of England lost the English people', they argue that the Church is heading in a different direction from society in general. But the same might be said of the Catholic Church, too, where one sees a greater divergence than ever before from what is now taken for granted in the wider society (especially the young) in prevailing moral assumptions.

However, one must be careful. The decline in attendance at mainstream Christian Churches is somewhat compensated for by the growth of evangelical groups. For example, the Pentecostal 'Redeemed Christian Church of God' (RCCG) has about 800 places of worship in Britain, with more being planned. The biggest of its churches, Jesus House in Brent Cross, North London, attracts more than 2,000 to its Sunday services (*The Guardian*, 30.12.16).

Moreover, the growing Muslim population maintains an active participation in the life of the mosques, partly, no doubt, because religious adherence and practice are sources for maintaining their social fabric as a community and their identity.

10 Context

The decline in the practice and the influence of mainstream Christian churches, however, must be seen within a wider European context. As Lieven Boeve (2007, p.13) argues,

> A culture has developed in Europe without precedent – in which God has disappeared from public awareness, either by way of denial or doubt with respect to God's existence, or as a result of the privatisation of the religious and the irrelevance of God for the public domain.

This sentiment and its implications are re-iterated by the Irish theologian, Dermot Lane:

> European culture is characterised by secularisation, individualisation and detraditionalisation. We are living in a post-Christian and post-secular world where religion is one item amongst others competing for attention in a world dominated by the influence of the media and the market.
>
> *(Lane, 2015, pp.28/29)*

In addition, Boeve refers to the absolute understanding of individual freedom which, paradoxically, leads to the dissolution of religious freedom (for example, wearing the cross or the hijab in certain public contexts). Recently, there was the case of the Northern Ireland family bakery that refused to accept a customer's order for a wedding cake, which would bear a slogan supporting gay marriage; the bakery claimed the right to refuse on the grounds of religious freedom, but was convicted nonetheless for breaking 'equality law'.

However, 'secular society' – embodying an underlying way of thinking about social, political, and moral matters – runs more deeply than is indicated by the decline in religious practices. Is there not in Britain, what Durkheim (1961, pp.3,11) referred to in relation to France, a 'secularisation of morality', thereby advocating 'a purely secular moral education', that is, one excluding all principles derived from revealed religion? This will be addressed in greater detail in Chapters 5 and 6.

Multi-cultural nature of society

When the 1944 Education Act required a daily act of worship of a mainly Christian character, it could not have envisaged that within a few decades there would be ten times as many Muslims as Methodists in Yorkshire! About 5% of the British population is now Muslim, many living in neighbourhoods which are predominantly of that faith with their mosques and their supplementary schools or Madrasas. There are sizeable numbers of other religious traditions – Jewish, Hindu, Sikh, and Buddhist.

Hence, there is the danger of the creation of a network of competing monocultures fostering separateness. Where there is a failure of the larger society to incorporate the minority religious communities and where, therefore, there is a growing

Contemporary political and cultural context **11**

sense of alienation especially amongst the young, often in impoverished economic circumstances, there is a danger of the rise of 'identity politics', the offering of 'meaning in life' through the possibly antagonistic relation to the wider society. We have seen several examples of young people, even of school age, travelling to the Middle East to fight under the banner of Isis.

Recently, for example, there have been well-publicised issues about some Community Schools in Birmingham as they in effect become schools for the children of the predominantly Muslim community within the inner-city neighbourhoods. They were accused of installing a particular version of Islamist curriculum and content of personal, social, and moral education, which went against the expectations of schools within the state system (Clarke Report, 2016). It was found to be necessary in what was called the Trojan Horse affair (in which there was an alleged take-over of twenty-one maintained schools in Birmingham by minority Muslim groups) to initiate an investigation, and to improve the accountability arrangements within the schools. Five schools (two secondary and three primary) received Ofsted inspections, which (despite previous complimentary inspections) judged the schools, in their encouragement of an Islamic ethos, now to be 'failing to prepare children for life in modern Britain', though finding no evidence of a 'conspiracy', which had been alleged in the popular press. One conclusion, however, was the need for greater accountability, though made more difficult as the schools had become part of an Academy trust, and thereby removed from local government responsibility.

That issue has been settled, but there are in addition a further 140 Muslim schools, not within the state system but mainly affiliated to the Association of Muslim Schools, and approximately 700 Supplementary Schools (or Madrasas) serving about 100,000 children. The Muslim Parliament of Great Britain has called for these to be subject to government inspection following the report on the problems in Birmingham.

On the other hand, there are many Muslim Faith Schools, especially those which have achieved or are seeking 'Voluntary Aided' status, which respond effectively to the needs of a Muslim population within the state system, partly because of 'the perceived secularism of community schools, including the perceived secularism of religious education' (see Barnes, 2014, p.39). The so-called 'secularism' of religious education is addressed in Chapter 5.

There have been, over the years, several significant reports addressing the problems arising from within the multi-ethnic communities of our cities and from the duty of the schools to play their part in addressing these problems. The Ouseley Report of 2001 entitled *Community Pride, Not Prejudice*, following riots in Oldham, warned 'of a socially segregated Britain and of a growing minority feeling alienated from mainstream society'. In what Ouseley saw as an increasingly segregated school system, society is becoming less cohesive, less a community.

The Cantle Report (2001) into community cohesion, following the race riots in 2001, warned of British society being increasingly divided along ethnic lines with segregation in neighbourhoods (and consequently schools). Such segregation

12 Context

leads to mistrust and alienation from within the minority communities. Therefore, it recommended that, 'all schools should consider ways in which they might insure that their intake is representative of the range of cultures and ethnicity in their local communities', and that at least 25% of pupils came from each community.

However, more recently, the Casey Review (2016) on integration argues that Britain is more divided than ever, especially where communities in the northern towns referred to are segregated on religious or ethnic lines, each living 'parallel lives'.

Although this chapter is focused on England and Wales, lessons might be learned from Northern Ireland, which is often cited as a society divided on religious grounds, the divisions of which are supported by a segregated school system but where there is a growing movement for 'Integrated Schools' (see Chapter 4 for an extended account, plus possibly lessons to be learnt for elsewhere). In these Integrated Schools, the different communities learn together, and each comes to appreciate the beliefs, aspirations, and fears of the other. The development of mutual respect despite differences would seem to be essential (see Moffat, 1993).

Changing moral climate

The moral climate, affecting the assumptions of the once prevailing religious ethos, would seem to have changed in several respects, both generally and in personal relationships. For example, characteristics of advanced capitalism through globalisation, ruthless pursuit of wealth, acceptance of ever greater inequality, destruction of environment and privatisation of public services would seem to militate against the values of equal respect, social cohesiveness, care for the environment, and public service.

Regarding personal relations, contrary to 2,000 years of religious belief and social acceptance, same-sex marriage is now permitted. Sexual relations outside the marriage state are now the norm rather than the exception. Such a radical change in practice and its underpinning beliefs make the traditional religious belief in the sanctity of marriage between man and woman look increasingly out-dated, and difficult to promote in a society where that is no longer the norm. How much more is that the case where religious bodies, through their schools, condemn abortion and the practice of contraception? A task of the inspectorate now is to ensure that schools, even those within religious traditions, are open in their teaching to these social and moral changes.

The question therefore arises. Can Faith Schools be supported where they teach a moral form of life (both civic and personal), which is increasingly at odds with the norms of the wider and secular society?

If, for one moment, one might shift from the exclusive focus on England and Wales to the changing picture of Ireland (see Chapter 4), the Catholic church is responsible for more than 90% of primary schools, despite the increasingly secular and multi-ethnic nature of society – a society which is no longer united, for example, over matters of sexual morality. Furthermore, the rising number of non-Catholics (in the 2011 census, 277,000 out of a population of 4.5 million declared themselves as atheist, agnostic, lapsed, or of no religion) often have no alternative to sending their children to Catholic schools; there may be no other in the area.

The question is raised, therefore, as to whether Faith Schools, which admit those of other faiths or none, can or should maintain, directly or indirectly, the teaching of moral norms and religious traditions which are not generally shared?

Concern over 'extremism'

Recent events in Europe and in the Middle East have given rise to the fear that there are people within our respective countries who are prepared to adopt extreme measures in pursuit of political and religious goals. The bombings in Paris in 2015 and in Manchester in 2017 are clearly the most obvious examples. But there is need for constant vigilance. There are many young people who have become radicalised by the social media, even to the extent of travelling abroad to join the 'wars' in Syria and elsewhere. And security has been stepped up within Britain, lest further massacres occur. This increase in radicalism leading to extremism is a recent social phenomenon which has had a profound effect on political control of the media and on the part which schools can and should play – indeed, on the very concept and aims of liberal education.

This has significantly affected the debate on Faith Schools since there is the belief that radicalisation emerges from some few Muslim schools which have escaped the vigilance of close national or local accountability. But it is seen to be a wider problem than that, such that all schools should take on responsibility for counter-acting the radicalisation of young learners. Therefore, the government strongly recommended through its 'Prevent Duty' scheme that the schools play an active part in eliminating radicalisation, and be constantly vigilant about its emergence. Former Prime Minister Cameron announced his determination to tackle what he saw as 'the scourge of radicalisation through efforts in schools, colleges and universities … to root out extremist ideology and ban hate speech' (Durodie, 2016).

Others argue for a different approach, namely, a central commitment to 'criticality', thereby equipping the students to resist extremist ideologies – in other words, a more fundamental examination of the aims of a liberal education as well as the teaching of religion.

Political challenges

It is not surprising, therefore, that controversies have arisen over the last decade in Britain (and now in Ireland) regarding the public support for schools within the state system, which have a religious affiliation. In an increasingly secular society, should the general taxpayer be supporting either schools promoting a religious ethos or a distinctive, if tenuous, religious ethos through assemblies and religious education lessons? Once again there are cries reminiscent of those directed at the reforms of the 1902 Act, which required local taxation to support the already existing voluntary schools. 'No Rome on the Rates' was the cry. Then Socialist

14 Context

Democratic Federation and later the Secular Defence League fought vigorously against any religious control over public education.

Thus, the Report of the Commission on Religion and Belief in Public Life (Butler-Sloss, 2015), entitled *Living with Differences*, called for a major overhaul of those areas of public life (which, in different ways, embody religious symbolism) to reflect the multi-cultural nature of national life. That multi-cultural nature of society embraces not only different religions but also non-religious cultures such as those promoted by humanists and atheists. The report picks out, in particular, such national and symbolic celebrations as that of the coronation of the monarch. In a society, which is increasingly less Christian (and, within that minority, less Church of England), it is seen that there can be no justification for an Established Church or for religion to have such a dominant place in our national life (as, for example, in the membership of the House of Lords or in the acts of worship required of all state-funded schools). 'Britain's landscape in terms of religion and belief has been transformed beyond recognition', says the report.

The report's central recommendation is that a 'statement' should be agreed of the principles and views, which foster the common good and which should underpin and guide public life, and that this should be the basis of a curriculum compulsory for pupils up to the age of 19. Recognising the significance of that diversity, Andrew Copson, chief executive of the British Humanist Society, in supporting the report, argued that

> vital to the future of Britain as a cohesive society will be the ability of people of all religions and non-religious beliefs and identities to act together for the common good.
>
> *(Reported in* The Guardian, *7.12.15)*

The conclusion drawn from recognising this need to create a 'cohesive society' is that (reminiscent of the arguments of the American philosopher, John Dewey, developed further in Chapter 11) there should be the 'common school', the school which will embrace all young people of different religious and non-religious backgrounds. This promotion of social cohesiveness through the creation of the common school is argued forcefully in the Cantle Report, *Community Cohesion* (already referred to), which, with reference to the race riots in Oldham, Burnley, Bradford, and elsewhere, recommended strongly that each school must be inclusive and admit at least 25% from each community within its area.

In particular, the criticisms from the secularists and the humanists tend to focus on matters concerned with social cohesion in a very diverse society and on the selection which is said to take place when there are different admissions arrangements. For instance, Jay Harman of the Fair Admissions Campaign (according to its newsletter of December 2015) claimed at the Comprehensive Future Conference, 2015, that the degree of selection on faith creates segregation not only religious and ethnic but socio-economic as well. Claims are made of skewed admissions, failure to meet the needs of the most disadvantaged, denial of choice in some areas, the exclusion of minorities and the increased fragmentation of the school system.

However, the criticisms are in a sense deeper than that. If the aforementioned claims were shown empirically to be untrue (and they are challenged in Chapter 3), there would still be a fundamental objection to there being Faith Schools in what now appears to be a secular society. In the *Quarterly Report* of the Accord Coalition, Rabbi Jonathan Romain speaks of the powerful pressure groups, particularly the Catholic Church, which lobby

> to maintain the various forms of religious discrimination that are not permitted elsewhere in public life.
>
> *(Romaine, 2015)*

In *public* life, as in France (see Chapter 4), there would seem to be no grounds for religious discrimination.

These claims need to be subjected to close scrutiny, for there are counter claims that religious-affiliated schools (inevitably with exceptions) have traditionally welcomed ethnic diversity and have seen themselves as providing a distinctive service to the disadvantaged and to the poor. Indeed, a recent survey by the Catholic Education Service showed that there were as many as 26,000 Muslims in Catholic schools (15 Catholic schools having a majority of Muslim pupils), very often preferring a context where a faith tradition is respected, even if that tradition be not that of Islam (*The Tablet*, 10.12.16). Furthermore, Muslim pupils outnumber Christian children in more than 30 Church schools, including a Church of England primary school in Oldham which had a 100% Muslim attendance (*Sunday Times*, 5.2.17). This we shall examine more closely in Chapter 6, but, prior to that in Chapter 3, we provide some figures to put the issues in perspective. A criticism against the Butler-Sloss report is that, although it had on its committee the Chief Executive of the British Humanist Society, it had no such representative of the Churches to put an alternative view, despite the fact that they are the trustees of a large proportion of the schools.

It is clear, however, that, unchallenged, the pressure from the secularists, led by the British Humanist Association, begins to permeate the general consciousness, facilitating the eventual abandonment of Faith Schools within the system financed by the taxpayer. The *Quarterly Report* of the Accord Coalition (No. 26, 2015) says:

> The last three months have been characterised not just by much activity on our part, but also by considerable support for our aims in the press, educational research groups and in political circles, including Parliament and the United Nations. Such build-up of support is a vital precursor to gaining political commitment for change … we are winning in the intellectual battle.

The recommendations were that

- all Faith Schools, supported by taxes, should select no more than 50% on religious grounds;
- religious education should be broad and inclusive;

16 Context

- religious education should be inspected by Ofsted, not by an inspectorate from within the respective faiths.

We saw the consequences of this secularist and humanist pressure when, in 2010, as part of the Coalition Agreement between the Tories and the Liberal Democrats, a 'cap' of 50% was put on the number of Catholics to be admitted to a Catholic school, where there was over-subscription for places within the catchment area. Subsequently, it was decreed that any new Faith School (which would have to be an Academy or Free School), if it were to receive public funding, must take no more than 50% on the basis of religious affiliation. Such a requirement was, however, rescinded in 2016 by the Conservative government, partly as a result of the lobbying by the Catholic Church and the Chief Rabbi, who publicly opposed a new Jewish Free School being established because non-Jewish children might make up 50% of its intake. Nonetheless, not all Jewish leaders agreed with the Chief Rabbi. In an open letter sent to the Education Secretary, 68 rabbis called upon her 'not to abolish the 50% admissions rule for faith-based free schools', believing that 'religious values can happily co-exist with social cohesion'.

Perhaps the incremental opposition to separate Faith Schools is succinctly put in the Comment page of *The Times*, 6.12.16: 'As Britain becomes more secular, it is time to separate education and faith'.

Such a recommendation has entered into the political party scene, and no doubt will be taken up elsewhere. The Liberal Party's Spring conference in 2017 backed the statement, calling for an end to religious discrimination in schools' admissions and that 'selection in admissions on the basis of religion or belief to state funded schools' should be phased out over the next six years.

School admission arrangements – the crucial issue

A crucial issue, therefore, lies in the requirements of the school admission rules. Every state-funded school has to have publicly available admission arrangements, agreed by the Office of the Schools Adjudicator or OSA (for example, catchment area, siblings already attending the school, or success in an entry examination in the case of Grammar Schools). These arrangements are drawn up by the 'admissions authorities'. In the case of Community Schools, the admission authority is the Local Authority. In the case of voluntary aided schools (mainly, but not exclusively, Catholic) the admission authority would be the religious trustees. In the case of Voluntary Controlled Schools (in the main Church of England), the admissions authority would be a partnership between the Local Authority and the Church. In the case of academies and free schools, the admission authority would be the sponsor – for example, a 'chain' such as Academies Enterprise Trust (AET). One can hazard a guess at the complications arising from the government intention to make all schools academies, thereby creating a much greater number of admissions authorities, each drawing up its own admissions criteria with increasing power to decide which pupils to admit.

However, in drawing up their respective admission arrangements, agreement of the schools adjudicator is necessary. That agreement has to meet the requirements set by parliament and the educational needs of the public that the school is to serve.

From time to time, the government will adjust such arrangements. For example, in order to meet concerns from the Accord Coalition about the religious basis for selection of pupils, government confirmed that it was to continue the policy of limiting new Academy Faith Schools and free schools from selecting more than half their pupils on faith grounds. A letter from Lord Nash, Education Minister, (reported in the Accord Coalition *Quarterly Report*, No. 26) stated:

> The Government regards the cap as an important way of supporting these schools to be inclusive and to meet the needs of a broad mix of families.

This, of course, referred only to new such schools, and did not affect already established schools, or indeed Voluntary Aided. But it was a significant development because, if the argument with regard to these schools is that a cap on admissions is an important way of supporting inclusivity, then the same imperative would seem also to apply to all (including established) Faith Schools. After all, a quarter of pupil places in the state system are at Faith Schools, and for a child not to be given a place in what in effect may be his or her local school (which may be a Faith School) would be clearly unfair.

In drawing up their admissions arrangements, the Admissions Authorities (local authority or sponsor) must make these arrangements explicit and be open to local objection. Such objections, if not accepted, could be put to the OSA. Paragraph 14 of the OSA's Admissions Code says:

> In drawing up their admissions arrangements admissions authorities must ensure that the practices and the criteria used to decide the allocation of school places are fair, clear and objective. Parents should be able to look at a set of arrangements and understand easily how places for that school will be allocated.

Two issues are raised by that paragraph.

The first is the question of 'fairness'. Would it be fair, for example, if a child who failed the religious test would then have to be parted from friends and neighbours and have to travel afar to a school which had vacancies? Ought not a Faith School, if it be the only local school, be open to those not of the faith who would otherwise be put at a disadvantage through lack of another local school?

The second issue lies in 'the games people play'. For instance, ITV's *Tonight* programme, called 'How to Get into a Good School', commissioned a poll in 2015 of 1,000 parents with primary school aged pupils. The poll revealed:

- 12.6% had pretended to practise a faith in which they did not believe.
- 23.7% said they would if they had to do so.

18 Context

- 13% had their child baptised purely to gain a school place.
- 11% had pretended their child had been baptised.

These figures relate to entry into Faith Schools generally, including the much larger group of 'voluntary controlled' under the trust of the Church of England. Indeed, in the light of such criticism, a letter was published in *The Guardian* from twenty members of the Church of England urging that the Church move towards operating open and non-religiously selective admissions arrangements.

> We are a group of Anglican clergy and laypeople urging that the Church amends its school admissions guidance, so that its schools no longer select pupils on grounds of church attendance.

There are no separate figures for the 'Voluntary Aided' Schools (mainly Catholic) where such 'gaming' should be easy to detect within the parish structure connected with the school, although the current requirement in some parishes of a 'Certificate of Catholic Practice' might be so construed. The Catholic Church, therefore, together with the Jewish and Muslim religious leaders would argue to maintain greater faith-based control over admissions, whilst at the same time being vigilant of 'the games people play' and also their responsibility for the poor and disadvantaged in their catchment area, whatsoever their religious affiliation. Even so, there is a dispute over individual parish priests vouching for parents' religious practices where the school is oversubscribed. Such a judgement would not, so it is argued, meet OSA's required admission arrangements to be clear, objective and procedurally fair.

However, a report in 2016 from the Sutton Foundation (Allen and Parameshwaren, 2016) claims that most socially selective primary schools are likely to be Faith Schools using the oversubscription criteria to select disproportionately wealthy pupils. According to the report, over 1,500 primary schools in England are 'highly socially selective' (especially Catholic schools), particularly in London and other urban areas. Other reports argue likewise. But this conclusion is strongly challenged, as detailed in Chapter 3. Reference is also made to the over complex oversubscription criteria, difficult for parents to navigate. It is recommended that Faith Schools should consider prioritizing 'pupil premium' applications ahead of others in their admissions criteria and that the admissions code properly enforced.

Nonetheless, the former Education Secretary declared that she wants to stop 'vexatious complaints' in order to unclog the admissions process, since the majority of the complaints against Faith Schools admissions come not from potential parents but from the Fair Admissions Campaign, supported by the British Humanist Association. A Memorandum of Understanding between the Churches and the government in April 2016 agreed that Academy conversions would take place only if the relevant Church authority was satisfied that the school's religious character would be maintained, for example, through Church-led Multi-Academy Trusts (MATs). This has provoked two kinds of opposition. First, regarding Voluntary Controlled Schools (mainly Church of England) this would mean the schools would come under greater Church control than hitherto. Second, especially with reference to Catholic Faith Schools, a spokesman for the National Secular Society declared (as reported in the *Catholic Education Service News*, 27.3.16):

> The Government's desire to protect the religious character of Faith schools makes a mockery of its promise to ensure all Academies are inclusive and welcoming to the communities around them. This Concordat simply ensures that faith-based schools will remain free to robustly assert a Christian ethos on a religiously diverse and largely religiously indifferent school community.

At the time of writing, there has been a reversal of the 2010 Coalition Agreement to cap Catholic admissions to Catholic schools at 50% when over-subscribed. This particularly affects the building of new Catholic schools where there is a demand for them. There are areas in London, especially West London, where children cannot secure a place in a Catholic school, a problem occurring in other places where Catholic populations have been boosted by immigration.

Summary of key issues to be tackled

Given this 'contemporary political and cultural context' (focused on England and Wales but raising issues that have much wider application) and in looking carefully at the arguments for and against the maintenance of faith-based schools, the book needs to attend carefully to:

- *Facts*: reconciling different figures concerning the extent to which Faith Schools, through their admissions, fail to accommodate a fair proportion of pupils from less advantaged and from minority backgrounds (see Chapter 3).
- *Secular morality*: its meaning and its seeming opposition to faith-based understanding (see Chapter 9).
- *Social cohesion*: the role of the school in promoting social cohesion and the implications of such an aim on promoting faith-based schools (see Chapters 8 and 11).
- *Discrimination in public services*: in a society, which, as Rabbi Dr Jonathan Sacks argued, is constituted, not simply of individuals but of different communities to which these individuals belong (see Chapters 8 and 11).
- *Philosophical issues I, educational aims*: viz. the reconciliation of 'liberal education' and 'secular society' with initiation into a distinctive religious tradition (see Chapter 9).
- *Philosophical issues II, knowledge, truth and rationality*: the rational foundation for religious understanding (see chapter 10).
- *Philosophical issues III, society and politics*: reconciliation of advocacy for 'a Common School' with that for separate 'Faith Schools', and thus parental rights to have children educated within religious traditions, though within the state system (see Chapters 11).

20 Context

- *Relation of the State* (in its responsibilities to ensure a good education for all): to
  - Local Authorities (and their arrangements for schools),
  - Academy and Free School Trusts, some of which are Faith Schools,
  - parental claims for education within their faith tradition,
  - the promotion of 'the common good' (see Chapter 11).
- *Admission arrangements*: which reconcile
  - parental rights for a religious tradition,
  - local schools for all,
  - service to the poor,
  - demands for social cohesion.

Many of these issues are raised in the report by Professor Linda Woodhead and former Secretary of State, Charles Clarke, which called upon Faith Schools and their sponsors to

> make further effort … to developing procedures which balance the rights of families of faith to have their children educated in that faith with other considerations of fairness to others and serving the whole local community.
>
> *(Woodhead and Clarke, 2015)*

References

Allen, R. and Parameshwaren, M., 2016, *Caught Out: Primary Schools, Catchment Areas a Social Selection*, Report for the Sutton Trust.

Barnes, L.P., 2014, *Education, Religion and Diversity*, London: Routledge.

Boeve, L., 2007, *God Interrupts History: Theology in a Time of Upheaval*, New York: Continuum.

Bullivant, S., 2017, *The 'No Religion' Population of Great Britain*, Twickenham: St. Mary's University.

Butler-Sloss Report, 2015, *Living with Difference*, Report of the Commission on Religion and Belief in Public Life, Cambridge: The Wolf Institute.

Cantle Report, 2001, *Community Cohesion*, Oldham Borough Council.

Casey Review, 2016, *A Review into Opportunity and Integration*, London: Department for Communities and Local Government.

Clarke Report, 2016, *Allegations Concerning Birmingham Schools: Arising from the Trojan Horse Letter*, London: HMSO.

Durkheim, E., 1961 (2016 edition), *Moral Education: A Study in the Theory and Application of the Sociology of Education*, New York: The Free Press.

Durodie, B., 2016, 'Securitising education to prevent terrorism or losing direction?', *British Journal of Educational Studies*, 64(1), p.21.

Lane, D., 2015, *Catholic Education in the light of Vatican II and Laudato Si*, Dublin: Veritas.

Moffat, C., ed., 1993, *Education for Ever for a Change*, Belfast: Fortnight Educational Trust.

Ouseley Report, 2001, *Community Pride, Nor Prejudice*, Bradford: Vision.

Romaine, J., 2015, *Accord Coalition Quarterly Report*, No.26, www.accordcoalition.org.uk.

Woodhead, L. and Clarke, C., 2015, *A New Settlement: Religion and Belief in Schools*, Westminster Faith Debates, p. 66. www.faithdebates.org.uk.

Woodhead, L. and Brown, A., 2016, *That Was the Church that Was*, London: Bloomsbury.

2

HISTORICAL BACKGROUND AND THE CURRENT POSITION

Introduction

In *Faith-based Schools and the State,* Harry Judge (2001, p.9) wrote:

> '[W]ithout the history (or rather histories), contemporary problems are unintelligible'.

Never could that have been truer than in the case of Faith schools. The grounds for their beginning and development, the relationship between the Church and the state, the consequent controversies which have surrounded their survival through the massive social and economic changes of 200 years, have shaped present assumptions and policies, though too often unawares. It is important as we face the future to understand how the present policy and practice in England and Wales are necessarily shaped by the past. But the controversies and changes no doubt resonate in other countries, where one also sees the struggle between secular and religion for the control of schools, and conflict over such control between the different religious groups. It is useful to see the various ways different countries have dealt with these controversies, as will be shown, though briefly, in Chapter 4, in Northern Ireland, Scotland, Ireland, France, and the United States.

19th century beginnings

Chapter 1 began by pointing out the religious foundations of the school system in England and Wales. But more needs to be said, both to understand the system and to raise important matters of principle which are at stake in our thinking about the future of the educational system generally and of Faith schools in particular.

22 Context

From the beginning of the 19th century there was growing interest by the state in supporting some form of elementary education for the majority of children. But, in so far as there was any provision at all, it was provided by parish-led communities. In 1811, the National Society for the Education of the Poor in the Principles of the Church of England (the National Society) was established, and, following the grants instituted in 1833 from the Privy Council, increased the number of schools within these parish communities throughout the country. By 1851, there were over 17,000 such schools catering for almost 1 million pupils. To support their schools, the Church of England established as many as 34 of the 40 teacher training colleges in England and Wales.

At the same time, beginning in 1814, the non-conformists, through the newly established British and Foreign School Society, were building their schools, not wishing their children to be inducted into the doctrines and practices of the Church of England. By 1851, there were 1,500 non-conformist schools, catering for as many as 225,000 pupils, mainly in the quickly developing industrial towns (Peterson, 1971, p.35).

The state's growing interest had several aspects. There was the general humanitarian one. But society also needed more literate and numerate citizens, especially as the franchise was increasingly extended. This became more urgent after the 1851 Great Exhibition when the industrial prominence of Britain was seen to be challenged by Germany and France, which had invested more in their educational systems.

There was, therefore, an inevitable clash between the state and the religious bodies which had provided most of the schooling, mainly through the National Society and the British and Foreign Schools Society. However, as they became increasingly dependent on the government's financial support, so there was a danger of the schools' distinctive religious affiliation coming under threat.

The problem and choice might be posed as follows:

(a) Since the taxpayer was increasingly paying for the schools, both new and old, and since some parents would not share the values and practices of the neighbouring denominational school, should there be a third type of school, a non-denominational school paid for completely from government grant?
(b) Since, however, the underlying ethos of the country was essentially Christian, was it important that such ethos be preserved and that the Church and non-conformists continue to be responsible for the national education through their schools?
(c) Since, in this last case, in many areas (if not all) the only accessible school would be religiously affiliated, should there be an opt-out opportunity – or what later became known as 'conscience clause'?

However, there were inevitably problems which seemed irresolvable, and, in one form or another, would remain so until the present day – perhaps much longer, given the issues which now are emerging over the maintenance through taxation of Faith schools.

Historical background and the current position   **23**

First, both the Church of England and the non-conformists resisted strongly the suggested non-denominational system: the Church of England wanting 'a Church system or none', and the Nonconformists, 'rather none than a Church system' (Peterson,1971, p.35). However, according to the report of the Royal Commission of 1818, the Church of England national schools were adopting a liberal position which would, it was thought, accommodate those of other branches of Christianity – the significance of which is developed in Chapter 5 ('Tradition I').

Second, the 'secular societies', as time went on, became a vociferous force for a universal, secular, and compulsory system of education. Looking across the Channel, they could see a national system of secular state primary schools achieved by 1850, influenced by France's political leader, Guizot, who, in 1833, tried to establish a national secular system, with religious instruction left to the priests and ministers. He argued:

> It is in general desirable that children whose families do not profess the same creed should early contract, by frequenting the same schools, those habits of reciprocal friendship and mutual tolerance which may open later, when they live together as grown-up citizens, into justice and harmony.
>
> *(Peterson, op. cit., p.26)*

The distinctive philosophy of such a secular position was developed by Emile Durkheim, as is shown in Chapter 9 of this book.

In 1907, the Secular Education League was formed, insisting that the teaching of religion was not the responsibility of the state. They were particularly vociferous over the 1902 Act. That Act confirmed that Church schools, if supported on the rates, would include the growing number of Roman Catholic schools. But 'No Rome on the Rates'!

However, progress was made on point (c) above. The matter was discussed in Parliament in 1820. According to Hansard:

> The Church catechism is only taught, and attendance at the established place of worship only required, of those whose parents belong to the establishment; due assurance being obtained that the children of sectaries shall learn the principles and attend the ordinance of religion according to the doctrines and forms to which their families are attached.
>
> *(quoted in Peterson, op. cit. p.35)*

An attempt to reconcile the differences was made in the 1870 Education Act, which established school boards throughout the country to arrange for the distribution of grants and to establish school board schools where there were no British National or British and Foreign schools. At long last it seemed that there were the non-denominational schools wanted by the secularists. In what is referred to as the 'Cowper-Temple clause' in the 1870 Act, it was stated that

24 Context

> No religious catechisms or religious formulary which is distinctive of any
> particular denomination shall be taught in the school.

Religious instruction was to be of a non-denominational kind based on the
Authorised Version of the Bible.

Furthermore, access to school entry should not require attendance at a place of worship or religious instruction. Hence, the 'dual system' of non-denominational school board schools, on the one hand, and, on the other hand, denominational schools, run mainly by the National Society and the British Foreign and Schools Society, but funded in the main by government grants directed through the school boards, was created. But even in the religiously affiliated schools, there was to be a 'conscience clause' where parents could remove children from religious assemblies and instruction.

One should not, however, underestimate the hostility that this arrangement and compromise gave rise to – which continued in different degrees for decades, always likely, even to this day, to resurface. The prospect of the non-religious people contributing from their taxes to religiously affiliated schools, particularly Catholic ones, gave rise to public meetings and protests. For example, one protest in Yorkshire led to 16 special trains being laid on to take the protesters, and even after the 1902 bill was passed, many Non-conformists refused to pay their taxes, thereby risking prison (Chadwick, 2001, p.477).

This organisational compromise in a developing national system of education between the religious bodies, responsible for the majority of the schools (by 1900 there were 10,000 parishes in which the only provision available was controlled by the Church of England), and the secularists, and between the religious bodies themselves, survived in its essence for over 70 years, until it was revised by the 1944 Education Act. But, as in the case of most compromises, it did not receive universal approbation. On the one hand, there was dissatisfaction, particularly from the non-conformists on the inclusion of the growing number of Catholic schools now in receipt of grants through the school boards ('Rome on the Rates') – a matter which will be returned to in the next section. On the other hand, many school boards did not opt for a completely secular regime where the general ethos of the locality, especially in rural areas, was a 'generalised' form of Christianity.

The rise of Roman Catholic schooling

The Catholic Church began to play an increasingly significant role in the provision of education with the establishment of the Catholic Poor-School Committee in 1847. It was this Committee which was given the task of negotiating grants for Catholic schools – grants which had been received by the National Society and the British and Foreign Schools Society since 1833. These, between them, were responsible for the emerging national system of elementary schools. Such negotiation was not without opposition both from outside the Catholic Church (anti-Catholic sentiment had not been totally quenched since the Catholic Emancipation Act of 1829) and from within. Indeed, Archbishop Ullathorne was deeply suspicious of government grants that might very well jeopardise the independence and distinctive ethos of the Catholic schools.

However, at the first synod of the province of Westminster, following the restoration of the hierarchy in 1850, it was resolved that

> the first necessity ... is a sufficient provision of education adequate to the wants of our poor. It must become universal ... to ... prefer the establishment of good schools to every other work ... We should prefer the erection of a school, so arranged as to serve temporarily for a chapel, to that of a church without one.
>
> *(quoted in Grace, 2016, p.21)*

Therefore, in the early years after the restoration of the hierarchy, Catholic schools were provided for Catholic children before their churches were built, usually with the generous help of low-income English and immigrant Irish Catholics. But the scale of new provision, which was required to meet the mainly poor population, would not have been possible without participation in the nationally funded system. Therefore, the Catholic Church, led by Cardinal Wiseman, was prepared to concede some independence, namely, the inspection by the newly created Her Majesty's Inspectorate (HMI), in order to participate in the funded system of elementary education. Such a concession, however, was not accepted by all. In a letter to Cardinal Manning, who was to succeed Wiseman at Westminster, Wiseman wrote of the school boards and of their perceived role in dispersing money:

> Their constitution, object and aim is to establish and maintain schools and propagate a system of education wholly in antagonism with Catholic education, and with all definite religious education.
>
> *(quoted by Judge, 2001, p.106)*

The 1870 Act, having established school boards to disseminate the grants to schools, including schools under the new school boards, in places not served by the National and British and Foreign Societies, confirmed the continued existence of 'voluntary schools', alongside the school board schools. But the partial independence of Catholic schools was at the cost of not receiving payment for the buildings and maintenance of its schools. The quite considerable sum required for building the schools, therefore, fell on the shoulders of parishioners, whose support was sufficiently generous for the number of Catholic schools to rise from 350 to 1,045 by the 1902 Act. This arrangement (the dual system) was confirmed in the 1902 Act and, to a great degree, in the 1944 Education Act.

20th century developments

Reference has been made to the 1902 Balfour Act, the main innovation of which lay in the abolition of school boards and the transfer of their responsibilities to

26 Context

the recently created county and urban local authorities. Thereby, local education authorities (LEAs) were created, which, being smaller in number (350 compared with the 2,650 school boards), had much wider remit in ensuring an equitable and adequate spread of school places within the different regions and districts. The denominational schools (much reduced as a percentage of the overall number of schools) remained heavily supported but now from local rates, with the LEA having some representation on the governing bodies. It was the early beginning of the partnership between central government, local government, and the voluntary bodies

It had been recognised by the 1895 Bryce Commission that the voluntary schools were in increasingly financial difficulties and were in need of public support. They depended on government grants. And, as Sidney Webb stated prior to the Balfour Act in the aptly entitled Fabian Society pamphlet of 1901, *The Education Muddle and the Way Out*:

> It is politically impossible to abolish these Voluntary Schools; and whatever we may think of the theological reasons for their establishment, their separate and practically individual management does incidentally offer what ought to be, in any public system of education, most jealously guarded, namely, variety, and the opportunity of experiment.
>
> *(Quoted in Judge, 2001, p. 43)*

Indeed, it is worthwhile being reminded of the number of voluntary schools providing elementary education and in need of financial support at the turn of the century. Of the voluntary schools in receipt of state grant, 11,777 were Church of England, 1,079 interdenominational (in effect, Non-conformist), 458 Methodist, 1,045 Catholic. There were only 5,788 board schools.

The Fisher Act of 1918 finally abolished fees for attendance at the public elementary schools, creating for the first time a universal and free 'primary education' (to anticipate the current term). At the same time, there was a growth of those continuing into a secondary phase of education. In 1922 R. H. Tawney published the highly influential *Secondary Education for All*. The Hadow Report of 1926 and the Spens Report of 1938 argued strongly for extending free secondary education for all. But that, together with proposals for extending the school-leaving age, created yet a further challenge to the role of voluntary schools within the overall system. Whereas the Balfour Act agreed to support the voluntary elementary schools, it did not legislate for the funding of wholesale building of new ones. Could the cost of building and maintaining new secondary schools be afforded by the Catholic Church? And, if not, would the Church therefore no longer be able to extend its educational mission into the secondary stage?

However, the 1936 Education Act, in anticipation of the raising of the school-leaving age, finally empowered LEAs to give grants of 50% to 70% to the building and maintenance of new senior schools within the voluntary sector. By 1939, 7%

Historical background and the current position **27**

of the elementary school population was educated in as many as 1,266 Catholic assisted schools.

The Church of England, however, whose National Society was responsible for educating the largest number of elementary school pupils, by contrast with the Catholics, saw its role, not so much in retaining a distinctive set of schools, as that of ensuring, in the more secularised system, the preservation of a Christian ethos and 'generalised Christianity' within the common school. Archbishop Temple (1942), wrote:

> Above all, let us not give the impression that our concern as church people is only with the adjustment of the dual system: we ought as Christians to be concerned about the whole of the education progress. I am quite sure that the raising of the school leaving age will of itself do more to make permanent the religious influence of the schools than anything that can be done with directly denominational purpose.
>
> *(quoted in Judge, 2001, p. 179)*

Judge (2001, p.54) sums up this particular stage in the historical developments of the relation between the state and the religious bodies,

> Church and State were irreversibly committed to co-operate at the national and local levels of government in developing an integrated system of elementary and secondary education within which the Voluntary schools would play an important part.

But also, that integrated system assumed, in the words of the Spens Report of 1938, that

> No boy or girl can be counted as properly educated unless he or she has been made aware of the fact of the existence of a religious interpretation of life.

Education Act 1944

The sentiment given by Spens was reinforced and given specific meaning in the preparation of the dual system to be enshrined in the Education Act of 1944. Bishop Henson of Durham spoke thus of the dual system:

> The Dual System, as it now exists, obstructs the complete triumph of the secularising tendency. It affirms an educational ideal which is larger in range, more intelligently sympathetic in temper, more congruous with human nature, than that which secularism embodies. It is a rallying point, to which the higher factors in the community can gather, and by means of which they can affect more or less directly the whole educational process.
>
> *(quoted in Chadwick, 1991, p. 179)*

28 Context

Therefore, a milestone in the progressive development of the national system was the 1944 Education Act. Universal and compulsory elementary education up to age 13 had been achieved by 1944. This Act legislated for secondary education for all up to the age of 15. Important for this book was the embodiment in that legislation of the three types of school governance, both at primary and at secondary levels, which, it was hoped, would reconcile the different and controversial religious and secular interests that had plagued the slow development of the national system since the first state support for education in the early to mid-19th century, and which was still strongly opposed by significant bodies such as the Co-operative Union, the TUC, the National Union of Teachers, and the Workers Education Association (see Simon, 1991, p.53).

The three types of school, therefore, in terms of their governance were:

- *voluntary controlled* (mainly Church of England) whose capital, maintenance and running costs were paid for by the state, two-thirds of whose management committee were appointed by the LEA but whose trustees (namely the respective diocese) retained some control over admissions and staffing;
- *voluntary aided* (mainly Catholic, but also some Jewish), 50% of whose capital and maintenance would be paid for by their respective religious communities, but who would have control over admissions, staffing, religious ethos and curriculum;
- *county or community* schools which would have no religious affiliation and whose admissions' arrangements included everyone in the local community, determined by the LEA.

However, a daily assembly of a religious nature was legally required of all county and voluntary controlled schools, together with an 'agreed syllabus', locally agreed, for the teaching of religion (except in the voluntary aided schools which would have their own distinctive syllabuses). The syllabuses, though of a generalised Christian nature, received approval in a manner which would have been inconceivable in previous decades.

But the 'conscience clause' of the 1870 Act was preserved, namely, that parents had the right to ask their children to be withdrawn both from the worship and from religious instruction.

Therefore, the 'dual system' (as the system of voluntary and county schools was called), continued the arrangements in much the same manner as had been provided under the 1870 and 1902 Acts of Parliament. Thus supported, the Catholic population within maintained schools continued to grow: 400,000 by the early 1950s, 500,000 by 1960, 750,000 in the 1970s – 9% of the school population and two-fifths of the voluntary school pupils (Judge, 2001, p.75).

But a word of caution. Butler, the Minister responsible for the 1944 Education Act, put in his diary in 1942:

> Political interest is shifting from the soul of man to his economic position which all seems very unhealthy.

Jewish and Muslim schools

In giving an account of the development of the relationship between Faith schools and the state, the focus has inevitably been on the Catholic and the Church of England schools, together with the non-conformist contributions, because they were at the centre of the changes which took place over the 19th and 20th centuries. The settlement of the 1944 Act, namely, the dual system, was the accommodation of these religious bodies, which, in fact, were responsible for a very large proportion of elementary/primary schools, and, subsequently, upon the raising of the school-leaving age, of the development of secondary schools. Such schools were universally referred to as 'Church schools'.

The shift of nomenclature to 'Faith schools' occurred because, first, the growing number of pupils within those Christian schools belonged to quite different religious traditions, and, second, these different religious traditions sought equally to have their own schools within the voluntary sector. Also, there had long been Jewish schools which had opted to be within the dual system as 'voluntary aided'. It is necessary, therefore, to introduce briefly these relatively small but essential parts of the voluntary schools sector.

Jewish schools

The Jews Free School in London was established in 1732. It taught secular subjects as well as specifically Jewish texts and traditions. But, just as the non-conformists and the Catholics did not want their children to be initiated into the Church of England version of Christianity, even more so with the Jewish population. Hence, major centres of Jewish population started from the mid-19th century onwards to establish their own private schools – to preserve their own Jewish identity and heritage.

At the same time, the school board schools created by the 1870 Act came to be much used by the Jewish population since many of the inner-city areas, where the immigrant Jewish population settled, were mainly Jewish – and hence, the local school population would be Jewish, too. For example, Castle Street Board School in London's East End had nearly 1500 pupils in 1883, 955 of whom were Jewish (Miller, 1991).

In 1853, the Manchester Jewish school received state funding on the same basis as the Catholic schools had done, but on the condition that the pupils were to read daily (not the King James' Bible) but Scriptures of the Old Testament – and would be subject to inspection by HMI.

However, the Jewish schools did not take much advantage of the state's aid for their own private schools (as distinct from the board schools), despite the fact that such aid would have been available through the adoption of voluntary status. One reason given was that the national system of compulsory and free education within the board schools would enable the Jewish children 'to acquire English habits of thought and character' – moving to greater integration of a Jewish population

30 Context

which was alienated in its poverty from the main society with its greater opportunities. The Jewish traditions and culture would be preserved through supplementary education, sometimes within the board schools, sometimes in the synagogues (see Miller, op. cit.).

There was, at the same time, concern amongst some about the gradual demise of the Jewish schools (i.e. those not within the state sector) as increasing numbers became more assimilated into the mainstream culture and as the supplementary education also declined. The (later) Chief Rabbi, Jonathan Sacks, entitled his book in 1994, *Will We Have Jewish Grandchildren*? Therefore in 1971, the Chief Rabbi, Lord Jacovobits, launched the Jewish Educational Trust to create new schools and to ensure the continuity of supplementary studies. Jewish education expanded considerably, partly to counteract the dangers of cultural assimilation – the loss of the distinctive Jewish tradition and of Jewish 'authenticity' (See Alexander, 1995)

The majority of Jewish schools now fall within the state sector as voluntary aided, thereby freely able (subject to inspection, as in all voluntary aided schools) to impress upon the learners 'important standards and values of Jewish belief', security in their Jewish identity, and 'confidence in their heritage', with close links to home and involvement in Jewish life through school (Felsenstein, 2000). The link between school ethos and the values and culture of the home was and is seen as an essential element in the relation between schools and the state, even within a national system of education.

Muslim schools

There are about 3 million Muslims in England and Wales. They are as denominationally divided as the Christians – into Sunni and Shia, but also with smaller groups outside the Sunni and Shia communities. Such divisions are no doubt as relevant to the establishment of Muslim schools as is, and was, the division between the major Christian groups in England. Significant, however, is the way in which the Muslim immigrants are concentrated in particular cities such as Birmingham, Bradford, Leicester, and Manchester, just as the Jewish immigrants had congregated in particular cities in the 19th century. Indeed, as with the early Jewish population, community and non-religiously affiliated schools in such areas became, in fact, predominantly Muslim.

To meet this, even in the community schools, many adjustments needed to be, and have been, made – for example, in dress codes, in the opportunities provided for religious practices, in the preparation of food provided, in language development, in the separation of the sexes. There is demand for separate schools for girls, just as that practice, once widely spread in England half a century ago, is fast disappearing. There is a demand from some parents for a 'confessional' teaching of Islam, not what had come to be accepted following the 1944 Act (through the Agreed Syllabuses) of a non-confessional understanding of different religious beliefs.

By the 1990s, there were as many as 60 independent Muslim schools, very often poorly resourced and not subject to inspection. Clearly, the Muslim population would wish to benefit, as the Catholic and Jews have benefited, from becoming voluntary aided. However, there were inevitably practical difficulties if, within the overall population, there was no need demographically for new schools to be built. The first application – in Bradford in 1986 – was thus turned down. Therefore, the growth of poorly resourced Muslim private schools continued. However, the Muslim communities have now taken advantage of the voluntary aided opportunities to gain some independence to create a distinctively Islamic ethos. The first two voluntary aided Muslim primary schools were established in London and Birmingham respectively in 1998. By 2014, 12 of the 140 Muslim schools had become voluntary aided.

However, complaints were made, and upheld by Ofsted, that some Muslim schools, both community and voluntary aided, were victims of attempts by a number of associated and 'hard-line Islamists' to introduce an Islamist ethos into the schools. This gave rise to several reports, including the report by Ofsted, into 21 schools in Birmingham referred to in the previous chapter. One report, commissioned by the Department of Education into what became known as 'the Trojan Horse affair', pointed to

> evidence that there were a number of people associated with each other and in positions of influence in schools and governing bodies, who espouse or sympathise with or fail to challenge extremist views – a co-ordinated attempt … to introduce an intolerant and aggressive Islamist ethos into a few schools in Birmingham.
>
> *(Clarke Report, 2016)*

This inevitably gives rise to concern over the existence of a separate category of religiously affiliated, voluntary aided schools, a matter not lost on the secular cause. But it should not do so. First, many of the schools were community schools, not Faith schools, but with a disproportionately large number of pupils and therefore parents from the Muslim community. Second, they were not typical of the range of Muslim schools, which, subject to the normal accountability through regular inspection, would not be open to such accusations. As with the Jewish and Catholic school, parents would wish for the ethos and the principles of their faith to be integrated into the life and teaching of the school, including an induction into the distinctively Muslim religious and ethical traditions. In the absence of such schooling, parents would (and indeed did do so) revert to home-schooling or to small, poorly equipped unregistered Faith schools, not publicly accountable and more open to extremist influence. These are at the time of writing being investigated by Ofsted.

But this is inevitably a problem when schools reflect immigrant communities which have become self-segregated, as indeed was the case with immigrant populations in previous years.

Wider implications

Such, however, are the changes in society that it is quite possible for yet other minority religious groups to demand voluntary aided status – Scientology, evangelical

32 Context

Christians, Jehovah Witnesses, Seventh Day Adventists, Sikhs, Zen Buddhists, and so on. Given the general principle that Faith schools should be entitled to public financial support, would the government have to distinguish between those claimants which should be supported and those which, for whatever reason, should not?

In a secular age

However, in a more secular age, as that is explained in Chapter 1 (and defined more precisely in Chapter 5), the objections to taxes supporting religious schools, which were raised in the 19th century and resurrected in the preamble to the 1944 Education Act, are surfacing once again. Those objections were hinted at during the discussions of the religious settlement of the 1944 Act. There were dissenting voices. The leader column in the *Times Educational Supplement* of October 1943 argues:

> As it is by no means certain yet that the basic philosophy of England will be in the future a Christian philosophy – which not unimportant sections of the community consciously and deliberately reject – any attempt to capture the schools for the systematic inculcation of the Christian view of life would be wrong and might well precipitate embittered conflict between rival religious and political parties for the possession of schools.
>
> *(quoted in Cairns, 1989, p.11)*

However, far from a precipitation of 'embittered conflict between rival religious parties', the likely failure to 'inculcate the Christian view of life' united religious denominations in their concerns about the increasing secular nature of schooling. Finally, gone were the opposing religious voices of the late 19th and early 20th centuries. According to the Free Church Federal Council Education Policy Committees in 1959 (whose member were once so vociferous about 'No Rome on the Rates')

> Christian of every church recognised with great anxiety that increasing numbers of children are growing up with no real contact with a church of any kind ... the Roman Catholics and the Anglicans are quite justified in being anxious about the education of their own and other children, and Free Churchmen must face the situation as it is now.
>
> *(quoted in Judge, 2001, p.223)*

What were the consequences?

The 'creeping secularisation' made the Catholic church more determined to preserve the independence of its schools within the national system, despite the spiralling costs of providing such schools, especially at the secondary level as the school-leaving age was extended finally to 16, exacerbated inevitably by the increase of those remaining at school in the Sixth Form. From the government's point of view, such was the importance attached to the voluntary sector in making the creation of universal secondary education possible, that the grant for capital building and maintenance was raised from the original 50% in 1944 to an eventual 85% in 1976.

The 1988 Education Act stipulated religion as a 'basic subject', but, unlike in all other subjects, no national guidelines over content and assessment were given. It was to be seen as teaching about religion and reflecting the 'local traditions of the area'. Religion no longer was equated with Christianity as it was in 1944. For example, the Birmingham local agreement was concerned with the teaching of world religions.

Nonetheless, the 1988 Act followed that of 1944 in stipulating daily collective worship, assuming that to be 'wholly or mainly of a broadly Christian character'. It would reflect the broad traditions of Christian belief without being distinctive of any particular Christian denomination. Moreover, in special circumstances the act of worship may not be Christian. Furthermore, such Acts of Worship could be in smaller groupings than whole school assemblies.

The assurance that there would be religious education, reflecting where necessary the 'local tradition', was entrusted to the local Standing Advisory Councils on Religious Education (SACRE). The 1944 Act permitted Local Education Authorities to set them up, but no details were specified as to membership or specific duties. The 1988 Act, by contrast, required each LEA to establish a SACRE with a membership which reflected the religious affiliations of the locality. Its function was

> to advise the [local] authority upon matters connected with religious worship in county schools and the religious education to be given in accordance with an agreed syllabus.
>
> *(DES, 1989)*

Those matters include the choice of materials, teaching approaches and the provision of teacher training. They also had oversight over the syllabuses in the schools within the LEA, and advised the LEA on the teaching of religion and on the act of worship as practised in the schools. They were the 'watchdogs' over the requirements of the 1988 Act, requirements of which were already loosely Christian. Further 'watchdogs' included the inspectorate, following the creation of Ofsted by the 1992 Education (Schools) Act, the duties of which included that of keeping the Secretary of State informed of the spiritual, moral, social and cultural development of pupils – though in this matter Faith schools could make their own inspectorial arrangements. For voluntary controlled schools this would include representatives from the local parish council, and for the voluntary aided Catholic schools, inspection would be devolved to the diocesan authorities. But in 2001, the Programme for Government indicated the commitment of government to address the needs of a changing (and more secular and diverse) society by establishing a forum on patronage and pluralism in the primary sector, considering the divestment of patronage and the inclusion of diversity.

34 Context

However, the evolution of thinking on this matter moves on. The leader column in *The Times*, quoted above, was prescient. Reference was made in Chapter 1 of this book to the Commission on Religion and Belief in Public Life (Butler-Sloss Report, 2015), which calls itself *Living with Differences*. It called for a major overhaul of those areas of public life (which, in different ways, embody religious symbolism), to reflect the multi-cultural nature of national life. Not only (so it was argued) does the differentiation of schooling on the basis of religious differences militate against 'living with differences', but also the daily act of worship of a 'wholly or mainly of a broadly Christian character is seen to militate against "living with difference"'. Ethnic and social diversity, so it is frequently argued, requires a common schooling without segregation on the basis of religion. This becomes even more important with the growth of Muslim schools, whether formally recognised as such within the voluntary aided sector of the dual system or as *de facto* Muslim schools, which were adopting distinctively Islamic practices and teaching that would not be acceptable in community schools. (This issue is developed further in Chapters 9 and 11.)

One response from the Catholics would be that, true to their origins of their schools in their 'service to the poor', those schools were disproportionately serving the disadvantaged and the ethnically diverse communities. There were and are, of course, exceptional cases, but, as the figures in the Chapter 3 show, the general picture is one of greater *ethnic* diversity than in the community schools.

Nonetheless, the mission of the Catholic Church to provide school places for Catholic children has inevitably, in some cases, led to priority being given to Catholic applicants to the exclusion of non-Catholic children. In a system where 'choice' is being extolled in a more market-led approach to 'driving up standards', this development has been attacked, and the rules changed. New free schools and academies (introduced by Michael Gove, then Secretary of State, in 2014), if of a particular faith, were to reserve 50% of places to pupils of a different faith or none. That requirement was rescinded in 2016. But it is important to be reminded, in recognition of the continuity of the controversies which beset the existence of Faith schools, that when, under Prime Minister Blair's Labour government, the expansion of Faith schools was encouraged, 45 Labour MPs argued that all Faith schools should recruit at least 25% of their pupils from a different faith or none.

Thus, one is now seeing a change in the relationship between Church and state – the hard-fought independence of the Catholic schools, for example, could gradually be eroded. Recent policy proposals to make all schools academics, beyond the responsibility of the local authorities, might further lead to a greater dependence of the schools on the state. Academies are, after all, under contract to the Secretary of State – they are in effect, contrary to the 1944 Education Act, government schools. Thus, their future lies increasingly on the views, even whims, of future Secretaries of State. What was a partnership between central government, local government and the voluntary bodies, which was integral to the dual system, is being eroded.

The 2010 Coalition Agreement, which insisted upon a cap on Catholics pupils in over-subscribed Catholic schools and as a condition for the creation of new

Historical background and the current position **35**

ones within the Academy and Free School 'system', has been removed under the premiership of Theresa May. But who knows how permanent this new agreement may be where the state is able to exercise such power?

Furthermore, there are diocesan proposals within the Catholic Church for the diocese to take direct control over all its schools with the authority 'to appoint and dismiss trustees' in what would be a Multi-Academy Trust (MAT). Under the plans, 600 Church schools would be run by large Academy Trusts. In December 2016, the Catholic Diocese of Westminster proposed that 180 schools join the MATs, with each Trust governed by a single board, which would act as the governing body for up to 15 schools each.

Consequences of this more secular age

The historical narrative given in this chapter reflects the changing place of religion, not only in the establishment of schools, but also in the content of religious teaching in the schools. Initially, the Anglican and Non-Conformist Churches were the only institutions able to meet the demand for elementary education for all, especially for the poor, for which government grants were awarded from 1833 onwards. But this itself contained the seeds of division, as the dominance of the Church of England was felt to be unacceptable first to the non-conformists, second to the small but powerful objections of the secularists, and finally to the growing contributions from the Catholics. Over the decades those differences were resolved through the 1870, 1902 and 1944 Education Acts in a dual system of county (initially school board) schools and voluntary schools within the state system, and in the division of the voluntary into controlled and aided.

The Catholics were, in England and Wales, as elsewhere (see Chapter 4 for an international perspective), determined to maintain their independence within the national system despite the cost of doing so. That was due to the fear initially that its religious tradition might otherwise be compromised by the dominance of Protestantism and later by the increasing secularism of society, reflected in the broadly conceived teaching and practice of religion in the voluntary controlled and the county schools.

Despite the success in so doing and the reconciliation of differences through the arrangements of the 1944 Act, the secularists are making more advances, especially in their opposition to the greater independence of the Catholic Church, but also of other religious bodies (Islamic, Jewish, Sikh, and Hindu) which have adopted voluntary aided status. There is,

- first, the belief that religious segregation into separate schools militates against a more cohesive society – there is a need for the 'common school';
- second, concern, particularly from the British Humanist Association, that admissions arrangements discriminate against more disadvantaged young people;
- third, that support for a specific religious ethos and teaching should not be paid for by the general tax-payer.

36 Context

The dual system within a 'national system locally maintained' is further vulnerable as a result of the demise of Local Authority responsibility for schools through the proposed forcing of Local Authority schools to become academics, outside Local Authority responsibility. The Chancellor of the Exchequer, in the 2016 Budget, announced that every 'state school' in England would become an Academy by 2022 (though the opposition was such that this intended change was postponed). This would mean the end of local responsibility for education as established in 1902, and possibly the end of parent governors. It is not clear how such 'academisation' of schooling will affect the ownership of land owned by the local authorities and the voluntary bodies, control over admissions and appointments, the teaching of religion and the curriculum in general, and accountability which will no longer be to their parishes and local communities.

Respect would be paid to the 'diocesan families of schools' in 'Academy trusts', though this would not include the 84 other Faith schools (Jewish, Muslim, and Sikh), 48 of which are maintained by the Local Authority and 33 are Jewish.

However, inevitably in this 'secular age', a spokesman for the National Secular Society argued:

> The Government's desire to protect the religious character of Faith Schools makes a mockery of its promise to ensure all Academies are inclusive and welcoming to the communities around them. The concordat simply ensures that faith-based schools will remain free to robustly assert a Christian ethos on a religiously diverse and largely religiously indifferent school community.
> *(Quoted in CES News, 2016)*

No doubt also inevitably in this 'secular age', religious education, despite requirements of successive acts of parliament, is no longer taught in many schools. According to the Report of the National Association of the Teachers of Religion, more than a quarter of England's secondary schools do not offer religious education (reported on BBC, 17 September 2017).

References

Alexander, H., 1995, *Jewish Education and the Search for Authenticity: A Study of Jewish Authenticity*, Los Angeles: University of Judaism.

Butler-Sloss, 2015, *Living with Difference*, Report of the Commission on Religion and Belief in Public Life, Cambridge: Woolf Institute.

Cairns, J.M., 1989, 'Religious education and the 1944 Education Act: missed opportunities', in Cox, E. and Cairns, J.M., *Reforming Religious Education*, London: The Bedford Way Series.

CES News, 27 March 2016, 'Churches get special relationship with regional School Commissioners', London: Catholic Education Service.

Chadwick, P., 2001, 'Anglican perspectives on Church schools', *Oxford Review of Education*, 27(4).

Clarke Report, 2016, *Allegations Concerning Birmingham Schools: Arising from the Trojan Horse Letter*, London: HMSO.

DES, 1989, Circular 3/89, London: HMSO.

Felsenstein, D., 2000, *Inspecting Jewish Schools*, London: Board of Deputies.

Grace, G., 2016, *Faith, Mission and Challenge in Catholic Education*, London: Routledge.

Judge, H., 2001, *Faith-based Schools and the State*, Wallingford: Symposium Books.

Miller, H., 1991, 'Jewish schooling in the UK', *Oxford Review of Education*, 27(4).

Peterson, A.D.C., 1971, (3rd edition), *A Hundred Years of Education*, London: Duckworth.

Simon, B., 1991, *Education and the Social Order 1940–1990*, London: Lawrence and Wishart.

Tawney, R.H., *Secondary Education for All*, London: The Labour Party.

Temple, W., 1942, *Christianity and the Social Order*, London: Penguin.

3

MAKING SENSE OF FACTS AND FIGURES

Introduction

As shown in Chapters 1 and 2, there is growing opposition to financial support for Faith schools within the state system. This is reflected in the Accord Coalition Quarterlies of the Fair Admissions Campaign, British Humanist Association (BHA), and major reports, for example: Butler-Sloss Report, 2015, *Living with Difference*; Sutton Trust Report, *Caught Out: Primary Schools, Catchment Areas and Social Selection* (Allen and Parameshwaren, 2016); Woodhead, L. and Clarke, C., 2015, *A New Settlement: Religion and Belief in Schools*. More recently, a report by the integration charity, *The Challenge*, claims that Faith schools, particularly Catholic primaries, lack social and economic diversity (www.tes.com/news/school-news/faith-schools).

In support of such opposition, statistics are given which purport to show that Faith schools:

- are less ethnically mixed, thereby not contributing sufficiently to social cohesion;
- tend to be socially selective, not taking a fair share of the socially disadvantaged;
- are not taking their fair share of children with special educational needs;
- tend to 'play games' in selection of pupils when the school is over-subscribed.

All this leads to the conclusion that Faith schools fail in the important educational task of serving the 'common good', which would be achieved through promoting social cohesion in an increasingly culturally mixed community and through taking their fair share of those from disadvantaged backgrounds.

It is important therefore to examine the data on which these claims are being made. In doing so, the account will focus particularly on the voluntary aided schools, because these often seem to be the main focus of criticism, and indeed these are the ones where there are detailed data. Nonetheless, difficulties arise in these critical accounts in their frequent failure to distinguish between the different kinds of Faith schools – Church of England, Catholic, other Christian, and other religiously affiliated schools (Jewish, Muslim, and a small number of Sikh, Hindi, and Buddhist).

Health warning

It is important, too, to heed a general 'health warning' about the use of statistics, produced by all parties to the debate, as will be indicated in the appropriate places in this chapter. Statistics deal in averages, and may (as argued by Harris, 2017) hide important variations within the sample, as, for example, in speaking of 'ethnic minorities', which embrace both recent immigrants and well-established second or third generation citizens. Furthermore, even where the statistics are not disputed, the significance of them may be, for example, where the number of children on free school meals (FSM) is used as the standard indicator of pupil deprivation,

It is also important to examine the language in which the objectors to Faith schools oppose their very existence. Such schools are accused of 'discrimination', of 'segregation', of 'manipulating' admissions. Such words are not merely descriptive but carry pejorative overtones. As Gerald Grace argued in response to the paper by the BHA (BHA, 2001), when referring to problems of 'segregated schooling' in Northern Ireland,

> [it] is an unfortunate feature of political and public discourse that the language of 'segregation' seems to be applied when parents make an educational choice based upon religion but not when it is based upon secular considerations.
>
> *(Grace, 2009)*

Schools, which give priority to those from religious backgrounds, for whom the schools were established, are not 'manipulating' the admissions, even if, in so prioritising, there is in fact a social bias.

Three areas of criticism

Ethnic selection

There are many schools, particularly in major northern cities, which do have a large majority of their pupils from ethnic minority groups. This is partly due to the fact that many such schools are the neighbourhood schools within ethnically segregated areas of our towns. However, it is also claimed that such a majority within the community schools is due to ethnic selection, particularly by Faith schools. Therefore, it is argued, all schools should, irrespective of religion, take their fair share of pupils from the ethnic minority population, because they are a major cause of selection on the grounds of ethnicity. Indeed, upon publication of the Casey Review (2016), a headline in *The Times* was 'Faith Schools encourage a form of apartheid'.

40 Context

In response to this argument:

One needs to refer to the census, carried out by the Catholic Education Service (CES, 2015), of all Catholic schools regarding the ethnicity of the intake to its primary and secondary schools. There was a 100% return rate from the 2,016 maintained Catholic schools in England (330 secondary, 1,667 primary, 14 tertiary, 5 all-through), which are 10% of the total number of schools in England and catering for 819,069 pupils (260,000 of whom were in sixth form colleges).

First, the schools were mixed in terms of religious affiliation. Of the total number, only 69% of pupils were Catholic (primary: 72%; secondary: 66%; tertiary: 38%).

Second, as indicated in Chapter 1, over 26,000 Muslim children attended Catholic schools, in some cases because their parents preferred attendance at schools where the ethos is one which respects religious faith and values. Indeed, 15 Catholic schools have a majority of Muslim children. Furthermore, Muslim pupils outnumber Christian children in about 20 Church of England schools, including one primary, which had a 100% Muslim population (*The Sunday Times*, 5.2.17).

Third, Catholic schools compared well with all other schools in terms of ethnicity, contrary to what many critics claim. Thus, the Catholic percentage of different ethnic groups, compared with schools nationally, was as follows:

	White British	White Non-British	Mixed/dual	Asian	Black	Chinese
All Catholic maintained	63	9	6	7	9.9	
All national maintained	71	5	5	10	5.4	0.4
Catholic primary	62	10	6	7	10	0.4
National primary	69	6	6	11	6	0.4
Catholic secondary	66	7	5	7	9	2.4
National secondary	73	4	4	10	5	0.42
Catholic tertiary	52	3	5	13	18	1

How is it, one might ask, that such evidence is neglected in critical reports such as that of the British Humanist Report (BHA, 2016), *Ethnic Diversity in Religious Free Schools*? The cause would seem to be that such reports lump all 'white' pupils together in their claim that Catholic schools are not ethnically diverse, ignoring the large number of Eastern Europeans in Catholic schools. The CES survey, to the contrary, uniquely examines the religious make-up of the pupils, thereby revealing a different picture of diversity. And that different picture should not be surprising. Regarding the contribution that Catholic schools make supporting ethnic minority pupils, it is worth quoting one claim (source unknown):

> Historically, the Catholic Church has largely been a church of migrants and the disadvantaged. They had to climb their way into English society through education. Also, there's a memory of when Catholics were marginalised in this country. So, they have a strong focus on helping the poor and the outsider.

However, one should not equate 'ethnic minority' with 'immigrants' or 'poverty'. Many of the early immigrants have integrated, and, having benefited from their education in the Catholic schools, are now highly educated and skilled – no doubt, thereby, affecting the *social* composition of those schools which admit a majority of 'ethnic minority pupils'.

Socially selective

The accusation of social selectivity is to be taken more seriously.

A Sutton Trust Research Brief (Allen and Parameshwaren, 2016), *Caught Out,* argued that most socially selective primary schools were likely to be Faith schools using oversubscription criteria (that is, when there are more applicants than there are school places) to select disproportionately better-off pupils. Thus, in over 1,000 primary Faith schools, it claimed that the proportion taking FSM (which is one popular criterion of disadvantage) is over 10% lower than that found in the neighbourhood from which they recruit, thereby leaving the Faith School population unrepresentative of the surrounding area. Furthermore, such socially selective primary schools are more likely to be found in London and other urban areas – often schools with a religious character that are said to have chosen to apply religious oversubscription criteria. Their intakes would be different from those of neighbouring schools. The evidence is that, whereas of the 7,504 primary Community schools only 6% are judged to be socially selective (that is, untypical of their catchment area), this would not seem so with Catholic or Church of England schools. For example, in terms of intake, the percentages of primary schools, which have a distorted intake untypical of the catchment area, are said to be as follows:

Catholic	Academy converted	196 schools	37%
	Academy sponsored	18 schools	56%
	Voluntary aided	1413 schools	32%
Church of England	Foundation	30 schools	23%
	Academy converted	277 schools	10%
	Academy sponsored	109 schools	9%
	Voluntary controlled	2075 schools	6%
	Voluntary aided	1728 schools	11%

The BHA, in its 'Fair Admissions' campaign (BHA, 2014), claims to have revealed how a large number of cases of selective state schools (particularly the voluntary aided) are breaking the law on admissions. Thus, according to Andrew Copley, chief executive of the BHA,

> We have been aware for some time … that the system by which schools religiously select their pupils is not fit for purpose. And while it is far from the case that every religiously selective school in this country is cynically manipulating the system or willfully ignoring the code in order to enhance

42 Context

> their intake, the level of non-compliance that we found indicates that such manipulation is certainly taking place in far too many schools.
>
> *(BHA, 2014, p.9)*

As stated above, there is a need here and elsewhere, in weighing the evidence for and against such claims, to be careful of the language used. It could be the case (but see '*in response*' below) that there is a lower proportion of less well-off children in Faith schools of whatever kind, without that being the result of 'cynical manipulation' or 'willfully ignoring the code'. Rather it could be due to the admission of pupils, not only from the neighbourhood, but also from the wider Catholic community, which sees the Catholic school as its neighbourhood school and to whose building cost that community has contributed. Faith-based admission might have the *effect* of skewing the socio-economic composition of voluntary aided schools, but that does not constitute evidence of malpractice.

The critique of religiously affiliated schools, particularly Catholic ones, continues. The Education Policy Institute (Johnes and Andrews, 2016) indicates that Faith schools take a lower proportion of the poorest children than other schools – only 12.1% of their pupils are on FSMs compared with 18% in the non-faith schools. Thus, small gains in attainment could come 'at the price of increased social segregation, with a risk of lower social mobility'. A further report into the proposals to rescind the 50% cap on faith-based admissions in over-subscribed schools argued that rescinding the cap would risk a reduction in social mobility. Indeed, it was argued, performance advantage of some Faith schools 'falls away when you look at their intake and the prior attainment of their pupils'. Such pupils were less likely to be from disadvantaged backgrounds than pupils at other schools.

Finally, these criticisms seem to be confirmed by a more recent report from the Sutton Trust on the 500 top comprehensive schools. Faith Schools are over-represented in these top 500 schools, but would seem to be the most socially selective (Cullinane *et al.*, 2017)

In response to these highly critical data, one needs to note:

First, contrary evidence comes from the Government's *Income Deprivation Affecting Children Index* (IDACI), which measures the level of disadvantage experienced by children aged 4–16. IDACI takes account of income deprivation in areas where children live. These are relatively small areas (about 1,000 dwellings). IDACI charts the proportions of pupils coming from the most deprived 10% of such areas, the next most deprived areas, and so on. It would seem to provide a more in-depth and nuanced community picture than FSM data, because it covers the whole population accurately, whereas FSM statistics only catch families on benefit. According to IDACI, in the most deprived 10% areas, Catholic primary schools cater for 18% of the children, compared with 14% in primary schools nationally, and the Catholic secondary schools cater for 17% of the students, compared with 12% in secondary schools nationally. As one moves to the next decile, the pattern is repeated – the

Catholic primary schools taking 14% (compared with 14.5% nationally) and the Catholic secondary schools taking 14%, compared with 11% nationally.

However, doubt has been expressed (see in particular Harris, 2017) about the value of the IDACI data on the grounds that, though referring to pupils from these closely defined geographical areas, the overall numbers in the Catholic schools are enhanced by those coming from outside the area, seeking admission to their nearest Catholic school (which for them is *their* 'community school') and who would not be socially disadvantaged. (The catchment area of a Catholic school is up to 10 times larger than the local neighbourhood school.) Therefore, it would be wrong to conclude that Catholic schools (the voluntary aided schools, on which there is clear data) are not taking their share of pupils in the most deprived areas. Rather, is it a matter of those schools taking students *also* from outside those areas as they, as Catholics, seek education within the school which is appropriate for their wider Catholic community. Indeed, paradoxically, by taking their share of the pupils from the most deprived areas and students from beyond those areas they may be supporting greater social cohesion. Furthermore, it does not necessarily follow from Catholic primary schools catering for a greater proportion of 'children from disadvantaged areas' that this entails a greater proportion of 'disadvantaged children', since not all children in disadvantaged areas are themselves disadvantaged children. Hence, back to the 'health warning', there is a need to be careful in interpreting the statistics. Furthermore, the Theos Report (Oldfield *et al.*, 2013), which has examined the different statistics, concluded otherwise, namely, that the evidence reviewed suggests there is little reason to think that Faith schools are more socially divisive than Community schools in reflecting the multi-cultural make-up of English communities and in promoting cohesion.

Second (in response to the criticism that a lower proportion of pupils in Faith schools are in receipt of FSMs), one explanation is that the figures quoted refer to those who actually take FSMs, not to the larger number who are 'eligible' but do not submit claims. It is argued on the basis of recent research (Bullivant , 2016, p.10), which itself refers to wider research studies, that, in areas served by Catholic schools, there are many, especially from ethnic communities, who are eligible for FSMs but who do not claim for various reasons including cultural. Pilot research in an area of considerable ethnic and cultural diversity, and focusing on 20 schools in the lowest two deciles of the IDACI index, reported from the head teachers that

> Cultural perception of welfare combined with language barriers and a poor understanding of the process of Free School Meals [were] most common as inhibiting FSM take-up among ethnic minority families.
>
> *(CES unpublished report, quoted in Bullivant, op. cit.)*

Furthermore, the work of Sahotah *et al.*, 2013, indicates that cultural and other factors may inhibit FSM take-up amongst certain groups who are disproportionately represented within certain ethnic minorities. Parental illiteracy or ignorance are frequently barriers to understanding the right to FSM or to completing the forms

44 Context

– a matter of some significance where those schools have (as indicated) a larger proportion of ethnic minority pupils. Such cautioning against reliance on FSMs as the measure of poverty was emphasized by Hobbs and Vignoles (2017), its status being seen as an 'imperfect proxy of low income or workless families, or one-parenthood'.

However, the inadequacy of the FSM measures, if they are accepted as such, may equally apply across all schools, and is not confined to the Faith schools. Moreover, it is surprising that, since FSMs attract extra funding for the respective schools (over £1,300 per year for primary pupils), the schools are not helping parents to complete the relevant forms.

Third, as Grace (2009) argued in response to the earlier research by Allen and West (2009), which compared characteristics of pupils at religious and secular schools in London, contrary evidence is provided by his research (Grace, 2002, pp.241–242) on 28 Catholic secondary schools in London which showed an average FSM entitlement of 37%. Nonetheless, acknowledgement is given to the strong possibility that, in the 10 'elite' Faith schools (five Catholic and five Church of England) within this London survey, covert selection did occur through pupil and parent interviewing procedures adopted.

Special educational needs

Amongst its many reports on 'how religiously selective schools have been found to break the admissions code', the Accord Coalition's analysis of the Department of Education (DfE) statistics reveals that, for every five pupils with a Special Educational Needs (SEN) statement, non-faith schools admit 1.44 whereas Church of England admit 1.23, and Roman Catholic 1.22.

In response:

Whatever the figures, it does not follow that the religiously affiliated schools 'have been found to break the admissions code' because the schools must and do accept all statemented children if the Local Authority believes the Faith schools are the best and most appropriate for the child's needs. Such is the requirement of the Office for Schools Admission (OSA) schools admissions code: Statutory Guidance for Admission Authorities, 2014.

Games people (and schools) play

There is a further accusation that many Faith schools (both voluntary aided and voluntary controlled together) are tempted to permit 'game-playing'. For instance, ITV's *Tonight* programme, entitled 'How to Get into a Good School', commissioned a poll in 2015 of 1,000 parents with primary school aged pupils. The poll revealed:

- 12.6% had pretended to practise a faith in which they did not believe;
- 23.7% said they would if they had to do so;

- 13% had their child baptised purely to gain a school place;
- 11% had pretended their child had been baptised.

In response:

This is a serious accusation, although its interpretation is rendered difficult by the lumping together of the different kinds of Faith schools. The large majority of Faith schools are voluntary controlled, not voluntary aided. Nonetheless, certainly in the case of the 'elite schools', as defined by Allen and West, the use of interviews in oversubscribed schools would open up the possibility of such 'game playing', and would need to be taken into account in the tightening up of admission regulations.

Conclusion

To what extent, therefore, do Faith schools contribute to the divisiveness of society on ethnic, social and religious grounds?

First, with regard to the provision for those pupils from the ethnic minorities, the accusation is clearly mistaken. One should note that in Catholic schools, over 30% are not Catholic, 37% of pupils are from ethnic minority backgrounds (7% more than the national average), and 17% are from the most disadvantaged households, 5% more than the national average (as reported in *The Tablet*, February 2016).

Second, with regard to Faith schools' failing to admit equally those from the poor and disadvantaged families, reference to the IDACI data would suggest a different conclusion. Catholic schools in the most deprived areas may indeed have a greater proportion of better off families, but that could be explained by the wider recruitment whilst still taking their fair share of children from the disadvantaged neighbourhood. The catchment area of the Catholic school would be much wider in many cases than that of the local community school. The IDACI data would not seem to make possible such detailed analysis. Moreover, Catholic schools in urban areas were established particularly in the late 19th century and early 20th to provide the needs of immigrant populations who were mainly Catholic and poor, and such schools continue to provide for subsequent groups of immigrants, including many Muslims who, in some cases, would prefer schools with a religious ethos rather than none.

One must, of course, beware the 'health warnings' given, and thus be cautious of statistics which deal only with averages, and which are liable to disguise wide variations, regional differences, and contrasts between urban, suburban, and rural areas. But no doubt some Faith schools are failing in their duty both to be open to those in need and to provide an education for those in their neighbourhood who otherwise would have to travel further afield to find a school place. Indeed, there could be tensions between the declared purposes of the Catholic schools, namely, to educate Catholic pupils whilst at the same time serving the poor and the marginalised – the two purposes once closely linked, but now no longer the case. But the majority would seem to take seriously their mission to serve those with special needs, immigrants and asylum seekers.

46 Context

There may well be 'game-playing' in some instances, providing fuel for those who wish to see the end of Faith schools within the state system. It is important, therefore, for all schools to clarify and to enforce the published admissions policies, which (as far as the educational mission of the Catholic Church is concerned – see Chapters 8 and 9) would make explicit openness to those in the neighbourhood who would otherwise be disadvantaged.

The responses to the critics of Faith Schools seemed to convince Nicky Morgan, when Secretary of State, that the operation of Faith schools was not a cause of unfair discrimination or social segregation. Complaints, referred to as 'vexatious', came mainly from lobby groups, particularly the British Humanist Society, not from the parents.

Recommendations

Admission policies should, therefore, embody the following principles:

- All Faith schools should consider the impact of their oversubscription criteria on pupil-premium children and those with special needs, and prioritise them in their admissions (irrespective of religious affiliation or none). Both Anglican and Catholic voluntary schools should remember that a declared aim of their respective Churches is 'to serve the poor'.
- Where there are cases when the Faith School is the only local school (such that failure to be admitted would mean pupils travelling to a distant school or separation from friends), the school should admit such pupils irrespective of their faith or none.
- The trustees of the Faith schools should be vigilant about the ways in which some parents, a little cynically maybe, take steps to gain admission to popular Catholic schools – for example, through late baptisms.
- Given that 30% of pupils in Catholic schools are non-Catholic (perhaps many having no religious affiliation), there is need for the school to make arrangements for such pupils to have their own religious worship and instruction, albeit as much as possible within a shared spiritual ethos.
- Each Faith School's Admissions Code (bearing in mind service to the respective faith communities which they were established to serve) should be clear, properly enforced, with complaints procedures transparent to the local community.
- There are instances where voluntary aided schools admit a cohort of students that does not reflect the social disadvantages of its area. They should heed the word of the first synod of the Province of Westminster in 1850:

  'the first necessity … is a sufficient provision of education adequate to the wants of our poor'.

  Or indeed of Vatican II's declaration on education, which urged Catholic schools

  to especially care for the poor, those who are without support and affection of a family, and those who do not have the gift of faith.

- It is the duty of the trustees to ensure their schools are serving their faith communities (which often stretch beyond their immediate neighbourhood), whilst at the same time making contribution to the poor and disadvantaged, irrespective of faith or none, within the local community. In so doing, they must guard against the temptation, affecting many schools, to manipulate the intake in response to pressure to demonstrate 'effectiveness'.
- There is a need to review, as objectively as possible, not only the accuracy of the statistical data, but much more the different interpretations given to them – in, for example, the different significances attached to the take-up of FSMs.

References

Allen, R. and Parameshwaren, M., 2016, *Caught Out: Primary Schools, Catchment Areas and Social Selection*, Report for the Sutton Trust, London: Millbank Tower.

Allen, R. and West, A., 2009, 'Religious schools in London: school admissions, religious composition and selectivity', *Oxford Review of Education*, 35(4).

BHA, 2001, *Religious Schools: The Case Against*, London: Humanities UK.

BHA, 2014, *An Unholy Mess*, London: BHA.

BHA, 2016, *Ethnic Diversity in Religious Free Schools*, London: Humanities UK.

Bullivant, S., 2016, *The Take-up of Free School Meals in Catholic Schools in England and Wales*, Twickenham: St Mary's University.

Butler-Sloss Report, 2015, *Living with Difference*, Report of the Commission on Religion and Belief in Public Life, Cambridge: Woolf Institute.

Casey Review, 2016, *A Review into Opportunity and Integration*, Dept. for Communities and Local Government, London: HMSO.

Catholic Education Service, November 2015, *Census Data for Schools and Colleges in England*, London: CES.

Cullinane, C., Andrade, J., Hillary, J., McNamara, S., 2017, *Selective Comprehensives*, Sutton Trust, London: Millbank.

Grace, G., 2002, *Catholic Schools: Mission, Markets and Morality*, London: Routledge.

Grace, G., 2009, 'Reflections on Allen and West's paper: Religious Schools in London: school admissions, religious composition and selectivity', *Oxford Review of Education*, 35(4).

Harris, J., 2017, *Commentary on 'The Take-up of Free School Meals in Catholic Schools in England and Wales'*, Unpublished Paper, given at Heythrop College, London.

Hobbs, G. and Vignoles, A., 2017, *Is Free School Meal Status a Valid Proxy for Socio-economic Status in Schools Research?* London: Centre for the Economics of Education, London School of Economics.

Johnes, R. and Andrews, J., 2016, *Faith Schools, Pupil Performance and Social Selection*, London: Education Policy Unit

Oldfield, E., Harnett, L., and Bailey, E., 2013, *More than an Educational Guess: Assessing the evidence in Faith Schools*, London: Theos.

Sahota, P., Woodward, J., Molnari, P., and Pike, J., 2014, 'Factors influencing take-up of free school meals in primary and secondary school children in England', *Public Health Nutrition*, 17(6).

Woodhead, L. and Clarke, C., 2015, *A New settlement: religion and belief in schools*, Westminster Faith Debates.

4

INTERNATIONAL PERSPECTIVE

Introduction

Many of the issues raised so far (and the arguments still to be pursued), although in the context of England and Wales, are both historically and currently similar to those raised elsewhere. But the very different responses which have emerged owe much to the different histories of these countries. In most cases, the origins of the state systems lay in the provision of education to the poor by religious orders and movements. Subsequent developments reflect, first, different political views about the relation of the state's responsibility for educational provision and for the curriculum, and, second, the status (if any) of Faith schools within the state system.

Therefore, with the increased concern of governments to ensure education for all, there inevitably arose questions about the relation of the state to the religious providers of education and indeed to the communities where parents sent their children to school.

That was the case, as we have seen the in 19th century England, and indeed remains an issue to this day. The present-day political aspiration that all schools should become academies, and thereby contracted directly to the Secretary of State (no longer, therefore, locally accountable) is yet the next move in shaping the relation of the state to the local school system, including the religious affiliated schools.

What follows shows how a few different countries, especially those within the United Kingdom, have addressed these problems, namely, the wishes of the different communities to have their own Faith schools, the problems emerging for those 'not of the Faith' for whom the Faith school is their local one, and the right of the state to shape the culture and the curriculum of all schools irrespective of the religious provenance of the particular school.

Northern Ireland and 'Integrated schools'

Ireland was partitioned in 1921, leaving the North a bitterly divided country of majority Protestants and minority Catholics. The 1923 Education Act sought to ameliorate the situation by providing for non-denominational County or 'controlled' schools. But the Protestant influence on the controlled schools remained dominant (see Nelson, 2004). The government succumbed to pressure from the Catholic Church to preserve control over their own schools, which, though state maintained, were to be administered via the Council for Catholic Maintained schools. Hence, there developed a dual system, with 91% of Protestant primary children attending controlled (mainly Protestant) schools and 88% of Catholic children attending Catholic maintained primary schools. Similar figures occur post-primary. Thus, the Catholics were able to maintain their distinctive cultural and religious identity, wherein, according to Gallagher (2005, p.158), in an aptly entitled book, *Faith Schools: consensus or conflict?*

> there was little or no organised contact between pupils in the separate schools and little evident enthusiasm for initiatives in this area … there was little evidence that contact between the teachers from the separate schools provided opportunities for them to explore issues related to social division or conflict or the role schools might play in contributing towards an amelioration of the conflict.

Northern Ireland, therefore, may seem to be a good example of the faults in separate Faith schools, but it is not clear that those faults, as with the context, can be generalised. The society was violently antagonistic, and the Catholics could see their own distinctive culture and identity as being threatened by a controlled school system dominated by the Protestant faith.

However, in 1981 the first 'Integrated school', Lagan College, opened. By 1989, there were 11 such schools mainly due to the initiative of parents. These were joint attempts by Catholics and Protestants to provide (or to transform) schools which would welcome pupils from both religious traditions and from none (see Moffat, 1993, p.164). The Education Reform (NI) Order 1989 was made 'to encourage and facilitate the development of integrated education', helped by statutory funding. Currently, there are over 60 grant-aided integrated schools, catering for about 7% of total pupils in Northern Ireland. Such schools are Christian schools which provide an opportunity for Catholic and Protestant children to be educated together, gaining respect for the respective beliefs and cultures.

There will be many critics who point to the existence of Faith schools as being partly responsible for the lack of social cohesion, indeed, for the very antagonistic relationships between the two communities. But, as Gallagher (2005, p.164) concludes,

> to suggest that the problem was caused simply because of separate schools, or could be cured by the removal of separate schools, seems to oversimplify the situation.

50 Context

This would be supported by John Greer's earlier large-scale survey of 2,000 pupils in 19 secondary schools (9 Catholic and 10 Protestant) which indicated that

> throughout the age range for both sexes and both denominational groups there was a positive relationship between attitudes towards religion and openness. The young people most favourably disposed towards religion were also most open to members of the other religious groups. This is an important finding, contradicting the notion that in Northern Ireland religiosity increases closedness to 'the other side'.
>
> *(Greer, 1993, p.458)*

Indeed, this is supported by government initiatives. Northern Ireland's Sharing Education Programme enables schools of different faiths to ensure that children from different backgrounds have the opportunity to mix. The National Citizen Service promotes a scheme in which 16–17-year-olds from different backgrounds work on joint community projects. Could these be useful examples for divided communities in England?

Addendum on the teaching of religious education

The Education Act (Northern Ireland) 1947 stipulated that the curriculum in state schools should be based on Holy Scripture but to 'exclude instruction as to any tenet which is distinctive of any particular denomination' (Armstrong, 2012, p.24). This, however, could create concern from the religious bodies. In 2008, the General Assembly of the Presbyterian Church in Ireland expressed the fears of the Protestant Churches that, with the emphasis on being more inclusive within the teaching of religious education (RE), 'their contribution and rights ... far from being respected and protected, are in fact being undervalued and ... systematically eroded' (quoted in Armstrong, 2012, p.35). The Catholic schools, however, were not enticed by such ecumenical intentions. Their programmes of religious studies would include preparation for the sacraments of Confession, Communion, and Confirmation. 'Formation as Christians' remained an essential aim.

Scotland and maintaining the Faith schools

By 2012, according to McKinney (2012), of the 2,708 schools in Scotland, 384 were Catholic (53 are secondary). There was also a small number of other religiously affiliated schools, including Jewish, and no doubt an increasing demand for them because of changing ethnic and religious landscape especially in cities like Glasgow (Mckinney, 2012, p.40). But there is a deeply rooted history as to how the present situation has developed.

After the Reformation 'Burgh schools' became the messengers of the Protestant faith. The Reformation project was highly successful in Scotland – working through the Burgh schools. But, as in England, the position changed, especially, in the second decade of 19th century when Irish immigration affected the population. The Catholic Schools Society was established in 1817 in Glasgow, and there was then a development of Catholic schools providing a very basic education, especially in Glasgow, helped by the further establishment of the Catholic Poor Schools Committee.

The parallels with England continued. The 1870 Forster Act in England, which established the school boards, was followed by the 1872 Education (Scotland) Act, which offered the opportunity for Catholic schools to join the school boards, thereby becoming eligible for grants. But the Catholic schools resisted the offer of becoming part of the local board schools, despite their poverty. They were, however, still able to benefit from government grants, and between 1872 and 1918 the number of Catholic schools in receipt of grants rose from 65 to 224.

It was the 1918 Education (Scotland) Act which enabled the aspirations of the (by then) 224 Catholic schools to be realised as they were established on equal terms with board Schools. In effect, they became state schools, losing control over curriculum and management, except for statutory power to approve teachers as to their religious beliefs and character and to appoint supervisors of RE. They were now part of a national system. But there was opposition from many that Catholic schools should not be paid for via the rates. And senior academics and politicians claimed that Catholic schools were, by virtue of their very existence, either unjust (staff who are not Catholic are denied promotion, etc.) or sectarian and thereby socially divisive.

There would seem to have been another sort of opposition growing, relevant to the concerns raised in this book. The report of the Scottish Education Department in 1947, *Secondary Education,* argued for a 'common school', not a system of schools based on religious affiliation, since that was most appropriate for a democratic society. And, as MacKenzie (1999, p.251) commented, in the pursuit of a common culture,

> the comprehensive school would be the mechanism for weakening social class and ethnic barriers in pursuit both of equality of opportunity and social equality.

However, the subsequent requirement of Local Authorities in 1965 to reorganise secondary schools along comprehensive lines did not apply the idea of the common school across the religious and secular divides, even though that was seen by many to be 'in the logic of the comprehensive ideal'.

Nonetheless, that 'logic' remained in the minds of many. As Mackenzie (op. cit. p.252) observes:

> Let there be no doubt, integration has re-entered Scottish political discourse. It is likely to remain in that discourse. It has been given added point by what is probably the most important development of all in Scottish education since the war: the decline in population,

52 Context

and thereby the creation of surplus capacity and the need to amalgamate schools across the religious and secular divide. However, Jones (1992) gives a detailed account of the determination of the Catholic Church not to permit amalgamation of its schools in Glasgow with non-denominational schools, even when that would make economic sense.

Walter Hume (2015, p.134), sums up the present situation by pointing to examples of campuses shared between denominational and non-denominational schools, but, as he concludes:

> these have generally been accompanied by a degree of controversy. At present, it is highly unlikely that any political party would risk the electoral consequences of making a purely secular system part of the its manifesto.

Addendum on the teaching of RE

The comprehensive review of the curriculum in the 2010 report *Curriculum for Excellence* confirmed RE as an essential component in the curriculum of all schools. Nonetheless, there remains a difference of approach and emphasis between the non-denominational schools and the Faith schools, particularly the Catholic, the direction of which was embodied within the 1994 publication, '5–14 Religious Education (Roman Catholic Schools)'. The guidelines included 'a greater focus on sacraments and liturgy, and personal search was understood to be within the context of Catholic Christianity for Catholic pupils' (McKinney, 2012, p.42).

Ireland and Catholic dominance

The dominant religion in Ireland has been Catholicism, and the Catholic Church has traditionally been responsible for providing the schools, although supported by government funding. Indeed, almost 95% of primary schools are Faith schools and 90% of these are under the trusteeship of the local Catholic diocese or the religious orders. However, of the approximately 740 post-primary schools, just over 50% are not under the trusteeship of the Catholic Church and its religious orders. The pressures to retain the Catholic faith dominance by powerful lobbies is reflected in the criticism by Professor Conway (of St Mary Immaculate College, University of Limerick) of government plans to introduce a new programme on religion, belief, and ethics, which would require denominational schools to teach a secularist understanding of religious faith.

Recently, therefore, Ireland has become an interesting example of the challenge from secularist forces to the dominance of Faith schools, from the decline in the religious orders, which had been responsible for so many of the schools, and from the failure of the Church leadership (according to Sean O'Connell writing in *The Furrow*, 'to confront the challenges of faith formation in what is now a post-Christian society').

In 1990, 81% of those identifying themselves as Catholic attended Mass at least once weekly. By 2006 it was 48%, by 2011 only 14% in the Dublin area. A rising number of young people around Dublin identified themselves as having no religion (*The Tablet*, 13.1.17).

Therefore, although historically a Catholic country, Ireland has become a more secular society. It has seen social and demographic changes which threaten this dominance of the Church over school admissions, especially in the primary age range, and, at secondary level, the nature of religious education and formation.

With reference to the primary level, there has been concern over the numbers of immigrants and non-Catholics that fail to get admission to their local school. It was reported, for instance, that

> hundreds of people have taken part in a protest in Dublin calling on the Government to strip the Church of its right to prioritise Catholics in its allocation of school place.
>
> *(The Tablet, 30.10.15)*

They were seeking a repeal of the Act which allows schools to operate the 'Catholics First Policy'. There were seen to be problems for minority religions, or of those of no religion, of getting their children into a Catholic school, even though there are few or no other choices in the vicinity – what has been referred to as the 'baptism barrier'. There is a call from voluntary human rights organisations (for example Equate) for an end to religious discrimination in state-funded schools. That is seen to create inequality both in access to school places and in respect for those of different beliefs. There are calls to remove Section 7(3)(c) of the Equal Status Act (2002), which permits schools to discriminate in their schools' policy. It calls, too, for the removal of Rule 68 of the 1965 *Rules for National Schools*, which imposes the 'integrated curriculum' imbued with religious values and which makes the refusal to attend religious instruction impossible.

Hence, the Education and Training Boards of Ireland met in September 2016 to consider the principles on which a system of public education might be based. How to reconcile effective planning nationally and locally with parental choice?

The Minister for Education and Skills, Richard Bruton, started a consultation 'on the role of denominational religion in the schools' admission process and possible approaches for making changes'. In a speech on 16 January 2017, he declared:

> It is unfair that a non-religious family or a family of different religion, living close to their local publicly-funded school, finds that preference is given to children of the same religion as the school [though] living some distance away. … It is unfair that parents, who might otherwise not do so, feel pressure to baptise their children in order to gain admission to the local school.

The Minister stated his intention to make changes first in the primary system where the problems are most acutely felt by families. Possibilities being considered (which may be of interest further afield) are:

54 Context

- *Catchment areas*: prohibiting religious schools from giving preference to children of their own religion, who live outside the catchment area, ahead of children not of that faith, who live inside the catchment area.
- *Nearest school rule*: this would allow faith-based schools to give preference to a child from a religious family only where it is that child's nearest school of that particular religion.
- *Quota system*: allowing a faith-based school to base admissions on religious affiliation in respect of only a certain proportion of places, the remaining places being allocated on other criteria (e.g. proximity to the school).
- *Outright prohibition*: thereby repealing all or key sections of the 2002 Equal Status Act.

Meanwhile, there has been created a new model of multi-denominational schools, namely, Community National Schools (CNS) – 11 at the time of writing but with more due to open. They aim to provide an inclusive education to all children, irrespective of religious belief. They offer a general religious education plus the opportunity for pupils of different faiths to separate also into their different faith groups for their distinctive faith formation.

Addendum on the teaching of RE

At the post-primary level, the 1998 Education Act relocated RE into the mainstream curriculum, with syllabuses agreed by the National Curriculum Council Agency (NCCA) for the Junior certificate in 2000 and for the Leaving Certificate in 2003, thereby placing RE in the public rather than the ecclesial sphere. By becoming an examination subject, RE attained greater status than had previously been the case. But inevitably it transformed the subject from one of personal formation into a more academic mould – teaching about religions. There was less opportunity for pupils to address the more spiritual, moral, and personal dimensions normally associated with RE.

As Carmody (2017) put it:

> It confronts the RE teacher with the dilemma of striving to find faith expression that respects traditional forms of religion including that of Catholicism while at the same time enabling the religiously diverse believer to face the situation of choosing to address the spiritual dimension of his or her life freely and responsibly.

France and the secular victory

In late 18th-century revolutionary France, there were edicts on universal free education, but without adequate arrangements for raising the money and ensuring it was spent on schools. A full national system was not established until 1833, with each commune obliged to pay for the upkeep through local rates. Nonetheless, well in advance of Britain, France showed its belief in funding universal free education, much influenced by the post-revolutionary commitment to egalitarianism but also to the pre-revolutionary 'enlightenment' ideas. The educational aim became that of forming the good citizens and unifying the nation around the values of liberty, equality and fraternity.

By 1869 the school population was about 4 million.

Despite, however, the secular aspirations of post-revolutionary France, about 70% of the girls' schools were run by religious orders and 10% of the boys' schools (Peterson, 1971, p.18). But the secular aspirations were strong. There was pressure from Prime Minister Guizot (as referred to in Chapter 2) to establish a secular education system, where religious instruction would be left to the religious bodies. With the onset of the Third Republic in 1870, there followed a period of bitter religious conflict. The ultimate solution was the establishment in 1881/2 of free secular ('*laique*') education with compulsory school attendance. It was still possible to have denominational schools, but with no financial assistance from the state. Later, in 1904, the religious teaching orders were suppressed. Teaching of religion was a matter for the family, not for the state. This strong secular arrangement has been roughly preserved in France, although in 1960 Catholic schools were enabled to enter into a contract with the state for financial funding so long as they conformed to national teaching programmes and examinations. Today, approximately 20% of pupils attend such private, though publicly subsidised, schools.

Therefore, the French education reflected the complete separation of Church and state in public policies and practice ('*laicite*'), as established in 1905, namely, (i) freedom of conscience, (ii) strict separation of religion from the state, and (iii) freedom to exercise any faith.

Consequently, it was seen to be important to establish a moral education in Republican values, replacing that of the Catholic Church. Such a moral education was developed at length by the sociologist, Emile Durkheim, in *Moral Education,* as explained later in Chapter 9 of this book. Indeed, in 2015, public school students at every level began a course in '*laicite* ethics', which included pursuit of liberty, equality, fraternity, rule of law in a democratic society, and anti-discrimination. This was supported by a number (150) of philosophical texts. Key to this aspiration was the role of the teacher, 'the Republic incarnate', bringing the secular ideal to life (Valland-Belkacen, 2015, p.17).

However, such a thoroughly secular ideal required the banning of head scarves in state schools in 2004 (as indeed 'all conspicuous religious symbols'), and the banning of the burqa in public places in 2010. This has inevitably created problems in schools where, for example, 75% of the pupils are Muslim, for whom such items of dress are important to their cultural and religious identity. To what extent does the secular ideal require the removal of every religious symbol in the pursuit of '*laicite*', where such symbols (e.g. mode of dress) are important for cultural identity in a situation which could not be foreseen when the Republican ideals were first formulated? But there remains the problem of integrating a growing Muslim population of 5 million.

56 Context

The United States and the common school

Between 1820 and 1920 over 33 million immigrants arrived in the United States, a large proportion, if not a majority, of them Catholics. This transformed cities like New York, where the population had risen from from120,000 in 1820 to 300,000 by 1840. About one half of the population had been born abroad and of these a half was Irish and Catholic. What had been a mainly Protestant country had become religiously divided, with harsh feelings towards the Catholic incomers. For example, in Philadelphia in 1844, riots were provoked by the concession that the Catholic Douai version of the Bible could be read in schools (Judge, 2001, p.64).

In the face of such a new and diverse population, not only of immigrants but also of those moving from rural communities into the cities, it was strongly argued for the need of 'the Common School' within the public education system. As Horace Mann declared:

> The common school is the greatest discovery ever made by man. In two grand, characteristic attributes, it is super-eminent over all others: first, in its universality, for it is capacious enough to receive and cherish in its parental bosom every child that comes into the world; and second, in the timeliness of the aid it proffers – its early, seasonable supplies of counsel and guidance making security antedate danger.
>
> *(quoted in Cremin, 1957, p.137)*

As with John Dewey at a later date, Mann was arguing for a common education in which, out of the cultural differences, a sense of common citizenship would arise, and civic virtues developed. As in the English compromise of the 19th century, there would be a Christian ethos, but one which transcended doctrinal differences, for it was the ethical ethos of religion which would be needed to underpin the virtues of citizenship and to overcome the sectarian rivalry.

But that sectarian rivalry remained strong, and there was an understandable and justified suspicion amongst the Catholics that the public school and its religious ethos, far from 'transcending doctrinal difference', would promote Protestantism. The Catholic Church, therefore, was keen to develop its own schools, not participating in the developing 'Common School'. The new and first Archbishop of New York, John Hughes, was determined to provide a place in a Catholic school for every Catholic child, and therefore, as in England, urged the parishes 'to build the school-house first and the church afterwards' (Judge, 2001, p.65).

However, many of these Catholic parishes, together with their schools, were essentially ethnically distinguished, as the immigrants from different countries lived within their national communities, preserving their distinctive cultures and languages, and thereby undermining (not only by religious affiliation but also by their cultural inheritance) the ideals of the 'common school'.

Unlike in England and Wales, there was no room for state support for schools which sought to preserve their religion-based independence. Hence, the Catholic parochial schools, concentrated much in the poorer urban areas, had to find the money for capital expenditure, teachers' salaries and running costs. It was a magnificent achievement. According to the 1916 Census report, in the United States there were over 200 colleges for boys with about 50,000 students, nearly 700 academies for girls with almost 100,000 students, and nearly 6,000 parochial schools with an attendance of over 1.5 million children (Judge, 2001, p.68).

This separation of the state (or states within the Federal system) from Church in the provision of public services, such that the preservation of Church schools could not be in receipt of public funding, was maintained and, when challenged, referred to the continuing interpretation of the First Amendment of the Constitution as that was declared in the 1791, which guaranteed religious freedom through the separation of the state from religion ('Congress shall make no law respecting an establishment of religion or prohibiting the free exercise thereof'). There were minor concessions, though much opposed, namely, in the granting of public aid to parents' expenses in the transport of their children to Catholic schools. But the opposition continued, as reflected in a popular book in 1948, entitled *American Freedom and Catholic Power*, which referred to the Catholic schools as

> a system of segregated schools under costumed religious teachers [and that] the struggle between American democracy and the Catholic hierarchy depends upon the survival and expansion of the public school.
>
> *(quoted in Ravitch, 1973, p.32)*

At the same time, the public schools were becoming more secularised. In 1963, Bible reading and the recitation of the Lord's Prayer were declared to be unconstitutional within the public-school system. Therein, however, lies an interesting twist in the narrative. The public-school system, which initially reflected a Protestant ethos, was becoming quite explicitly secular, as religion became excluded in different ways from the spirit and content of the school. A specific case was inevitably the teaching of evolution. This provoked the increasing opposition of the Evangelical Christians who, therefore, developed their own private schools, in which, for example, creationism not evolution, could be taught. There was increased concern that an anti-religious form of secularism was permeating the public-school system. Indeed, even Cardinal Spellman was outraged at what was happening in the public system despite that system having no place for Catholics.

> I am shocked and frightened that the Supreme Court has declared unconstitutional a simple and voluntary declaration of belief in God by public school children. The decision strikes at the heart of the Godly tradition in which America's children have for so long been raised.
>
> *(quoted in Judge, 2001, p.127)*

Others were 'joining' the Catholic Church in challenging the rigid separation of state and religion in the shaping of education.

58 Context

Certainly the 'wall' between state funding and Church financial responsibility for its schools came to be breached in several, often small, ways such as the payment of transport costs and subsidies to instruction. The Elementary and Secondary Education Act of 1965 aimed at the reduction of poverty through the schools and supported endeavours (including those in the Catholic schools) which provided support for the disadvantaged – even to the extent in some states of subsidising teaching of 'secular subjects'. And the introduction of vouchers to 'buy education' in private (therefore Catholic) schools was much debated under various Presidencies in the 1960s and 1970s, though ultimately defeated.

Therefore, the separation of state and religious interests (now strongly endorsed by the Evangelical Christians) was continually, and remains, upheld.

However, it should be noted that, as the inner-city population of immigrants became established and more prosperous, so they moved from the urban centres, with fresh waves of poor immigrants replacing them. Though largely black and non-Catholic, Catholic schools in such locations continued to serve the local community working on the principle expounded by the Second Vatican Council, namely:

> First and foremost, the Church offers its educational services to the poor, or those who are deprived of family help and affection, or those who are far from the faith.
>
> *(Congregation for Catholic Education, 1977, para. 58)*

But without government money and with the decline in religious orders which subsidised these services, those schools are having to close, removing, therefore, a most valuable social service.

Hence, the principle at stake is whether US support for Faith schools, which are open to the poor and providing a public service otherwise not being provided, offends the First Amendment.

Conclusion

This very brief 'tour' around countries within and without the United Kingdom, though necessarily brief, shows the persistent conflict in the provision of education.

First, between those who wish to preserve, within the public system, a religious provision of education for people of religious faith and those who insist upon an exclusively secular basis for educational provision which is open to all.

And second, between those, on the one hand, wishing to promote a religious education, which accommodates different denominations and religions, and those, on the other hand, who emphasise a religious formation within a particular tradition.

The issues arising, therefore, from this brief comparison across several educational systems are:

- the extent to which an inclusive concept of RE can accommodate the diversity of denominational and theological differences (see Chapters 6 and 7);

International perspective **59**

- the power and authority of the state to determine the philosophical basis of public education, irrespective of the religious affiliations and values of the constitutive communities (see Chapter 11);
- the possibility of a coherent secularist morality as a basis for social values and citizenship, as in the case of France (see Chapter 9);
- the universal concern for social cohesion within ethnically and religiously mixed societies, and the role of the school in its promotion, as in the promotion of the 'common school' in the United States (see Chapters 8 and 11);
- the ways in which different aspirations might be reconciled in shared schools, as in the case of Northern Ireland's 'integrated schools' (see Chapter 12);
- the effect of increasing secularisation of what had been a uniformly religious context for educational provision, as in the case of Ireland (see Chapter 5); and
- the extent to which in the common school (perhaps necessitated by population changes) the spiritual dimensions, preserved by the Faith school, might continue and contribute to the school as a whole (see Chapter 12).

References

Armstrong, D., 2012, 'Northern Ireland', in Barnes, L.P. (ed.), *Religious Education in the UK and Ireland: debates in Religious Education*, London: Routledge.

Carmody, S.J., 2017, 'Irish Second Level Religious Education in search of a paradigm', unpublished paper given at Heythrop College, London, September.

Congregation for Catholic Education, 1977, *The Catholic School*, Vatican City: VEV.

Cremin, L.A., 1957, The *Republic and the School: Horace Man on the Education for Free Men*, New York: College Teachers Press.

Durkheim, E., 1961 (3rd edition), *Moral Education: A Study in the Theory and Application of the Sociology of Education*, New York: The Free Press.

Gallagher, T., 2005, 'Faith Schools and Northern Ireland', in Gardener, R., Cairns, J., Lawton, D. (eds.), *Faith Schools: Consensus or Conflict?* London: Routledge.

Greer, J.E., 1993, 'Viewing the "other side" in Northern Ireland', In Francis, L. and Lankshear, D.W. (eds.), *Christian Perspectives on Church Schools*, Leominster: Gracewing.

Hume, W., 2015, 'Scotland: an overview', in Brock, C. (ed.), *Education in the United Kingdom*, London: Bloomsbury.

Jones, P., 1992, 'Education', in Linklater, M. and Denniston, R. (eds.), *Anatomy of Scotland*, Edinburgh: W. and R. Chambers.

Judge, H., 2001, *Faith-based Schools and the State*, Wallingford: Symposium Books.

MacKenzie, M.L., 1999, 'Catholic education in Scotland: a phenomenological approach', in Conroy, J.C. (ed.), *Catholic Education: Inside Out, Outside In*, Dublin: Lindisfarne Books.

McKinney, S., 2012, 'Scotland', in Barnes, L.P. (ed.), *Religious Education in the UK and Ireland: Debates in Religious Education*, London: Routledge.

Moffat, C., ed., 1993, *Education Together for a Change*, Belfast: Fortnight Educational Trust.

Nelson, J., 2004, 'Uniformity and Diversity in religious education in Northern Ireland', *British Journal of Religious Education*, 26.

Peterson, A.D.C., 1971, (3rd edition) *A Hundred Years of Education*, London: Duckworth.

Ravitch, D., 1973, *The Great School Wars: New York City 1805–1973*, New York: Basic Books.

Valland-Belkacen, N., 2015, in Duclert, V. (ed.), *La Republique, Ses Valeurs, Son Ecole*, Paris: Folio, p.ix.

PART II

Religious education

5

THREE TRADITIONS

The idea of a 'tradition'

A tradition is a general and inherited (from the Latin 'handed down') way of thinking, which shapes how one sees the world and responds to experiences of different kinds. It is what Charles Taylor (2007, p.323) refers to as

> the generally shared background of understandings of society, which make it possible to function as it does. It is 'social' in two ways: in that it is generally shared, and in that it is about society.

Taylor refers to the ways in which people imagine their social existence, how they fit together with others, how things do, and should, go on between them and their fellows.

Such shared background is embedded in everyday behaviours – shaking hands on meeting, saying 'please' and 'thank you', queuing for buses – which, in this or that community, reflect values of politeness and caring. It is a way of thinking and behaving which has become internalised, affecting civic and moral judgments, and affecting the significance given to events. But it is extended, too, to what Taylor refers to as the 'cosmic imaginary' which

> makes sense of the ways in which the surrounding world figures in our lives ... in [for instance] our religious images and practices ... in our moral and aesthetic imagination.

> *(ibid.)*

For example, in the way in which we view the natural environment, either as material to be exploited for human benefit or as that which has been entrusted to human beings as its guardians.

64 Religious education

Tradition, therefore, embodies the background assumptions, which are generally accepted within civic society, but also within the different communities or associations that constitute that larger society – the 'tacit knowledge' not usually made explicit, which has evolved over time but which can too easily be taken for granted. Michael Oakeshott (1962, pp.56ff.) shows how political life and thinking are shaped by traditions which have evolved though retaining continuity. Such an evolution arises from adaptation to new circumstances or to refinements that meet criticisms, internal as well as external. Therefore, the current ways of thinking and behaving cannot be fully understood without reference to their historical roots and development, and that is why it is important, in addressing Faith schools, to have given an account in Chapters 1 and 2 of the historical origins, and responses to changing circumstances, of Faith schools. Furthermore, coming to understand that tradition – and to be an insider – is

> to learn how to participate in a conversation: it is at once initiation into an inheritance in which we have a life interest, and the exploration of its intimations.
>
> *(op. cit., p.62)*

Traditions inevitably change with circumstances, because the social fabric in which they were nurtured changes. But, where traditions run deep, they adapt rather than discontinue – characterised possibly by a *tradition* of critical enquiry which we take for granted, and which, however, by no means universally prevails, but which enables traditional modes of life to adapt to changing circumstances and to ensure continuity of those traditions, albeit reformed. In this and Chapter 6, it will be shown how religious education, its embodiment in Faith schools, and the criticisms of them are embedded in different but changing traditions.

In many respects, a tradition is akin to the notion of 'culture', a common framework of thinking and behaving within a community which is imbibed through membership of that community and which shapes how one sees the social and moral worlds which one inhabits. In some contexts, such a 'common framework' is referred to as the 'ideological background' which underpins a mode of thinking and reasoning, as in the background assumptions of rationality which characterised the Enlightenment, or, as in the case of understanding scientific revolutions in terms of distinct 'paradigms', argued by Thomas Kuhn (1970).

A tradition, therefore, embodies values and modes of judgment which are not necessarily explicit in the consequent thinking and behaving of those who have inherited it. This is the case of the apprenticed craftsman (as that concept was traditionally understood and so powerfully described by Sennett, 2008), who has been initiated not only into the skills of doing a job in a particular way but also into an appreciation of the standards whereby such work is judged successful. It is the case with the researcher in the humanities and the sciences, whose work is informed by the inherited standards and values of academic research acquired through training within a community of researchers. This is the case (most important for the argument of this book) with those who follow religious views of the world and of human destiny.

However, it is equally the case, as I shall argue, with those who, in pursuit of a secular ideal, reject a religious account of the universe. Their values, modes of judgment and practical habits of behaviour have themselves been internalised through living within a secular community whose members participate in that tradition, and where possibly an underlying materialism (or 'naturalism', as shall be argued in Chapter 10) affects their judgment.

One role of philosophy is to make explicit the assumptions which form a tradition, as is intended in the more philosophical Chapters in Part III, thereby providing clearer insight into its riches but also its limitations. Of course, such a philosophical examination will itself reflect a particular tradition of thinking – as, for example, in the dominant position which 'analytic philosophy' once had within the philosophical scene in post-war Britain.

Religious traditions and Faith schools

Different religions reflect distinct traditions of what it means to be, and to develop, as persons – or, put in modern parlance, 'distinctive anthropologies'. These arise from generations of spiritual insight and philosophical deliberation. Those 'meanings' may be articulated more or less explicitly. But they may be embodied in liturgy, in practices of various kinds, in symbols and representations, and in theological and philosophical attempts to articulate and make explicit the respective traditions. In so doing there will be interactions between different religious beliefs and practices as one sheds light on another. There is, in other words, a tradition of reasoned criticism and argument enabling religious practice to adapt and develop.

To understand the current issues over Faith schools, one needs to see them representing those distinct traditions, with their respective moral codes of conduct, spiritual appreciation of the world, and respect for others as persons, thereby, introducing the next generation to what it means to be human within that tradition – the insights, the distinctive practices, the consequent modes and habits of virtuous living. Such traditions will have a history and can be understood only through a familiarity with that history, not only of key events but also of changing theological debate and philosophical articulation of the underlying beliefs. To teach within such traditions is then (to borrow Oakeshott's language) to introduce them to a 'conversation between the generations' and to a mode of belief and of living which is articulated in those conversations.

Within society, there have been and are, understandably, those who do not share in such traditions and, indeed, who would seek to eliminate them from their representation in public life, and in particular, the state's support for them through the schooling system. However, even such opposition (especially that of the 'secularists') does itself speak from within traditions which have a history, and which need to be understood and then exposed to critical scrutiny.

66 Religious education

Furthermore, we need to understand the shaping of our education *system* in terms of the *political* tradition (changing, maybe, as reflected in Chapter 2) within which the state has taken responsibility for the provision of education – in particular, the evolving way in which that system has accommodated differences within the civic community over the place of religion in the control and practice of schooling. How are we to understand the role of the state (its powers, its authority) in relation to the wishes of parents and the local communities concerning the education and upbringing of the next generation? Such questions in political philosophy will be approached in Chapter 11. But by contrast, one might see how very different traditions in France and the United States determine the relationship between the state and schools, as was shown in Chapter 4. Should the state, as well as ensuring that there should be school places for all children, also determine what those children should learn, and, more particularly for the purposes of this book, determine the extent to which religious communities and parents should be able to control the kind of education which they want for their children?

In the pursuit of that question, it is necessary to clarify how the historical developments described in Chapter 2 characterise the present system and how different traditions underpin the differences within it. The 1944 Education Act's division of schools (within 'a central system locally maintained') into voluntary controlled, voluntary aided, and community schools must be understood within three, though frequently interacting, traditions. And their defence must be understood in that light.

Tradition I

Religious and spiritual education broadly conceived

It is important in viewing the religious education landscape to distinguish between, on the one hand, a perspective, rooted in and articulated by religious belief and spiritual appreciation, yet accommodating significant differences between denominational and theological communities, and, on the other hand, a more detailed and confessional tradition. Here, within the context of the voluntary controlled schools, as introduced in Chapter 2, an attempt is made to explain the first (and evolving) tradition.

'Voluntary schools' arose historically from the provision of elementary schooling for the poor by the Church of England (mainly) and by the Dissenters (or non-conformists) from early in the 19th century. As the brief history detailed in Chapter 2 points out, Board schools were established by the 1870 Elementary Education Act to extend the provision of elementary education to places where the voluntary schools were unable to provide. This created the distinction between voluntary and board schools, and, with that distinction, controversies arose over the place of religious teaching in schools. As we saw, the controversies were not just between religious and no religious teaching, but (within the broadly Christian community) the nature of that religious ethos and teaching. The non-conformists did not want the voluntary schools to be promoting the distinctive doctrines and tenets of the established Church.

However, according to the report of the Royal Commission of 1818, as we saw in Chapter 2, the Church of England National schools were adopting a *liberal*

Three traditions **67**

position which would accommodate those of other branches of Christianity, and indeed those who were generally indifferent. This was made explicit in the 1870 Education Act in what was called the 'Cowper-Temple clause', namely, that

> no religious catechisms or religious formulary which is distinctive of any particular denomination shall be taught in the Board Schools.

Positively, this clause provided for the instruction in a *broad, non-denominational* form of Christianity. The majority of schools, under the trusteeship of the Church of England, though working within a Christian ethos, opened themselves to everyone. Their Christian task was to further the education of all, especially the poor, irrespective of their religious or non-religious interests and affiliations. They sought to be inclusive, respecting differences but against the broadly accepted traditional Christian ethos of society in general. That ethos was reflected, for instance, in the general closing of shops on a Sunday ('the Lord's Day'); in businesses closing on Good Friday; on Sunday being a 'day of rest' from work. The Established Church continued to manifest itself in national events of importance such as the Coronation of the Monarch and the Opening of Parliament. Schools would begin the day with an assembly at which there would be a prayer and a hymn. The Nativity play would be staged in primary schools. All this was but the unquestioned cultural or traditional background to schooling. Biblical references in literature and conversation would be familiar. The ethos in society would be described as generally Christian, as, therefore, would be the ethos of the schools, but open to all under the aegis of the Church of England. There would be, for example, understood rules of appropriate sexual behaviour derived from the Christian roots of our culture.

Thus, one can understand the *cri de coeur* of Lady Olga Maitland in a speech in the House of Commons in 1962, 'the time has come to stop being apologetic about being a Christian country, we should not allow unbelievers to undermine our traditions'.

The 1944 Education Act, therefore, required every school, whether voluntary controlled, voluntary aided, or community, to have a compulsory daily act of worship of a *broadly Christian nature*, from which pupils could be exempted if that were to be the will of the parents. The teaching of religion would be according to agreed syllabuses, which were to be agreed by conferences convened within the respective local education authorities, on which would be representatives of different Christian denominations and (later) different religions. Initially, however, many such syllabuses would be explicitly Christian, as in the Surrey syllabus of 1947 which stated in its Preamble that its general aim was to give children

> knowledge of the common Christian facts held by their fathers for 2000 years [and to help them] to seek for themselves in Christian principles which could give purpose to life and a guide to all its problems.
>
> *(Barnes, 2014, p.57)*

68 Religious education

Such knowledge, with its 2,000 years of evolution, would be very much bible based – the common text across denominations.

Such a conception of schooling, rooted (but very broadly) in Christian beliefs and culture, and yet open to diversity, constituted a tradition in which the learners could become aware of the sacred, of a spiritual dimension to life, though not one so thoroughly 'embedded in and reinforced by a total way of life … enacted in rituals' as described by Jonathan Sacks (1997) of the Jewish inheritance. Rather, in so being, it had within itself openness to other religious beliefs, and indeed to those of none, without discarding the essentially moral purpose of education. Indeed, 'inclusivity' was the value which characterised its conception of schooling, arising from the original mission of the National Society to provide elementary education for all, especially the poor. As stated by Bishop Henson of Durham in 1939 (quoted in Chadwick, 2001), 'the dual system obstructs the complete triumph of the secularising tendency'.

This tradition has been articulated in several major reports from the Church of England.

The Durham Report of 1970, *The Fourth R*, argued for the importance of the Church schools in the national system because of the values, derived from the Christian inheritance, which were embodied in our culture, and which need to be reinforced within our communities. Such values would militate against the kind of individualism which increasingly marks the society. The schools provided this most important national service.

The Dearing Report, 2001 (significantly entitled *Way Ahead: Church of England Schools in the New Millennium*), placed their schools at the centre of the Church of England's mission to the nation, serving particularly those in social and economic need. Those schools should be distinctively Christian institutions in fostering its service to others, the intrinsic value of each individual, the redemption of all, no matter what lives they had lived, and

> a spiritual dimension to the lives of young people, within the tradition of the Church of England in an increasingly secular world.
>
> *(p. 3)*

Such noble ideals may not be confined to Christianity, but they are substantiated by the distinctively Christian narrative in the person of Jesus Christ and developed in the scriptures, which should permeate the school and the teachers' commitment to them. Non-Christians should feel comfortable and reassured in such a context.

At roughly the same time as the Dearing Report, the Church issued a report which saw that the churches (working together in an increasingly secular world) would ensure 'the long-term continuity of a strong Christian presence'. Within a tradition so described, there was an alternative vision for society.

> Globalisation and the ascendancy of consumerism have emphasised personal choice, but have not so far generated a balancing sense of community or a

coherent sense of responsibility for sustaining the earth's own well-being or for the quality of our civilisation. In a world of shifting sands, many parents have welcomed the stability offered by schools that offer an enduring alternative to the growing secular values of society … It is about forming people who, however academically and technically skilful, are not reduced to inarticulate embarrassment by the great questions of life.

(Church of England, 2002)

The Chadwick Report (2012), marking the bicentenary of the National Society and interestingly entitled *Going for Growth: Transformation for Children, Young Persons and the Church*, similarly argued for its schools (approximately 5,000, serving nearly a million pupils) to be 'witness to their own religious foundation whilst serving increasingly secular and multi-faith communities'. The schools need to celebrate their *distinctive Church ethos*, sharing an *'enduring narrative'* in the values promoted, namely, the absolute value of each young person, the importance of fostering caring relationships, respect for the created order (namely, the environment), service to the community, belief in the redemption of all as reflected in the virtue of mercy, whilst at the same time being responsive to parents and their surrounding communities who may not share the background Christian narrative. In particular, its education should be imbued with the distinctive view of what it means to be human, based on Church wisdom.

This harks back to the worries expressed by Chadwick (1997) in her reflections on the 1988 Education Act, which she saw as a threat to the spiritual dimension of an education,

> dominated by a secularist viewpoint indicative of an increasingly utilitarian and materialist approach to education in which market economics would become the overriding ethos of schools.

Part of the Church's task is to model and teach what this growth into God's likeness (as shown in the scriptures and Church tradition, but also in other religious traditions) means for that journey of faith. Crucially, it involves accompanying children and young people of all faiths and none in their search for self and identity, recognising that the search will not always result in the Church's way. Indeed, it was seen as the duty of such Faith schools (in the words of Lord Runcie when Archbishop of Canterbury, quoted in *National Guidance to Diocesan Boards of Education on Admission to Church of England Schools*) to

- Nourish those of the faith;
- Encourage those of other faiths;
- Challenge those who have no faith.

I suggest, therefore, that here is a distinct tradition behind the maintenance of the voluntary controlled schools – a tradition in the sense that it represents a service

70 Religious education

to the general community (not confined to those within it who are of a particular religious persuasion) but rooted in a Christian narrative which has been 'handed down', and is deeply ingrained in minds and rituals of the Church. Furthermore, as indicated in the reports referred to, this tradition is to be contrasted with the gradual secularisation of society.

Very similar sentiments were expressed by Thomas Groome (1998) in *Educating for Life*, reflecting on his work in Catholic schools run by religious orders in the predominantly Muslim context of Pakistan. He was intrigued by how the system of education, which showed none of the symbols of Christianity but which instead provided religious education in Islam, had a

> humanising philosophy that clearly had its grounding in Christian faith and yet remains open to all and without any trace of evangelizing to Christianity.
> *(Groome, 1998, p.10)*

And earlier he argues, regarding the distinctive ethos:

> They promote the value of the person, emphasising the equal dignity of boys and girls – exceptional in this society; they encourage a positive outlook on life and challenge the fatalism that pervades the surrounding culture; they build up a sense of school community and promote friendship across class and ethnic divide. They encourage pupils to develop a personal spirituality; to commit to justice and peace, to respect those who are different.
> *(p.10)*

Tradition II

Common School and the secular tradition

We have seen, in Chapter 2, the opposition (from those who espoused what was referred to as a 'secular view' of society) to the faith-affiliated provision of education paid for by the taxpayer. Such opposition becomes more acute as society, generally speaking, becomes more secular. However, it is important to distinguish four different shades of meaning in the use of the word 'secular' – 'shades' because they do merge into each other but need to be distinguished for the purposes of this book.

First, in general, it conveys simply that the modern Western world is free, in its practices and social beliefs, from any connection with faith in (or adherence to) God. Religion thus becomes largely a private matter, no longer an integral part of social life, as for example in people's link to the parish or (as in earlier days) to the guilds or to religious feasts. There is an indifference to religion and to the way it permeates social life.

Second, however, Taylor (2007, pp.25–43) traces the 'freedom' emerging over centuries from what he refers to as the long period of 'enchantment' (in which people would have had a deep sense of the connection between the physical and the spiritual, between humanity and nature, and between themselves in community) to modernism and the 'age of enlightenment' – expressed by Immanuel Kant as

> man's release from his self-incurred tutelage ... inability to make use of his understanding without direction from another.
>
> *(quoted in Gearon, 2013, p.142)*

And to the dominant materialist (and thereby scientific) understanding of the universe (developed further in Chapter 10). Such a secular *tradition* in education was outlined by Durkheim in his book *Moral Education* (developed at length in Chapter 9 of this book), where he states:

> The last twenty years in France have seen a great educational revolution which was latent and half realised before then. We decided to give our children in our state-supported schools a purely secular education [that is, an education] not derived from revealed religion, but that rests exclusively on ideas, sentiments and practices accountable to reason alone – in short, a purely rationalist education.
>
> *(Durkheim, 1961, p.3)*

Therefore, 'secular' in many respects came to signify more than indifference. The Secular Education League, formed in England in 1907, insisted that the teaching of religion was not the responsibility of the state, and indeed that the state should not be funding schools which supported religious faiths. It was within that spirit that school board schools were conceived in 1870, enhanced in significance as non-denominational elementary schools by the 1902 Act, and confirmed under the title of 'Community schools' in 1944.

However, 'secularists' go further in pointing to what they see as a *contradiction* between confessional and secular education. Such an argument was put by Paul Hirst who saw education, properly speaking, to lie in the development of reason and thus in the introduction of young people to those areas of thought which have publicly agreed rational grounds for belief. As a result of this

> there has already emerged in our society a view of education, a concept of education, which makes the whole idea of Christian education a kind of nonsense and the search for a Christian approach to, or philosophy of, education a huge mistake.
>
> *(Hirst, 1965)*

Therefore, what is to be taught should be settled independently of any questions about religious belief. The deliberate *passing on* of such beliefs is not in itself an educational process and should be left to the parents and religious ministers. Indeed, the provision of a distinctively religious environment, and therein the teaching of religion, is to be seen as a matter of indoctrination.

72 Religious education

Third, there is stress on individual freedom and personal autonomy. As described by Owen Chadwick (1975, p.29) in his book entitled *The Secularisation of the European Mind*, a further feature of this secularisation is the view of liberty 'increasingly seen as personal possession, to enable self-realisation', and therefore freed from the moral constraints and reference points of an inherited religious tradition. The connection is made with the development of the free market in the globalised economy, put succinctly by Copley (2005, p.30), as 'economics has become the theology of a materialist society'.

Fourth, there has emerged, within this post-religious, secular world, a 'post-modernist' understanding of the world, reflected in (and reinforced by) the globalisation just referred to, namely, the dominance of markets and competition where the individual person, no longer autonomous, is reduced to a calculation, to a metric, in the new language of management. Thus, in this respect, there has emerged a dramatic change in 'a world view', including the implicit understanding of what it means to be a person – and therein the decline of 'the personal'.

Therefore, it is important to remember the distinctions (though they shade into each other) between

- secular in the sense of general indifference to religious modes of life (and thus to significant 'reference points' in society);
- secular in the sense of a materialist understanding of the world, giving rise to hostility to religious education, since, having no rational basis, such teaching is said to entail indoctrination;
- secular in the sense of personal liberty unconstrained by previously held religious and moral reference points;
- secular in the depersonalisation of persons in public and private spaces (illustrated in Ken Loach's film *I, Daniel Blake*).

Regarding the first sense

Put positively (that is, not principally in hostility to religious affiliation), one argument is that in a pluralist society there is a need for a place (for example, the Common School) where people from different communities (religious or none) can cooperate and engage in dialogue without being constrained by a religious framework which they may have no appreciation of. Thus, the 'Common School', as conceived by Horace Mann in the United States or John Dewey (1938, pp.55–56), would make all or no faiths welcome to encourage dialogue between the holders of different beliefs in order to foster a common culture and citizenship.

Regarding the second sense

There prevails a *tradition* of secularism within education which is more than religious indifference and which has emerged gradually from the period of the Enlightenment according to which human perfection lies in the development of the rational mind without reference to God and religion. Thus, as was noted, Durkheim (1961, p.6), in his essays on moral education, refers to a 'purely rational education', which is a 'transformation' and a 'secularising of education' and which has been in process for centuries'. In place of the religious dimension, there is the working towards a more general social good. However, here, as in all traditions, there are foundational beliefs (for example, about the nature of reason and of freedom), which are assumed and which go unquestioned (a matter to be discussed in Chapter 10). Nonetheless, in rejecting the existence of God within the secularist tradition, may it not be felt that there is a gap to be filled? As John White, formerly a colleague of Paul Hirst and indeed author of a book entitled *Education and Personal Well-being in a Secular Universe*, in suggesting how it might be filled, asks:

> Has the time come in our increasingly secular society to assimilate religious contemplation to thinking about other man-made characters such as Doctor Zhivago or Faust?
>
> *(White, 2002, p.111)*

Quite clearly there is seen to be a need to take away the statues of the saints and replace them with those of good humanist sympathisers. Indeed, such religious overtones were difficult to avoid, even amongst the most ardent pursuers of the secular state. The London Positivist Society, founded in 1867, opened a 'positivist temple' in Chapel Street in London's East End. Perhaps this reflects *The Dialectics of Secularisation*, the title of a book by Habermas and Ratzinger (later, Pope Benedict XVI), 2006, to which further reference is made in Chapter 10. However, within this *second sense*, a more definitive humanist and anti-religious case is represented. The Humanist Philosophy Group (2001), from a distinctive philosophical and moral position, with overtones of the Enlightenment, would oppose not only religiously based schools but also the teaching of (as opposed to the teaching about) religion. Indeed, they would attribute blame for many social divisions (for example, in Northern Ireland) to the central place occupied by religion in the organisation of schooling. More significantly, following Hirst's argument, the pursuit of the development of reason as an educational aim, is seen to exclude religion because religious arguments and statements are believed to lack a rational basis in terms of not being open to verification. To act, therefore, as though religious propositions were to be held as true would be to indoctrinate. This opposition is put most strongly by Richard Dawkins, namely, that modern society required a 'truly secular state', from which followed that there should be state neutrality 'in all matters pertaining to religion, the recognition that faith is personal and no business of the state' (*New Statesman*, 19.12.11).

Regarding the third sense

Freed from the constraints of religious teaching, in the absence of inherited moral reference points, and influenced by the importance attached to personal autonomy,

74 Religious education

people are encouraged to do what pleases them, to choose their form of life and destiny, to find their own distinctive ideals of self-fulfilment – so long as such freedom does no harm to others. There is no longer to the same extent as used to be the case the widely shared understanding of what constitutes the life worth living.

Regarding the fourth sense

'The secular age', freed from a religious perspective, and even questioning the confidence of the rationalists (in what Taylor referred to as the 'post-modern understanding of the world'), leads to a world without 'moral horizons' – indeed, the 'depersonalisation' of what is human. There has evolved a language through which, in the absence of the once prevalent religious and spiritual ethos, a distinctive interpretation of the social and moral worlds has emerged (Taylor's 'cosmic imagery', already referred to). Dominant in recent years has been the language of 'management control' through which the relation of state to schools and teachers has been transformed. The practice of education, through the high-stakes testing regimes, is dominated by a particular form of language: of targets, performance indicators, audits, efficiency gains, even the science of 'deliverology', all reflecting a distinctive utilitarian understanding of human development and educational structure – very much within a market-based approach to improvement. It largely goes unquestioned in the managerial assumptions borrowed from the business world and economic orthodoxy. Being unquestioned, it forms a tradition of thinking with its own values and language which shape our understandings of educational success.

Tradition III

Voluntary aided – a third tradition

James Arthur, bearing in mind this secularisation of society, argues that schools are inevitably affected when they have lost their connection with the religious community. There would seem to be a need, therefore, for schools to provide this religious critique of the secular. But a general religious identification (no doubt such as that depicted in 'Tradition I') 'erodes the religious uniqueness of the particular denomination's contribution' (Arthur, 2006, p.136). Hence, the need for more denominational (indeed, 'confessional') related schools, namely, what have come to be called 'voluntary aided'.

The significance in England and Wales of the description 'voluntary aided' in contrast to 'voluntary controlled' was that the trustees of the former, although in receipt of government funding through the taxes, retained greater control over the running of the schools and its religious nature. These were for the most part Catholic schools, which had grown immensely from the middle of the 19th century, mainly as a result of Irish immigration. The bishops retained control over appointments, governing bodies, selection of staff. and admissions. But, in return, they had to provide the school buildings and their maintenance, which they achieved by considerable sacrifice from the (mainly poor) Catholic congregations. Following the 1944 Education Act, the cost to the Church was 50% of the construction of new buildings and their maintenance, a sum which was gradually reduced and presently is 10%. Indeed, it was the policy of the Church to provide Catholic schools before they had built their churches, such was the importance attached to education.

There were also Jewish schools, though not many, which similarly sought to preserve their distinctive values and understandings within the national system. And more recently there has been a growth of Muslim (as well as a few Sikh and Hindu) schools claiming voluntary aided status.

However, the Catholic Church is possibly the largest provider of schools worldwide with almost 150,000 primary and secondary schools serving over 50 million pupils in very different ethnic and cultural social settings. In addition, it has established many institutions of higher education, a rationale for which was given in John Henry Newman's *The Idea of a University*.

Justification of the right to offer this provision within a national system might refer, oddly enough, to Durkheim's claim to the importance of the 'sacred' in our understanding of human life, in the challenge it offers to the profane and mundane exigencies of everyday life, and in the alternative to secular modes of thinking and living such as those outlined above. What makes the creation and continuity of these arrangements a distinctive tradition is the inherent understanding of the nature and the aims of education. As Durkheim (1971, quoted in Grace, 2016a, p.19), argued in *The Elementary Forms of the Religious Life*, it would be considered a most important aspect of the educational enterprise to preserve the spiritual form of life, with its concepts of the transcendent, the divine, and the sacred, through which we come to value things in a distinctive way, especially their relation to the 'profane' in human societies.

The former Chief Rabbi, Jonathan Sacks, provides a telling account of what such a distinctive tradition means to being a Jew – and, furthermore, how the preservation of such traditions contributes to the common good. Any complex society such as ours is

> a confusing mixture of reasons and associations, which emerge, like a great river from its countless streams and tributaries, out of a vast range of histories and traditions.
>
> *(Sacks, 1997, p.55)*

But each of these 'streams and tributaries', in order to contribute to the general good, needs to be preserved yet developed through further insight. A profound tradition will embody the moral narrative and 'philosophical tools' for such further insight. Within the Jewish tradition, for example, the idea of social contract gives way to that of *covenant*, and thus to a very different account of relationships and obligations, of responsibilities and loyalties, and of the common good. This account is embedded in practices and rituals that have to be understood *from the inside*. It cannot be grasped from an outsider's theoretical attempt to give an account.

76 Religious education

> This is a morality received not made. It is embedded in and reinforced by a total way of life, articulated in texts, transmitted across the generations, enacted in rituals, exemplified by members of the community, and under-written by revelation and tradition. It has not pretensions to universality. It represents what a Jew must do, in the full knowledge that his Christian neighbours in Mainz are bounded by a different code.
>
> *(Sacks, op. cit., p. 89)*

However, there are warnings of the loss of a tradition and of the moral and social values which it embodies unless it is protected, and that explains the defence of Faith schools against attacks from without. There were as many as 33 Jewish schools within the maintained system of England and Wales in 2002. As Jacob Neusner in his book *Conservative, American and Jewish* argues:

> Civilisation hangs suspended, from generation to generation, by the gossamer thread of memory. If only one cohort of mothers and fathers fails to convey to its children what it has learnt from its parents, then the great chain of learning and wisdom snaps. If the guardians of human knowledge stumble only one time, in their fall collapses the whole edifice of knowledge and understanding.
>
> *(quoted in Sacks, op. cit., p. 173)*

As the post-modern vision of the human person transforms society into a collection of depersonalised units, to be manipulated within a globalised and market economy, so such a critique becomes essential. How might one preserve the personal dignity and the sense of each person's supreme importance, irrespective of their talents, strength, money, or social position?

The voluntary aided schools, therefore, would claim, as their raison d'etre within the broader system, to provide a form of education which has a distinctive narrative which illuminates our understanding of human nature and of the place of each human being within the divine order of things. The upholders of such a view would be deeply suspicious of handing the nurturing of the next generation to a political system which may have no wish to protect it, and no way of providing insight into it.

Furthermore, part of that tradition would be a questioning of the right of the state to intervene in the exercise of that educational tradition. The state rightly enables financially, and in other ways, 'education for all', but, in so doing, it needs to recognise that the populations within the state are not just aggregates of individuals but *members of communities with their distinctive cultures and values* – a point developed in Chapter 11. Indeed, the preservation of such difference might be considered to enrich the wider community – in the words once again of Jonathan Sacks, emerging 'like a great river from its countless streams and tributaries, out of a vast range of histories and traditions'.

The Catholic Church (the provider of the vast majority of voluntary aided schools) claims that the rights of the family are superior to those of the state in providing the education of their children, and that therefore, they should be able to maintain their distinctive Catholic schools within the overall education system (Pius XI, 1929). The same applies to other religious groups such as the Jewish and Muslim families. Indeed, two central tenets of Catholic social teaching (to be developed further in Chapter 11) are those of 'solidarity' (mutual support and respect) and 'subsidiarity' (devolving from central power whatever can be conducted by the different communities). Education – enabling the young to develop as persons – needs to reflect the deep-seated traditions through which human development is defined.

That distinctiveness of such religious educational traditions, as shall be argued in Chapter 9, lies in the particular understanding of the aims of education, of the development of the distinctive human qualities and virtues, of the inherited narrative which inspires the pursuit of 'the good life', of the sort of society and community which responds to human needs. Such a tradition would be critical of state control of schools (as opposed to state support for schools) as a form of totalitarianism – as an imposition of values, which assume a purely secular understanding of human life and which might be seen as alien within the long-standing faith tradition. In providing such a distinctive tradition, the education would be an extension of, and support for, the values and beliefs of the families and the communities from which the children come.

However, that (as any) tradition evolves in response to changing circumstances. A working party on Catholic education in a multi-racial, multi-cultural society (aptly entitled 'Learning from Diversity: A Challenge for Catholic Education'), canvassed for welcoming minority religious and ethnic groups into Catholic schools – a matter to be developed further in Chapters 8 and 11.

This book is written chiefly with reference to the *historical* development of Faith schools in England and Wales – and hence the focus, within the Tradition III, upon those Faith schools within the Catholic Church. However, the same issues arise, and a similar defence may be made, with regard to Muslim and to Jewish schools – and references to these will be developed in subsequent chapters. For instance, the Muslim population within the United Kingdom is approximately 3 million – and growing. One has seen how the secular attack on the presumption of faith has been reflected in the attempt to remove religious symbolism from public places – the wearing of the cross by certain employees and the prevention of Muslim women from wearing the veil. This, indeed, is more actively pursued in France, where on many beaches in the south, the burkini has been forbidden. Modesty, once in the list of virtues, is obviously no longer seen as a virtue in the secular world. The assumption so often is that there is something incongruous, if not subversive, within our civic society, of this distinctive religious tradition, and certainly not to be nurtured at public expense within the state system of education. But in an interesting book, *Generation X: Young Muslims Changing the World* by Shalina Janmohamed (2016), speaking of 'Generation M' (namely, those born in the last 30 years in the United Kingdom), asserts that

> one over-riding characteristic … is that they believe that being faithful and living a modern life go hand in hand, and there is absolutely no contradiction between the two.

78 Religious education

That concept 'of being faithful' is well explained by Saeed Shah:

> Muslim scholars emphasise that Muslim culture represents the worldview of faith … A faith or religion is, broadly speaking, a set of beliefs or practices generally held by a human community, involving adherence to certain beliefs and rituals that generate a specific culture.
>
> *(Shah, 2016, p.41)*

There is a mode of thinking, enacted in the details of daily life and underpinned by beliefs, which are based on the narrative of the Qu'ran but which have been refined and developed through the critical thinking of philosophers and mystics over the centuries. Where such religion and culture are inseparable, it is one of the 'countless streams and tributaries, out of a vast range of histories and traditions' of which the former Chief Rabbi spoke. Clearly, this must characterise the idea of an educated person within such a community – for instance, in the teaching of history, of a culture revealing the profound critical contributions of Islamic philosophers to Western thought, of poetry, of the mystic traditions within Islam and indeed of the contributions to science inspired by this tradition.

For this reason, the educational traditions of the Islamic and the Jewish enter into the defence and justification of Faith schools in subsequent chapters.

Conclusion

Our understanding of the physical, social, and moral worlds which we inhabit develops from general backgrounds and assumptions which support and justify such understandings. These backgrounds and assumptions constitute traditions, which themselves have been internalised from the different communities to which people belong – scientific, artistic, historical, literary, religious. Such traditions inevitably evolve through changing social and physical circumstances and through criticism both internal and external to them.

Particularly relevant to education are those traditions which embrace a form of life, constitutive of different communities within civic society. Where such forms of life do embody enriching traditions of moral and intellectual life, affecting what are seen to be the aims of education, it would seem to be the duty of the state to help such communities to maintain and to enrich such traditions so long as they contribute to the common good.

The key issues, therefore, which lie at the centre of the controversy over publicly funded Faith schools are:

- Given the diversity of beliefs in society about what constitutes human development, and thus an 'educated person', how far has the state, in publicly funded schools, the authority to enable a particular view (e.g. secular in its various manifestations) of the 'educated person', which may not match the distinctive traditions within the broader community?

- Given that such diverse traditions of what constitutes personal maturity need to be respected, may it not be appropriate (when such communities so wish it) to support separate schools which embody those diverse traditions and challenge the prevailing secular ideology?
- Or alternatively, given the diversity of religious traditions which have emerged in recent years in our society, should there not be ways in which these diverse traditions might be maintained within a 'common school' rather than through the creation of a diversity of Faith schools, which might be seen to endanger the pursuit of a common citizenship?
- Given the close connection between 'education' and 'development of reason', is education compatible with teaching a religious understanding of the world which (it is claimed within a secular tradition) cannot have a rational basis?
- Given that one claimed purpose of education is the development of personal autonomy based on reason, is not the early initiation (or nurturing) of young pupils into a faith tradition a matter of indoctrination rather than education?

We return to these underlying philosophical questions in Part III.

References

Arthur, J., 2006, *Faith and Secularisation in in Religious Colleges and Universities*, London: Routledge.

Barnes, L.P., 2014, *Education, Religion and Diversity*, London: Routledge.

Chadwick, O, 1975, *The Secularisation of the European Mind in the 19th Century*, Cambridge: Cambridge University Press.

Chadwick, P., 1997, *Shifting Alliances: Church and State in English Education*, London: Cassell.

Chadwick, P., 2001, 'The Anglican perspective on Church schools', *Oxford Review of Education*, 27.

Chadwick Report, 2012, *Going for growth: transformation for children, young persons and the Church*, London: SPCK.

Church of England, 2002,

Cooling, T., 1994, *A Christian Vision for State Education*, London: SPCK.

Copley, 2005, *Indoctrination, Education and God*, London: SPCK.

Dearing Report, 2001, *Way Ahead: Church of England Schools in this New Millennium*, London: Church House Publications.

Dewey, J., 1938, *Experience and Education*, Illinois: Southern Illinois University Press.

Durham Report, 1970, *The Fourth R: The Report of the Commission on Religious Education in Schools*, London: SPCK.

Durkheim, E., 1961 edition, *Moral Education: A Study in the Theory and Application of the Sociology of Education*, New York: The Free Press.

Durkheim, E., 1971, *The Elementary Forms of Religious Life: A Study in Religious Sociology*, London: Allen and Unwin.

Gearon, L., 2013, *Master Class in Religious Education: Transforming Teaching and Learning*, London: Bloomsbury.

Grace, G., 2016, *Faith, Mission and Challenge in Catholic Education*, London: Routledge.

Groome, T., 1998, *Educating for Life*, Texas: Thomas More.

80 Religious education

Habermas, J. and Ratzinger, J., *The Dialectics of Secularism on Reason and Relations*, San Francisco: Ignatius Press.

Hirst, P.H., 1965, 'Morals, religion and the maintained school', in *British Journal of Educational Studies*, 14.

Humanist Philosophy Group, 2001, *Religious Schools: The Case Against*, London: BHA.

Janmohamed, S., 2016, *Generation M: Young Muslims Changing the World*.

Kant, I., 1784, *What is Enlightenment?*, quoted in Gearon, L., 2013, *Master Class in Religious Education: Transforming Teaching and Learning*, London: Bloomsbury.

Kuhn, T., 1970, second edition, *The Structure of Scientific Revolutions*, Chicago: University of Chicago Press.

Lane, D., 2015, *Catholic Education*, Dublin: Virago.

MacIntyre, A., *God, Philosophy, Universities*, London: Continuum.

Oakeshott, M., 1962, *Rationalism in Politics and Other Essays*, Indianapolis: Liberty Fund.

Pius, XI, (Pope), 1929, *Divini Illius Magistri*, Vatican City: LEV.

Sacks, J., 1997, *The Politics of Hope*, London: Jonathan Cape.

Shah, S., 2016, *Education, Leadership and Islam*, London: Routledge

Sennett, R., 2008, *The Craftsman*, London: Penguin Books.

Taylor, C., 2007, *A Secular Age*, Harvard University Press.

White J., 2002, *The Child's Mind*, London: Routledge.

6

RESPONSE TO THE SECULAR AGE

In search of its soul

Religious education (RE) has been described by Andrew Wright (1993, p.5) as the 'Cinderella subject' – indeed, a subject 'in search of its soul'.

There is a paradox here.

On the one hand, we saw in Chapter 2 how RE had been preserved by the 1944 Education Act, together with the requirement for a daily act of worship. The background assumption was that, whatever the decline in practice, Britain was basically a Christian country in terms of its history and culture, providing and supporting moral understanding and a code of conduct. The Christian story, as encapsulated, for example, in the Beatitudes and in the inheritance from the Old Testament of the Ten Commandments, provided the background to deliberations on how one should live.

Furthermore, a daily assembly of a religious nature was legally required of all community schools, together with an 'agreed syllabus' of a generalised Christian nature, locally agreed. The 1988 Education Act reinforced religion as a 'basic subject', though without national guidelines over content and assessment.

Hardly, then, a 'Cinderella subject'.

On the other hand, difficulties arose (as indicated in Chapter 1): first, from the decline, both culturally and practically, of Christianity, as is the case in much of Western Europe; second, from the growth through immigration of other religious groups (particularly, but not exclusively, those of Muslim faith); third, from an increasingly secular and humanist opposition. As a result, according to David Bell, when Chief Inspector for Schools, 76% of schools were failing to meet their legal requirement. Religion was no longer strictly equated with Christianity as it was in 1944, as witnessed by the guidance to the local Standing Advisory Councils on Religious Education (SACREs), which required the 'agreed syllabuses'

82 Religious education

> to reflect the fact that religious traditions in Great Britain are in the main Christian whilst taking account of the teaching and practice of the other principal religions represented in Great Britain.
>
> *(DES, 1988, Section 3)*

It came, fairly generally, to be seen as teaching *about* religion and reflecting the 'local traditions of the area'. The Act of Worship, though reflecting broadly the traditions of Christian belief, would not be distinctive of any Christian denomination, and in special circumstances may not be Christian. It was as though the subject, though compulsory, but bereft of any special denomination, had had the stuffing taken out of it.

There is clearly a conflict here between, on the one hand, those for whom RE (given the nature of religion as a way of life underpinned by a set of beliefs and with a distinctive narrative) must be seen as a personal formation and as an introduction to a spiritual tradition and community which is manifest in a range of practices, and, on the other hand, those for whom religions are but part of the social and cultural landscape that a well-informed person should be familiar with.

Such a state of affairs would seem to demand 'a new settlement for religion and belief in schools' as outlined by the former Labour Secretary of State for Education, Charles Clarke, and Professor Linda Woodhead – but in keeping, no doubt, with the Dearing and Chadwick Reports referred to in Tradition I of Chapter 5. They spoke of curriculum weaknesses in secondary schools being often related to a lack of clarity about the purpose of the subject at Key Stage 3 ('confusion in purpose in the minds of the teachers') – for example,

> uncertainties about the relationship between fostering respect for pupils' beliefs and encouraging open critical investigative learning in RE.
>
> *(Clarke and Woodhead, 2012, pp. 29–30)*

How might one reconcile in one subject such a diversity of views?

The current general debate

At the time of writing this book, the Religious Education Council of England and Wales (of which Humanist UK is a member) has set up a new commission to review the legal, educational, and policy frameworks of RE, indeed the nature, purposes and scope of the subject. It has now (September 2017) issued its interim report and is beginning consultation on various matters, including the very name of the subject to reflect its inclusion of non-religious world-views, including that of humanism. It sees the subject as equipping pupils to develop their own beliefs in the light of their reflection on these different world views.

Furthermore, REforREal (2015) produced a report on the *Future of Teaching and Learning about Religion and Belief,* which

> explores the role of schools in equipping young people with the knowledge and skills to engage effectively with religion and belief diversity in schools, in their community, and in future workplaces, and in wider social contexts.

Clearly there are difficulties where that Christian background can no longer be counted upon, where the practices of the Christian faithful seem alien, and where the narrative is unfamiliar. Moreover, many of the pupils come from actively different traditions (Muslim, Jewish, Hindu, Sikh) with their own narratives and practices which define the communities from which they come. Is it possible or even meaningful to abstract from those differences some common element which can be the basis of curriculum content, especially where, added to the mix, are the many who actively disassociate themselves from any religious interest? The liberal society, the product of the 'enlightenment' and increasingly secular in its understanding of what it means to be human (as explained in Chapter 5's Tradition II), would find little space for the teaching of a specific faith's understanding of that humanity, or indeed in maintaining religious references in traditional practices, as in the case reported in the *Daily Express*, 'Carols out of tune in schools', where such carols had to be doctored for fear of upsetting Muslim pupils with references to the birth of Jesus (*Daily Express*, 21.12.92). The secular vision is seen as the only one acceptable.

What, therefore, is required for RE once again to find its soul? The problems have not been ignored by the teachers of religion in our schools, nor indeed by the reports referred to under Tradition I in Chapter 5. Much thought has been given by the SACREs, by professional associations of teachers, by the reports of inspectors, and by the faith communities. But, by 2013, the funding of SACRE had been reduced, as also had the number of local education authorities full-time officers supporting their SACRE and agreed syllabus. The number of RE training places in universities had been slashed by 50% by 2013, and bursaries for RE trainees cut.

One might, therefore, reflect on some of the different ways in which the teaching of religion is, or might be, conceived, namely,

(i) teaching about different religions;
(ii) appreciating the significance of religious beliefs and experience;
(iii) religious engagement with controversial issues;
(iv) making sense of religion;
(v) 'religious literacy';
(vi) spiritual insight and formation.

In addition, religious understanding cannot ignore the link between such understanding and the promotion both of the common good and of care for the environment. This will be examined in Chapter 8, *Service to Society*.

Teaching about religions

Certainly, there is room for teaching *about* different faiths as part of the social and multi-cultural world we inhabit, rather than promoting a particular faith perspective. There would seem to be no room in the Common school for the 'confessional' form of religious education, reflected in Tradition III of Chapter 5, which had been, howsoever lightly, implicit within the 1944 settlement. Positively, however,

84 Religious education

knowledge of the different religions practised within the multi-ethnic community would be seen as valuable. After all, as the Pew Research Centre pointed out in 2010, 84.6% of world's population adhere to a religious faith. Hence, ignore religion at your peril.

Indeed, as a reaction to wars and acts of terrorism, partly seen to result from what was referred to by Huntington (1996) as a 'clash of civilisations', there was much pressure internationally for schools to include in the curriculum an account of different cultures, much of which required an understanding of the religious beliefs shaping such cultures. For example, the Organisation for Security and Cooperation in Europe (OSCE, 2007) produced guiding principles on teaching about religions and beliefs in public schools (as explained by Gearon, 2013, pp.16–24) showing how such understanding should lead to greater harmony and respect across the different cultures. United Nation agencies increasingly recommended RE as a way of supporting its policies for promoting peace and tolerance. In 2009, a Faith and Education Seminar at the Commonwealth Headquarters in London argued for the heightened place of RE

> to promote tolerance, respect, enlightened moderation and friendship amongst people of different races, faiths and cultures, as well as explore initiatives to promote mutual understanding and respect in the Commonwealth.
>
> *(Gearon, 2013, p.24)*

Therefore, a parliamentary cross-party argued that, since different religions were often portrayed inaccurately, RE could break down the prejudice which is based on ignorance.

> Pupils belonging to minority faiths need to feel that their way of life is understood and its true worth appreciated. We believe that in a multi-racial and pluralistic society there must be dialogue between those holding different beliefs, and growth in mutual understanding, not the widening of inherited divisions.
>
> *(Parliamentary Report, 2012)*

Assemblies, still required by legislation (though not necessarily whole school assemblies), might well be more broadly conceived, the character of which to be decided by the schools' governors to reflect their educational concerns and the cultural context of the school – for example, promoting multi-cultural respect and understanding. Indeed, the Humanist Society of Scotland (2016) proposed that

> All pupils in attendance at a maintained school shall on each school day take part in a period of reflection which addresses their spiritual, moral, social and cultural development.

Welcome though these international influences are, and have been, there are drawbacks in seeing them as the *essence* of RE.

First, it is treating the value of RE to lie in its being but a 'means to an end', thereby undermining its intrinsic worth and importance. As the REforREal Report (2015) said,

> Perhaps we should question whether RE bears too much of an instrumental responsibility – its instrumental purpose distracting from religious education proper.

Second, the introduction to the several different religious beliefs and traditions might be, as argued by Copley (2005, pp.119–120), criticised as a 'pic'n mix' tour of religion', trivialising each faith's claim to truth. Can such an approach provide the insight into the meaning and significance of a particular religious tradition or into a religious perspective shared across different religions? One would not, for example, enable students to understand and appreciate literature by a quick 'Cook's tour' of the 'great books and poems'. More, then, would seem to be required.

Appreciating the significance of religious beliefs and experience

Appreciating the significance of religious beliefs would involve more than 'laying out the facts'. It would seek to show, from the point of view of the 'insider', how and why religious beliefs and practices are taken seriously by different communities, the way in which they are seen to make sense of experience, the significance of a spiritual dimension in people's lives, albeit within different traditions. Such teaching would help pupils to grasp the distinctively religious languages – their 'phenomenological understanding of reality'.

The term 'phenomenological understanding', emerging from the philosophical tradition established by Husserl, was popularised within the realm of RE over several decades by Professor Ninian Smart, for example, in his *The Religious Experience of Mankind* (1969) and *Dimensions of the Sacred: An Anatomy of the World's Beliefs* (1999). There he argued that even an outsider to a particular religious faith could, given sensitivity to the experience which shape it, make sense of it, show empathy towards what that faith seeks to convey, and be able to present it intelligibly. Indeed, the Swann Report in 1985, *Education of Children from Ethnic Minority Groups*, argued that the phenomenological approach provided

> the best and only means of enabling all pupils, from whatever religious background, to understand the nature of religious belief, the religious dimension of human experience and the plurality of faiths in contemporary Britain.

Religious engagement with controversial issues in society

The study of philosophy is increasingly popular in the sixth forms of secondary schools. It is one of the few opportunities for students to engage in critical examination of the background traditions and beliefs which underpin moral assumptions,

86 Religious education

understanding of self and of other minds, and what counts as knowledge – in the arts, physical and social sciences, and religion. But, more often than not, that opportunity to do philosophy takes place in religious study classes – making that subject popular irrespective of the states of belief or unbelief within the class. The philosophical reflection and critical appraisal probe beneath the everyday, often unreflective, assumptions. Has life some meaning or purpose other than what is obvious on the daily round of tasks? On what grounds are certain moral rules or virtues to be pursued? What is signified by the changing concept of marriage and the controversies within society over those changes? On what basis might we invoke 'the dignity' of each human being against the impersonal forces manifest in an increasingly unequal society?

Gearon (2014, p.43) puts the matter well in summarizing the role of philosophy in religious education:

> Philosophy of religious education is, then, associated with not simply the encounter with philosophical themes – philosophical arguments for or against God, religious experience, and so forth – but a *method* of making judgments on religious truth, however this truth is conceived. Religious education has focused on the re-integration of philosophical themes and methods as a way of doing religious education.

Thus, RE could be the forum in which matters of human concern, yet deeply divisive within society, are explored through systematic discussion and by reference to what is seen as relevant evidence. Such evidence would be extracted from texts (including religious texts), poetry, literature, science, history. For example, what constitutes a 'just war' is a matter which divides society but on which opinions and beliefs should be formed through, say, engagement with St Augustine's criteria for a just war, with the war poets of the 1914–1918 conflagration, with the historical and political backgrounds to wars. The Humanities Curriculum Project, developed under the patronage of the now disbanded Schools Council, provided an 'Integrated Humanities' as a basis for examining the issues of importance which divide people in society and in which religious understanding played a significant part (see Stenhouse, 1975, *passim*).

Other areas for class deliberation in which the religious dimension could and should be introduced would be 'the prevalence of poverty in the world', 'relations between the sexes and the nature of marriage', 'the role of the State vis-à-vis the different ethnic and religious community practices', 'the prevalence of racism', 'environmental damage and our duties to nature' (to which deliberation the 'Jewish voice', as described by Rabbi Jonathan Sacks, 2002, pp. 161ff., is so important). To what extent is the dignity of the human person diminished in what Charles Taylor (2007, p.10) refers to as the post-modern world, in which religion is side-lined and in which the dignity of the human person is assailed through de-personalisation, through the managerial language of market capitalism and consumerism, or through violence and bullying within the social media?

To engage with an open mind on such reflections arising from everyday life and its problems, and on the messages from different sources which purport to provide answers, might well call upon a religious form of discourse, which itself can be pushed to greater depth (for example, concerning the dignity of each human being irrespective of ethnicity, social class or gender). One would then be entering into a different sort of 'language game'. For many, these considerations might well be the threshold of a sense of the religious dimension to life. But more needs to be said about this 'making sense'.

Making sense of religion

Despite the general decline in religious practice, there is not to the same extent a decline in the questions which are raised by religious belief and practice. According to Ofsted (2013)

> Most pupils recognise the value of RE and nearly two-thirds of them left school with an accredited qualification in the subject in 2012.

Hence, according to Clarke and Woodhead, not only would RE encourage students to recognise and respect diversity, and develop knowledge about a range of beliefs, but also

> an ability to articulate and develop one's own values and commitments, and the capacity to debate and engage with others.
>
> *(op. cit. p.34)*

The Schools Council, in arguing years ago for the continuing importance of religious education within a growing secular ethos, suggested that RE was the subject 'to address the elements of mystery in life, particularly that created by the awareness of death'. It would appeal to the need in children who have 'a deep sense of wonder and awe', a 'genuine search for meaning in life', and a sensitivity to the 'deeper aspects of human experience of which religion speaks'. For Whittle (2016), following the writings of the philosopher and theologian, Karl Rahner, it is the development of this sense of mystery which opens up the possibility of a theological response. The Ofsted Report (2013) on RE criticised RE teaching for too often failing to explore fundamental questions about human life and belief.

Such education, in seeking critically to understand the diverse nature of understanding within different religious traditions, would begin to engage with the distinctive types of religious experience – what philosophers of religion refer to as an experience of 'transcendence', as experienced not only through religious texts but also through aesthetic and moral experience and through art, poetry and music. Such understanding (even if, upon investigation, it is rejected) would open up the distinctive nature of a religious form of life. The Ofsted (2007) report, *Making Sense of Religion* argues that

88 Religious education

> RE should 'engage pupils' feelings and emotions' as well as promote respect
> for the commitments of others while retaining the right to question critically.
> [It] provokes challenging questions about ultimate meaning and purposes of
> life, belief in God and the evaluation of different viewpoints. It is not just an
> academic exercise.

The different religious traditions, despite significant differences in what they claim, would not be seen to be completely incompatible, but similar in the attempt to transcend self-centredness in our understanding of human affairs and to open up a sense of mystery in our experience of material reality. Key texts in the Old and New Testaments, in the Qu'ran, in the Torah, and in other religious writings would *show* the sense of mystery and transcendence.

Indeed, the non-statutory guidance for RE in English schools in 2010 put the matter clearly.

> Religious education provokes challenging questions about the ultimate
> meaning and purpose of life, beliefs about God, the self and nature of reality,
> issues of right and wrong, and what it means to be human.
>
> *(DCSF, 2010, p.6/7)*

Perhaps it is this exploration of what it means 'to be human' (in what Clarke and Woodhead, quoted above, referred to as encouraging 'open critical investigative learning in RE') which gives RE a special and important place in the school curriculum, to which of course literature, poetry, and history also contribute. Such an *exploration* is central to the different religious claims, but unfortunately restricted in schools by an examination system and the need to 'hit targets'.

Religious literacy

Such exploration and investigative learning requires, according to the Butler-Sloss Report, 2015, a degree of 'religious literacy', by which is meant a gradual understanding of the language of religious discourse, namely, the distinctive concepts through which religious beliefs and practices are described and understood. In particular, that discourse would include such concepts as the 'spiritual' and the 'sacred', which introduce a different dimension to our experience of the world, namely, a divine presence – God as both the continuing creator of the universe and our ultimate destiny.

But to understand such concepts requires learning a particular 'language game', that is, the proper use of an inter-related set of concepts connected with social practices which have emerged over time. Such 'literacy' would extend beyond that of 'God' to a range of concepts such as (within Christianity) 'sin' and 'redemption', 'prayer' and 'sacrament'. But what in particular would appear to give distinction to those 'challenging questions about ultimate meaning and purposes of life' from the religious perspective lies in the sense of the 'sacred' and the spiritual dimension to life – something which 'transcends' empirical understanding and experience of the world, and which is reflected in feelings of awe and in a realisation that there is more to understanding and appreciation of the universe than is to be captured in the sciences.

Inevitably, and quite rightly, questions arise concerning the role of reason, and the truth- value of claims made, in so depicting this religious dimension. The concept of God and of a divine presence requires close analysis, and the reasons for belief articulated and explored – as, indeed, they have been through the major religious traditions and by philosophers. In this, the three major monotheistic religious traditions, rooted in the early testaments of the Bible (Judaism, Christianity, and Islam), and developed through centuries of philosophical analysis and reasoning, provide detailed accounts of the meaning of God and of the relationship of God to humanity. To such issues (that is, to the theoretical problems in the knowledge status of religious claims) we must return in Chapter 10.

To engage in such a form of enquiry may not be confused with a 'confessional account' of religious education as described in Tradition III of Chapter 5. The aim is to develop in the students an understanding of what it *means* to believe in God and to *live* a religious form of life – to appreciate how others (Jews, Christians, Muslims, and those of other religions) come to see matters and pursue certain moral purposes in the way that they do. This is well illustrated in Dr Saeed Shah's account of religious discourses and practices from an Islamic perspective in which she explains the intrinsic link between the pursuit of knowledge, the 'complete world view', the ultimate awareness of the divine presence and the idea of the 'good life' – that is, the life shaped by virtue (Shah, 2015, chapter 2). For some, of course, it may lead to yet further exploration and thereby to religious belief and practice. For everyone, however, it is hoped it will lead to wider tolerance and interest based on understanding, namely, seeing matters and practices from others' points of view, appreciating and respecting the lives and practices of their religious friends and acquaintances.

Spiritual insight and formation

Much is said in educational pronouncements, not necessarily in connection with a religious form of life, about spiritual experience and spiritual development. Both the 1944 and 1988 Education Acts required all schools to develop the spiritual well-being of their pupils. Such development would traditionally have been identified with a religious perspective as in the Judaic theology of creation:

> The breath of Yahway, that is the spirit of God, who brings order out of chaos and life out of dust of the earth and continues to sustain that gift of life in existence.
>
> *(quoted in Polkinghorne, 1986, p. 86)*

Or as in the Christian Gospels where the 'spirit' comes down on Jesus at his baptism and is the in*spiration* of the disciples.

90 Religious education

However, in the more secularist context, such a connection is severed. The National Curriculum Council in 1993 explained spirituality as follows:

> [Spirituality] has to do with relationships with other people and, for believers, with God. It has to do with the universal search for individual identity – with our response to challenging experiences such as death, suffering, beauty, and encounters with good and evil. It is to do with the search for meaning and purpose in life and for values by which to live.
>
> *(NCC, 1993, p.2)*

It may appear that 'spirit' and 'spiritual' are words which so easily come to mean whatever it is convenient for people to make them mean once they have departed from a religious conception of the world. However, their use does seem, generally speaking, to suggest openness to an account of experience which cannot be reduced to a purely empirical and material account of the world. It would, for instance, refer to that sense of awe, transcending the 'the elements of a mundane life' arising from art, music, or poetry. Listening to a Bach concerto or a Mozart Mass gives rise to what might be called a 'spiritual experience'. And music and art have always played a central part in religious ritual and liturgy, embodying a spiritual dimension and thereby transmitting it. Similarly, one can be 'uplifted' by some noble act or a morally led life that one has observed or which is recounted in literature. One is in*spired* and thereby gives a *spirited* account of what one has witnessed.

Indeed, to pursue the spiritual in this broader, if ill-defined, sense might be seen as a reaction against a narrow vision of education which leaves the 'person' (in terms of ideals and values) unaffected. Such a spiritual dimension, if taken seriously as schools have been instructed to do, would (or should) temper the stress upon passing examinations as the main aim of education, emphasising instead the sort of person one is to become – one's authenticity in terms of the moral values one a*spires* to and the way of life committed to. Such a spiritual dimension would be contrasted with the increasing materialism and hedonism in what is sometimes called the 'post-Christian Society' (Methodist conference, 1997, p.37), or what Chadwick (1997) refers to as 'an increasing utilitarian and materialist approach to education'.

But how might one connect these spiritual appreciations and yearnings with that recognition of 'the sacred' in our understanding of the world and our experience of it? How might the teacher move from that sense of the spiritual (as articulated by poets, musicians and artists or as reflected in the accounts of brave and noble lives) to that religious sense of the spiritual which recognises the sacredness of life to be derived from a sense of the divine, namely, God as the purported source of life and as (through the prophets) the inspiration as to how one should live? To what extent does 'religious literacy' (that is, being able to use and interconnect key words such as 'sin', 'redemption', 'grace', 'prayer', 'sacred', 'sacramental'), lead to a depth of understanding?

Too often so-called 'understanding' is disconnected from the experiences which it is supposed to be an understanding of (as indeed so often is the case in the formal teaching of science or social studies). Coming to understand often requires gradual participation in the practices which embody such understanding, even such everyday practices as 'shaking hands' or saying 'please' and 'thank you'. One might say that a form of life has to be lived in order to be known. Is not the young child developing a particular relationship, appropriate for certain situations, through engaging with such customary greetings? And may not the child be coming to see the spiritual dimension to life through participation in those rituals and practices which have come to express that dimension over the centuries — what might be referred to as 'the initiation thesis'? Such a thesis is attributed by Eamon Callan to the late Terry McLaughlin who argued that

> the initiation of children into religious practice could secure an understanding of religion unavailable, or at least less readily available, in the absence of initiation, and that the relevant understanding enabled or enhanced in some way autonomous choice regarding religion.
>
> *(Callan, 2009)*

Interim conclusion

Such an 'initiation', namely, a coming to understand and appreciate (in a paraphrase of Durkheim):

> things which are superior in dignity and power to the elements of mundane life, to things set apart, to concepts of the transcendent and divine, and to the ultimate destiny of persons, to what is holy, ineffable and mysterious, is the beginning of the argument for Faith schools.

References

Bell, D., 2015,

Butler-Sloss Report, 2015, *Living with Difference*, Report of the Commission on Religion and Belief in Public Life.

Callan, E., 2009, 'Why bring kids into this?', in Haydon, G., *Faith in Education: A Tribute to Terry McLoughlin*, London: University of London Institute of Education.

Chadwick, P., 1997, *Shifting Alliances: Church and State in English Education*, London: Cassell.

Clarke, C. and Woodhead, L., 2012, *A New Settlement: Religion and Belief in Schools*, Westminster Faith Debate.

Copley, T., 2005, *Indoctrination, Education and God*, London: SPCK.

Cooling, T., 1994, *A Christian Vision for State Education*, London: SPCK.

DCSF, 2010, *Religious Education in English Schools; Non-statutory Guidance*, Nottingham: DCSF Publications.

DES, 1988, *Education Reform Act*, London: DES.

Durkheim, E., 1961 edition, *Moral Education*, New York: The Free Press.

92 Religious education

Gearon, L., 2013, *Master Class in Religious Education*, London: Bloomsbury.

Gearon, L., 2014, *On Holy Ground: The Theory and Practice of Religious Education*, London: Routledge.

Humanist Society of Scotland, 2016, *Religion in Law Report*, Edinburgh: BHA

Huntingdon, S.P., 1996, *The Clash of Civilisations: The Remaking of the World Order*, New York: Simon and Shuster.

Methodist Conference, 1997, 'Use of Methodist Premises by People of Other Faiths', Report of the Faith and Order Committee.

NCC, 1993, *Spiritual and Moral Development; A Discussion Paper*, York: NCC.

Ofsted, 2007, *Making Sense of Religion*, London: Office for Standards in Education.

Ofsted, 2013, *Realising the Potential*, London: Office for Standards in Education.

OSCE, 2007, *Toledo Guiding Principles on Teaching about Religions and Beliefs in Public Schools*, Warsaw: OSCE/ODHR.

Parliamentary Report, 2012, *RE and Good Community Relations*, London: HMSO.

Polkinghorne, J., 1986, *One World: The Interaction of Science and Theology*, London: SPCK.

REforREal, 2015, *The Future of Teaching and Learning about Religion and Belief*, London: Goldsmiths College.

Sacks, J., 2002, *The Dignity of Difference*, London: Continuum.

Shah, S., 2015, *Education, Headship and Islam: Theories, Discourses and Practices from an Islamic Perspective*, London: Routledge.

Smart, N., 1969, *The Religious Experience of Mankind*, London: Macmillan.

Smart, N., 1999, *Dimensions of the Sacred: An Anatomy of the World's Beliefs*, Berkeley: California University Press.

Stenhouse, L., 1975, *An Introduction to Curriculum Research and Development*, London: Heinemann.

Swann Report, 1985, *Education of Children from Ethnic Minority Groups*, London: HMSO.

Taylor, C., 2007, *A Secular Age*, Harvard University Press.

Whittle, S., 2016, *A Theory of Catholic Education*, London: Bloomsbury.

Wright, A., 1993, *Religious Education in the Secondary School*, London: David Fulton Publishers.

7

RELIGIOUS EDUCATION

An extended vision

Introduction

The possible transition, referred to in Chapter 6, 'from spiritual appreciations … to the recognition of the "sacred" in our understanding of the world' is far from easy, although appreciation of how others may hold to such a vision and may experience such a feeling of sacredness could no doubt be developed through skilful teaching, dialogue and exposure to the experiences and way of life enjoyed by the adherents of a religious tradition. Indeed, as will be explained further in Chapter10, what Ninian Smart influentially argued for within the phenomenological tradition was an 'attitude of informed empathy' which 'tries to bring out what religion means to religious actors' (quoted in Gearon, 2014, p.107).

Indeed, the Agreed Syllabuses from 1944 had revealed a great change of emphasis. Increasing attention was paid in them to worship, and the aim of the teaching was declared to be that children should understand and accept the Christian faith and follow the Christian way of life. It was hoped by some that school worship and religious instruction would lead pupils to become and remain full members of a worshipping community outside the school.

There were few dissenting voices until the 1960s on this more 'confessional nature' of religious education. But we have seen how the foundations to thinking about the physical, social, and moral worlds, which we inhabit, have become predominantly secular – affecting what it means to be a person, what constitutes the common good and what are the goals worth striving for in life. Furthermore, we have seen one feature of a secular world (the fourth sense as explained in Chapter 5) to be the reduction of human life and achievement to that which is easily measured in the now dominant language of management.

Religious traditions: Distinctive visions and challenge

However, religious traditions, which have evolved through many generations, embody a different vision, articulated in a different language, and challenging what they see as an impoverished understanding of what it means to be a person. Central to such traditions – whether Jewish, Muslim, or Christian – has emerged a way of seeing the world as embodying spiritual presence, not reducible to a purely material explanation, whether that be in a distinctive idea of what it means to be a person, or in the sense of wonder in the natural environment (unless besmirched by a human exploitation), or in the human search for meaning and for life-purpose which cannot be reduced to material profit and success. Such traditions provide different 'horizons of understandings' for making sense of, and interpreting, one's encounters and experiences. What have been referred to, especially in Chapter 5, as the 'background understandings' or 'horizons of significance' cannot be escaped, for such must characterize, too, the secular views of humanity and of society – the basic understanding of what it means to be human, of the common good within society, and of the norms of good behaviour.

Such religious and moral 'horizons' or traditions have emerged from key persons, figureheads, who manifest the ideals of faith in a human form. For the Jews, these are the prophets as retold in the Old Testament and the Torah, which embraces every aspect of human life; for the Christians, Jesus Christ but seen, through the New Testament, as continuous with the Jewish narrative; for Muslims, Muhammad as revealed in the Qu'ran and the Hadith, but with roots along with Judaism and Christianity in Abraham's narrative. Through such texts and persons are revealed distinctive forms of life, expressed through detailed narratives of how life should be lived, through the articulation of the ultimate end to which such living leads, and through identifying the means for approaching the state of perfection that is shown in such narratives (for example, the 'five pillars' of the Muslim faith, the life of prayer and sacraments for the Christians, the understanding and the following of the Torah for the Jews). The Bible is to be seen as a rich and profound account of man's search for, and growing understanding of, God, developed through critical reflection over thousands of years.

It ought to be a matter of wonder, even to the unbeliever, how such narratives and ways of living have survived and flourished over many centuries. In so doing, these narratives have not remained static. Indeed, each incorporates a long tradition of rational argument, reconciling the revelations shown in the narratives with a central philosophical inheritance rooted principally in Plato and Aristotle.

An essential ingredient in that tradition of rational argument is the understanding of rationality as a deliberative process which can transcend the reality of sense experience, as when one seeks a deeper explanation of the experiences for which a language (different from that referring to empirical reality) arises, and is pursued and is dissected in discussion. In *The Idea of the Holy,* Rudolf Otto (1923) shows how such transcendence of the empirical world is itself a product of rationality, making possible a fundamental experience irreducible to any other.

Therefore, there would seem to be a strong argument for different religious communities, as they face the taken-for-granted assumptions which an increasingly secular society promotes, to seek to ensure that education has the wider brief of initiating the next generation into the religious tradition which they have inherited – the way of life with its distinctive narratives, its moral traditions, its liturgical practices embodying a sense of the sacred, but also its internal and developing dialogue about its beliefs and practices, as they respond to the problems of the modern world.

It is, of course, assumed within the prevailing secular society that the maintenance of such traditions inculcates beliefs and ways of experiencing the world which would not have been arrived at through the purely rational appraisal of evidence – such a rational appraisal being the aim of education in a liberal society. The mark of the autonomous person is that he or she should make up his or her own mind on such matters. But the concepts of 'autonomy', of 'indoctrination', and of 'liberal society' need to be examined critically – and will be in Part III. Here it is necessary to refer back to Chapter 5 and to the centrality of 'tradition' in all our thinking, including that of the secularists. Such traditions provide the foundation for the way in which we see the world, make sense of experience, formulate a moral perspective, define personal growth and fulfilment, and defend a particular vision of human life and destiny. As is argued in Chapter 5, the secular view is one tradition amongst others. Hence, there is a need either to protect the respective faith views within the community school or to maintain the Faith schools for those who see the distinctive faith understanding of human development as an essential part of education, but in danger of being watered down, ridiculed or neglected in an often hostile or indifferent secular context.

Such a distinctive understanding of human development and of its religious dimension, was stated by Durkheim in *Elementary Forms of the Religious Life* (paraphrased by Grace, 2016, p.1) to be of

> [t]hat which is sacred … refers to things which are superior in dignity and power to the elements of mundane life, to things 'set apart', to concepts of the transcendent and divine, of souls and spirits, and to the ultimate destiny of persons. The sacred is holy, ineffable and mysterious.

If education is concerned with the growth and fulfilment of the total person within a distinctively human society – intellectual, moral, and spiritual – then those who belong to a tradition which provides the background to such a development would wish it to enter into the educational life of the school. But part of that initiation into, and a strengthening of, such a tradition would be the deepening of understanding of that faith, the questioning of its presuppositions, the growing appreciation of its spiritual inheritance.

Such an understanding and appreciation, as in so many things in life, is not achieved by a purely didactic approach. It is, as Rabbi Jonathan Sacks states (quoted earlier in Chapter 5) a morality received not made. It is embedded in and reinforced by a total way of life, articulated in texts, transmitted across the generations, enacted in rituals, exemplified by members of the community, and underwritten by revelation and tradition.

(Sacks, 1997, p.89)

Indeed, is not all distinctively human development (that is, becoming more human) of this nature? We acquire moral principles and virtues through living within a moral community – with its distinctive practices for expressing gratitude, caring, love, fortitude. Indeed, the society based on humanist principles has its own 'secular saints' and its own distinctive narrative. Thus, it can be seen that

'the whole of the school ... assists and promotes faith education – a school has as its purpose the students' integral formation.

(SCCE, 1987)

What then in a nutshell would be distinctive of Faith schools that goes beyond the community school in response to a secular age, not simply in provision of religious education as such, but in the embodiment of a particular educational ideal?

'Whole of the school' and faith education

The following illustrates how different kinds of Faith schools (namely, voluntary aided) within Tradition III (see Chapter 5) might embody such a view of education.

Muslim Faith schools

The considerable rise in the Muslim community in England and Wales has been quite recent, due to immigration and to children born of those who arrived especially from the former colonies in Africa in the 1960s and then from the Far East, especially Pakistan and Bangladesh. As was the case of Irish immigrants in the second half of the 19th century, they were mostly poor and concentrated in major cities in relatively segregated communities. In addition, the new arrivals had little command of English. They met much prejudice, indeed Islamophobia, from the indigenous population, and the children generally underperformed in the community schools which they attended, leading the community to believe that the state system of schooling was failing their children (as has been well researched by several studies – for example, those by Hewer, 2001, and Shah, 2012) as well as providing a secular view of the world. As Merry and Driessents argued (quoted in Shah, 2012, pp.51–55),

For the small but growing number of Muslims who seek out an Islamic education for their children, public schools represent moral permissiveness and lower academic achievement, others are dismayed with the extent to which schools ignore the cultural and religion identities of Muslim children.

But in addition, and as the case with any world-wide religious community, the Muslim population sees itself as part of not just the civic society but the much larger Ummah (over 1.5 billion people constituting a community beyond geopolitical boundaries), which provides an identity transcending the local community with a distinctive understanding of what it means to be and to grow as a person. The need, therefore, for their own schools arises from the perceived failure of the state system, the prejudice which they experienced and the preservation of their distinctive Islamic culture. Indeed, such successful schools would enable the learners not only to be good Muslims but also to enter into the main community and to contribute to it, bringing to the political and civic life of the state the contribution from the values of the Ummah. Without, however, the contribution from the state, as is the case with voluntary aided schools, the Muslim community would be restricted to poorly resourced and unaccountable private schools or madrassas, often attached to the local mosque.

There is much in parallel here with the growth of the Catholic schools in the late 19th and early 20th century, and it would have been inconsistent with government policy (evolved, as outlined in Chapter 2, from 1870) not to extend voluntary-aided status to the Muslim schools, which meet conditions set by the government.

What then is distinctive of such schools, given that they too must offer the National Curriculum and be subject to external accountability, as is the case with all state-funded schools? They would introduce the pupils to the Ummah – to its distinctive civilization (history, literature, arts, and languages), to its spiritual traditions (for example, Sufi mysticism), to its theological account of human nature and destiny (namely, 'tawhid' – 'oneness with God'), to the major texts (the Qu'ran and Hadith) through which that account is given, to the 'taqwa' or way of life (ethical code, values, and virtues collected in the Sunna and dictated by the Prophet), and to the social and economic structures reflecting those values.

Inevitably, there would be aspects of such a schooling which may not be generalizable across the state system of schools (for example, the segregation of females from males, although that remains a feature of both the state and especially private schools). But it is difficult to see how such a way of life does other than make a valuable contribution to the broader community which, as Sacks (1997, p.55) says, is

> a confusing mixture of reasons and associations, which emerge, like a great river from its countless streams and tributaries, out of a vast range of histories and traditions.

The situation is, in some respects, similar to that of the Catholic schools in the late 19th century, which, often in a fairly hostile environment, led to greater integration rather than fragmentation. Having their own schools within the state system helped

98 Religious education

to move Catholics out of their initial isolation and to become more confident and able to contribute to the civic society more generally.

Catholic Faith schools

The Catholic community, one of several which make up our society and which has, together with other Christian denominations, contributed over the centuries to its development, is the product of 2,000 years of critical reflection upon the life of Jesus Christ and upon the exposition of that life, first, within those early Christian communities (as reflected, for example, in the Acts of the Apostles), leading to a distinctive anthropological understanding of what it means to be fully human, that is, to seek a particular human ideal. Given, as will be argued in detail in Chapter 9, that 'enabling us to be human' is a principal aim of education, then such understanding of this inheritance must be an important aspect of schools in which members of that community and that tradition (the third sense, as explained in Chapter 5) wish their families to be educated. Such an 'anthropological turn' would be particularly central to the educational ideals of the Catholic community.

'Anthropological turn' is the term used by Karl Rahner, theologian and philosopher, and introduced by Sean Whittle (2015, p.96) into his *A Theory of Catholic Education*. It is a *theological* response arising from the *philosophical* reflections upon the understanding of experience of different kinds but above all upon the sense of mystery when one pursues significant questions about 'meaning' – a *meta*physical attitude which suffered from, but was not defeated by, 'the age of enlightenment'. Such a response, providing a very different 'horizon of significance', is made possible by the philosophical deliberations encouraged through (though not solely) religious education, which then is able to articulate it as it has been developed in the practices, liturgy, prayer-life, moral pathways, and codified teachings of the Church.

Just as that development has been profoundly philosophical over the centuries (particularly integrating the different treatise of Aristotle), so it can be related to the serious philosophical engagement of the students as they reflect systematically upon their lives, aspirations, and experiences – each systematic reflection being 'transcended' by yet further questioning and provisional answers. From such questioning, there can arise a sense of mystery, namely, where the positing of a transcendental Being emerges for many. Such an answer has been the subject of theological and philosophical thinking over the millennia and leads to a different and contrasting vision of human nature and destiny from that of secular society.

What, then, would be the distinctive nature of the religious experience and teaching within such schools, in conjunction with or following from such philosophical deliberation? According to Philip Robinson, who advises the Catholic Education Service,

> The core purpose of RE in Catholic schools is to ensure that all pupils have a good knowledge and understanding of the Catholic theological tradition. [From] studying RE, pupils will be able to engage critically with big

questions about doctrine, religious practice, the interpretation of Scriptures and other Church documents as well as wrestling with the philosophical and ethical questions about which the Catholic theological tradition has something important to say.

(Robinson, The Tablet, *6.5.17)*

Such systematic study would necessarily involve the acquisition of the 'religious literacy', referred to in Chapter 6, through which that understanding is achieved and furthered – key concepts, for example, of 'incarnation', 'eucharist', 'sacrament', 'sin', 'redemption', 'Trinity'. But it would lie also in the ethos, the spiritual atmosphere, of the school. This was described by one teacher in a Catholic school as 'not just a subject but a way of being' where, for example, one learns about 'the Beatitudes in the corridor, morality in history' (Nicholson-Ward, *The Tablet,* 1.10.15). The Faith permeates the overall formation of the person – an essential element in an educational process which is geared to personal fulfilment.

But it would include, too, what Grace refers to as the 'spiritual capital', which the principals and teachers in the schools draw upon in sustaining a sense of mission, purpose, and hope when faced with many difficulties and in maintaining a distinctive ethos in their schools, integrating faith principles and practice with secular knowledge and skills required by the state (see Grace, 2013).

That overall distinctiveness of such a Faith school, as analysed by Stephen Tierney (Executive Director of Blessed Edward Bamber Catholic Multi-Academy Trust), would seem to lie in the following:

- *curriculum,* namely, the organisation of learning (both theoretical and practical) which would provide a comprehensive account of what it means to be human and to grow as a person, as that emerges in the narrative of the specific faiths;
- *moral ethos,* namely, interpersonal relations, institutional values and sense of duty shaped by virtues such as justice, mercy, caring, humility, fortitude, kindness, as developed within the faith traditions, (for example, the 'Imitation of Christ' – the title of a popular prayer book);
- *theological understanding,* namely, a grasp of the key ideas and teachings of the particular religious traditions;
- *liturgy,* namely, the practical manifestation of the religious understanding as enacted in words and in rituals;
- *prayer,* namely, personal and regular recognition of the divine presence, assisted by words inherited from within that tradition;
- *collective worship,* namely, orientation of the community in prayer and in the recognition of the divine presence;
- *philosophical understanding,* namely, a critical examination of the central ideas, rooted in traditions of philosophical and theological argument; and
- *counter-culture,* understanding humanity and community in a way that runs counter to the materialism, pursuit of profit, and consumerism often characterising secular society.

Religious education

One must, of course, be careful. The critics may well point to faith-based schools which fall short of such ideals – accusations of abusive behaviour or pursuit of academic success at the expense of a broader vision. But in the words of Psalm 130, 'if Thou, O Lord, should mark iniquities, Lord, who shall endure it?' Part of the valid religious picture to be passed on (so clear from the Old and the New Testaments) is that of an imperfect people striving to serve, often failing, but with a sense of hope.

Jewish Faith schools

As Helena Miller (2001) explains in her paper, 'Meeting the challenge: the Jewish schooling phenomenon in the UK', there has been a rapid increase in Jewish schools in Britain over the last few decades, accommodating (by the year 2,000) approximately 55% of Jewish children aged 5 to 18, with a view to ensuring the continuity of the Jewish faith and the Jewish community. Of the 100 or so Jewish schools, over 40 are voluntary aided. As with Muslim and Christian schools, there are denominational differences – mainly between those under the United Synagogue, which has the Chief Rabbi as its religious authority, and those under the Jewish Community Day School Board. But whatever the differences, central to the distinctive aim of education, which shapes such schools, is the nature of the relationship between the Jewish ideas of holiness (namely, the Judaic concept of 'connection to God') and the dynamics of their teaching and learning practice. As Steinberg (1947) explained 'to Judaism uniquely amongst religions the processes of learning are sacred and study a holy pursuit'.

Isaac Calvert expands on this:

> [T]hose who teach and learn within the Jewish tradition (a cultural/religious paradigm that allows for educational practices, concepts and structures to be treated as sacred) have access to pedagogical techniques, learning methodologies and other insights to which contemporary educational sensibilities have been relatively unaware, and from which they could benefit both theoretically and methodologically.
>
> *(Calvert, 2017)*

One such 'learning methodology' is that of 'story-telling', the encapsulation of deep insights in accessible and powerful stories, which give access to that which, in its full essence, is inaccessible. Another is the musical inheritance. Furthermore, there is a rich textual tradition (the Torah), which is drawn upon. This interacts with a living spoken tradition of oral Torah and its lived practices. Entry into such a long-standing and rich tradition is through participation in the readings and the practices, which encompass nearly every aspect of human experience. It is here above all that one can see the strength of 'tradition', as stated in one of the Mishnah's most well-known tracts:

> Moses received Torah from Sinai and passed it down to Joshua, And Joshua to the Elders, and the Elders to the prophets, And the Prophets passed it down to the men of the Great Assembly.

Central, too, as in the case of all the major religions, is the idea an experience of 'holiness' – a disposition (reflected in personal experience, in text and narrative, in ritual and in place) related to God.

Interim conclusion

The general account of religious education given in this and the previous chapter, and especially the account and specific examples of such education in Faith schools, raise critical questions of a philosophical kind – concerning the ethical basis of the educational aims of such schools, the justification of the knowledge claims being made, the obligations of the public authorities to support educational goals which are not generally shared.

These concerns are crucial and require more systematic philosophical examination than is possible in the exposition so far given. To those concerns, we return in Chapters 9, 10, and 11.

But there is one further aspect of the initiation into a religious tradition (and thus religious education) which has not been dealt with, and to which, in Chapter 8, we must turn. That is, the contribution made (through upholding the distinctive religious traditions within Faith schools) to the 'common good'. The moral requirements of religious practice are not of purely private importance and concern. They have a social aim and impact. That deserves a further chapter. Furthermore, its significance is enhanced by the accusation, frequently given, that the pursuit of separate Faith schools undermines the common good rather than enhancing it.

References

Calvert, I., 2017, Unpublished doctoral thesis, University of Oxford.

Durkheim, E., 1971, *Elementary Forms of the Religious Life: A Study in Religious Sociology*, London: Allen and Unwin.

Gearon, L., 2014, *On Holy Ground: the theory and practice of religious education*, London: Routledge.

Grace, G., 2013, 'The distinctive nature and challenge of school leadership', paper commissioned by the National Council of School Leadership, UK.

Grace, G., 2016, *Faith, Mission and Challenge in Catholic Education*, London: Routledge.

Hewer, C., 2001, 'Schools for Muslims', *Oxford Review of Education*, 27(4).

Miller, H., 2001, 'Meeting the challenge: the Jewish schooling phenomenon', *Oxford Review of Education*, 27(4).

Otto, R., 1923, *The Idea of the Holy*, Oxford: Oxford University Press.

Sacks, J., 1997, *The Politics of Hope*, London: Jonathan Cape.

SCCE (Sacred Congregation for Catholic Education), 1987, *The Religious Dimension of Education in the Catholic School*, Vatican City: LEV.

Shah, S., 2012, 'Muslim Schools in secular societies: persistence or resilience', *British Journal of Secondary Education*, 34(1).

Steinberg, 1947, *Basic Judaism*, Harcourt: Brace and World.

Whittle, S., 2015, *A Theory of Catholic Education*, London: Bloomsbury.

8

SERVICE TO SOCIETY

Religion and social education

An account of religious education which confines itself, as often is the case, to the development of the sense of sacredness and transcendence, or which focuses on a spiritual dimension, or which locates these within an historical narrative (whether that be of the Bible, the Qu'ran, or the Torah) does not complete the story. Thus, Durkheim (1971) argued for the intrinsic relation between the religious idea of the sacred in our lives and the human society.

> If religion has given birth to all that is essential in society, it is because the idea of society is the soul of religion.
>
> *(quoted in Grace 2016, p.2)*

The great religious traditions, therefore, had distinctive views about the kind of society to be created or developed, and about the contribution such societies should make to the welfare of its members,

> the ways in which people imagine their social existence, how they fit together with others, how things go on between them and their fellows.
>
> *(Taylor, 2007, p.419)*

For instance, religious traditions (howsoever they may often fail in practice) have a central place for such virtues as justice, caring, and respect for others whatever their background. The exercise of such virtues raises critical questions about the economic world order which shapes our lives. Indeed, such traditions should, and indeed do, provoke those who, taking them seriously and aiming to live within them, engage in social reforms of different kinds. They are witnesses to the sense of the sacred in the human society and thereby to the dignity of each person, irrespective of background or indeed of personal failures. That is why the Dearing Report, 2001, for example, placed the Church of England schools at the centre of their *mission to the nation*, serving particularly those in social and economic need.

This 'service to society' should be seen not simply as a consequence of religious education as described in the previous chapter but as a living manifestation of the religious vision revealed in the nurturing of religious faith. Such service to society might be encapsulated in the following:

- special regard for the poor and disadvantaged;
- social teaching which benefits all within society; and
- care for the environment.

The following three subsections develop these aspects of 'service to society' as an essential element in the religious education of young people – and one which would underline for them the social relevance of religious faith.

Special regard for the poor and disadvantaged

John Astley, writing from the Anglican tradition (Tradition I, as explained in Chapter 5), points out that

> the Christian idea of schooling, when construed in terms of a service and ministry, should encourage us to recover our focus on the poor.
>
> *(Astley, 2013, p. 106)*

Gerald Grace, in referring to the 'foundation charter or mission statement for contemporary Catholic education', states clearly the original purpose of the Catholic school within this Christian idea (and the danger of forgetting it), namely, since it is motivated by the Christian ideal, the Catholic school is particularly sensitive to the call for a more just society and it tries to make its own contribution towards it. That contribution emphasises a commitment both to solidarity and community through its educational practice and a commitment to the service of the poor, irrespective of their faith or none.

> First and foremost, the Church offers its educational service to the poor, or those who are deprived of family help and affection, or those who are far from the faith. Since education is an important means of improving the social and economic conditions of the individual and of peoples, if the Catholic school were to turn attention exclusively or predominantly to those from the wealthier social classes, it would be contributing towards maintaining their privileged position and could thereby continue to favour a society which is unjust.
>
> *(SCCE, 1977, quoted in Grace, 2016, p. 71)*

104 Religious education

Furthermore, it is very critical of those who fail to follow this demand:

> [I]n some countries … the Catholic school runs the risk of giving counter-witness by admitting a majority of children from wealthier families. … This situation is of great concern to those responsible for Catholic education because first and foremost the Church offers its educational services to the poor, or those who are deprived of family help and affection or those who are far from the faith.

This would seem to be particularly pertinent to the Faith schools debate in Britain, if the weight of evidence shown in Chapter 3 would suggest that some Catholic and other Faith schools appear to be more socially selective than neighbouring schools. This is by no means universally true, and even where admissions do seem skewed to better-off families, this may be due, not to a deliberate policy of social selection, but to the naturally wider catchment area of the parishes which the schools serve. But even in such cases, given the explicit mission of Catholic education as pronounced in the document quoted, ought they not to be seeking out those, even when not of any faith, who are disadvantaged in different ways? Are they really living up to their religious vocation?

Social teaching which benefits all

There are three aspects of social teaching which are at the core of religious traditions and which are in danger of being undermined within the secular world in which we live: first, the dignity of each individual; second, the centrality of the family in upholding that dignity; third, the promotion of the 'common good'.

First, however, it is important to refer back to Chapters 1 and 5 as to what is meant here by the 'secular world'. 'Secular' sometimes means simply the absence of a religious reference and background. At other times, it refers the more systematic philosophical position, stemming from the 'Enlightenment', in which there is no need to refer to religion in the explanation of the universe – reason, not revelation, explains all that is to be explained. A third meaning pointed to the belief in the pursuit of autonomy – personal freedom divested of the moral horizons which traditionally had been points of reference. But a fourth meaning (which we have in mind here) is a world which is divested of 'the personal', often in the pursuit of profit and of material well-being irrespective of personal or social consequences. This is referred to by Dermot Lane (2015), following the new anthropology of *Laudato Si*, as the myths of modernity increasingly prevail, namely, individualism rather than mutuality, unlimited progress, competition rather than co-operation, compulsive consumerism, the unregulated market. It is enhanced by the increasing dependence on technology which replaces human intercourse and personal interaction. The dignity of each person is undermined.

Hence, the basis of 'social teaching' within a religious tradition must be the retrieval of 'personal dignity', a 'sense of communal solidarity' and respect for constitutive associations, especially 'the family'.

Personal dignity

This arises from

- emphasis on the humanity, and thereby the dignity, of each person (irrespective of background, ethnicity, social standing or economic need);
- provision of the essentials for living a distinctively human life (home, clothes, warmth, food, support when in need, and basic education);
- opportunity to participate in those communal decisions which affect such provision;
- freedom, both negatively (in the sense of not being prevented from pursuing one's own goals so long as no harm to others), and positively (in the sense of being empowered to see what leads to fulfilling ends, and to act accordingly).

Only then are persons treated as 'ends in themselves', that is, not disposable when not fitting into prevailing values or not being simply the means to someone else's aims. Such a sense of personal worth or dignity is at the heart of the Christian story in which all are redeemed through Christ's sacrifice on the cross, at the heart of the Jewish heritage and identity which needs to be preserved, and at the heart of the teaching of the Qu'ran. That said, the centrality of the dignity and worth of each person irrespective of ethnicity, social class or religion is not necessarily obvious in all cases from the respective religious practices.

It is for these reasons that teachers in the different faiths are (or should be) critical of an economic system which, often in the pursuit of profit and in deference to the 'free market', is prepared to deny individuals the essentials for dignified living. The pursuit of profit within the labour market too often drives down what should be the just reward for the labour undertaken. The general principle, shared (I suspect) across the different religious faiths, was put forcefully by *Rerum Novarum*:

> Let it be granted that, as a rule, workmen and employer should make free agreements, and in particular should freely agree as to wages. Never the less, there is a dictate of nature, more imperious and more ancient than any bargain between man and man, that the remuneration must be enough to support the wage earner in reasonable and frugal comfort. If, through necessity or fear or worse evil, the workman accepts harder conditions because an employer or contractor will give him no better, he is the victim of force and injustice.
>
> *(Papal Encyclical, 1891)*

'Persons' – their sense of worth irrespective of gender, class, ethnicity, ability – should be at the centre of educational aims. That is partly driven by religious understanding of what it means to be, and to grow as, a person, and partly through a critique of the social and economic structures which obviate such personal respect and development.

Pursuit of the 'common good' (solidarity)

Social teaching, therefore, must arise from what is needed to ensure respect for human dignity for all. Under what conditions can individuals live a life of dignity and fulfilment? Clearly that requires giving up some independence of action (the pursuit of one's own desires) where these impinge upon others' legitimate aims for a satisfying and fulfilling life. It recognises that we are all members of community and that personal growth arises from interaction and relationships with others. Hence (as shall be explored in greater detail in Chapter 11), there is need for political associations through which personal lives endure some restrictions for the benefit of everyone but through which the individuals might attain the moral and intellectual attainments otherwise not possible. The political community is legitimated by its enabling the personal development of its members and by its being consented to by those members.

Such 'social teaching' is part of religious education because it shows the ways in which each person may and should contribute to those conditions in society which enable everyone, but in particular the least well off, to live a fully human life, namely, the economic and political conditions for such a life and the charitable works necessary where the economic conditions fail individual members.

Subsidiarity: The centrality of the family

The state (or the political entity) is given its power and role, by those governed by it, to enable its members to meet their needs, to live fulfilling and distinctively human lives and to overcome conflicts between individuals pursuing their personal goods. The exercise of such power embodies the principle of justice which maximises the possibility of all to flourish.

But within such a political community there are not only individuals, but also associations where the citizens come together to promote their particular interests and aspirations. Such associations include the various religious and humanist communities, which contribute to the discussions on what constitutes human flourishing. There should be no necessary opposition between the higher order political body and the various associations which are contained within it. 'Subsidiarity' was the concept which underpinned the social teaching of *Rerum Novarum* and subsequent encyclicals. It is explicated in *Quadragesimo Anno* (Papal Encyclical, 1931), as follows:

> It is an injustice, a grave evil and disturbance of the right order for a larger and higher association to arrogate to itself functions which can be performed efficiently by lower and smaller societies.

In particular, one should refer here to the family which

> is anterior both in idea and in fact to the gatherings of men into a commonwealth [and which] must necessarily have rights and duties which are prior to those of the latter, and which rest more immediately on nature.

The stability of the family is central to religious traditions, with certain rights to its preservation and with obligations of others towards it within society. Within the Christian tradition, marriage is a sacrament – a commitment before God to mutual love and respect and to the provision of a stable home for the upbringing of children.

One is seeing, however, in the more secular society, which has emerged, an undermining of the concept of the family as a permanent life commitment. People live in partnership without that commitment sanctified through the sacrament of marriage. Divorce is increasingly common. Sexual relationships are freed from their place within the marriage state and from permanent commitment. The consequence of such secularisation provides further need, amongst the religious community, for reinforcing through education the importance and sanctity of the family.

Care for the environment

We are witnessing profound ecological changes which have serious consequences both for human beings (witness the serious famines in many parts of the world) and for wildlife. Social teaching cannot ignore the problems emerging. That, however, requires the development of a profound respect for the environment, of human understanding of the changes, and of a sense of responsibility for that environment and its preservation.

There are interrelated causes for these problems – on the one hand, the destruction of nature to meet immediate human consumer demands, but, on the other hand, the economic motivation and models which are pursued to meet those demands. The answer, therefore, must be a change in what human beings see to be important – a longer term vision of, and a profound respect for, the environment. Such a human transformation is clearly expressed in the papal encyclical 'Laudato Si'.

> Many things have to change course, but it is we human beings above all who need to change. We lack an awareness of our common origin, of our mutual belonging, of a future to be shared with everyone. ... The modern self-understanding of man is a major part of the ecological crisis. ... There can be no ecology without an adequate anthropology.
>
> *(See Lane, 2015, for reference and further commentary)*

There is need, therefore, for what Lane (p.22) refers to as a 'new anthropology ... more chastened and humbled ... to respond to the ecological crisis of the 21st

108 Religious education

century' – a sense of stewardship, not one of domination. Education should seek a better understanding not only of how the environment is changing, but also of the responsibility of human beings for those changes – an *acceptance of stewardship* – and of the demand which nature makes on our respect for it.

Perhaps, too, this integration of such social teaching into Faith schools would help the students to appreciate the significance of the religious perspective in an increasingly secular society. It needs to be recognised that handing down the super-structure of Catholicism in creeds and catechisms without dialogic attention to the existential context and experiential agonising of humanity in the 21st century will not work, and is not working (Lane, 2015, pp.65/66).

Conclusion

Religious education cannot ignore an account of the relationship between the individual, the wider society, and the environment – in particular, how the dignity of each person (central to recognition of his or her humanity) requires interrelated-ness with others within community. It cannot ignore, therefore, the political and social questions about the sort of community which is fitting for the recognition of each person's right to a worthwhile, free, and dignified life. This requires

- social teaching which looks critically at prevailing economic models in the light of their impact on community and human dignity;
- critique of the 'individualism' which is reflected in pursuit of profit irrespec-tive of personal impact, fragmentation of community, increased inequality, and decline in public services and responsibility;
- support and promotion of those associations which are integral to the wider society, especially the family; and
- sense of stewardship for the environment in place of the dominance through which governments and individuals consume and destroy.

Within a tradition of religious education, articulated by the different faiths, there is an alternative vision for society as indicated by the Dearing Report (2001, p.14).

> For globalisation and the ascendancy of consumerism have emphasised per-sonal choice, but have not so far generated a balancing sense of community or a coherent sense of responsibility for sustaining the earth's own well-being or for the quality of our civilisation. In a world of shifting sands, many parents have welcomed the stability offered by schools that offer an enduring alterna-tive to the growing secular values of society.

The religious response takes us into the realm of ethics (see Chapter 10), namely, the need to examine yet again what it means to be and to develop as a human being within the created world. This is expressed in the idea of a revised 'anthropology', a deeper sense of what it means to be human arising from all the areas of knowledge which contribute to that understanding. To this, then, we must turn in the first of the three chapters which address the philosophical issues emerging in what has been said about religious education.

But the religious response takes us also, as already hinted at, into social and political philosophy concerning the nature of society and the common good, the relation of the state to subsidiary associations within it, and in particular the rights of the family within the educational system. That will be the concern of Chapter 11, the third of the three chapters addressing the philosophical questions which have arisen.

References

Astley, 2013, 'Church schools and the Church's service to the poor', in Worsley, H.J. *Anglican Church School Education: Moving Beyond the First Two Hundred Years*, London: Bloomsbury.

Dearing Report, 2001, *Way Ahead: Church of England Schools in this New Millennium*, London: Church House Publishing.

Durkheim, E., 1971, *The Elementary Forms of Religious Life: A Study in Religious Sociology*, London: Allen and Unwin.

Grace, G., 2016, *Faith, Mission and Challenge in Catholic Education*, London: Routledge.

Lane, D., 2015, *Catholic Education in the light of Vatican II and Laudato Si*, Dublin: Veritas.

Papal Encyclical, 1891, *Rerum Novarum*.

Papal Encyclical, 1931, *Quadragesimo Anno*.

SCCE (Sacred Congregation for Catholic Education), 1977, *The Catholic School*, London: CTS.

Taylor, C, 2007, *A Secular Age*, Cambridge: Harvard University Press.

PART III

Key issues emerging

The need for philosophy

9

ETHICS

Education and its aims

Introduction

Chapter 5 gave an account of three different traditions within which the publicly funded system of education in England and Wales has evolved. Although these countries constitute a 'limited case' within the international scene as that is exemplified in Chapter 4, such an account reveals the different ways in which belief systems enter into our thinking about education and its aims. The provision of education, therefore, requires prior consideration of what we mean by 'education' and, in particular, its aims.

Aims of education

What do we mean by 'an educated person in this day and age'? What are those values and virtues, the obligations, the kind of knowledge and understanding, the social qualities and skills which we regard as characteristic of the educated person that we are trying to develop through the context of the school?

No school can be neutral in regard to such questions. What is taught and how it is taught, the relationships encouraged between pupil and pupil and between pupil and teacher, all embody (howsoever inadvertently) answers to those questions.

It could be the case (yet to be shown) that importantly different responses to such questions from within the different religious and secular traditions and practices (in part referred to in Chapter 5) might be seen as justifications for different kinds of school within the state-funded system, in keeping with their different values and ideas of 'the educated person'. If such a justification is not accepted, then families might well argue that, despite having paid their taxes to support the public system, they are denied the educational opportunities for preserving the sort of life which embodies those values.

114 Key issues emerging: The need for philosophy

What then counts as an educated person in this day and age?

The importance of the question is reflected in the letter sent by the principal of a large high school in Boston, in the United States to newly appointed teachers.

> Dear Teacher
> I am the survivor of a concentration camp.
> My eyes saw what no man should witness:
>> Gas chambers built by learned engineers.
>> Children poisoned by educated physicians.
>> Infants killed by trained nurses.
>> Women and children shot and burned by high school and college graduates.
>>> So, I am suspicious of education.
> My request is: Help your students become human.
> Your efforts must never produce learned monsters, skilled psychopaths, educated Eichmans.
> Reading, writing, arithmetic, are important but only if they serve to make our children more human.
>
> *(Strom, 1981, p. 4)*

At the heart of education and its aims must be those qualities and attributes which make us distinctively human, and indeed more so. They are not simply academic achievements, such as those acquired by the principal's 'learned engineers', 'educated physicians', 'trained nurses', and 'college graduates'. Indeed, if they were, then those of poor academic ability would be deemed ineducable and thereby less open to distinctively human development.

On 'being human' and becoming more so

To some extent, our understanding of what it means to be human evolves through the insights provided by the human and material sciences, through the humanities and philosophical deliberation, through reflection on the practical demands and choices arising in one's daily life, and indeed through theological and religious scholarship. That is why reference is frequently made to 'human anthropology' (see Lane, 2015, pp.33ff. and Rahner, 1972), namely, the different and interacting contributions to the ways in which one might understand what it means to be human – and thus the aspiration of the principal, quoted above, to make our children more so.

In what follows, I wish to argue for four key features of what it means to be human, and thus to become more so.

Moral seriousness

The first characteristic of being human, which would have been in the principal's mind, is the development of a 'moral sense' and 'moral purpose': that is, the capacity

Ethics **115**

and the tendency to think seriously about what constitutes a worthwhile life and the obligations and duties which arise from that – for example, not submitting to one's own whims or pleasures irrespective of the consequences to other people. Such a person would have learnt to respect both the dignity (intrinsic worth) of oneself and also the dignity of others. Moral sense would thus be developed in relationship with others, recognising and respecting their interests and concerns. The 'learned engineers', the 'educated physicians', the 'trained nurses', and the 'high school and college graduates' may well have the *knowledge* associated with 'the educated person', but it was exercised in defiance of any moral sense. That clearly had not been developed in their so-called 'education'.

That life of duty and of fulfilling obligations needs to be informed and supported by virtues – the dispositions to pursue the right path: *modesty* in exercising appraisal of one's achievements; *humility* in the face of correction; *courage* in pursuing one's considered course; *honesty* in facing problems encountered; *perseverance* through challenging circumstances; *justice* in the treatment of others, and so on, which constitute a 'form of life'.

To be fully human, then, is to have developed this moral sense: of deliberating what goals are worth pursuing in life; informed by relevant duties and obligations to others; and marked by appropriate dispositions or virtues. Such development of serious deliberation, and of the appropriate duties and dispositions, is the purpose of moral education, and, as Durkheim argued, the school is the ideal place where deliberations over what is worthwhile can be pursued and where the habits leading to the relevant duties and virtues can be developed – preferably under teachers who reflect that sense of duty and those virtues (Durkheim, 1961, chapter 2).

Personal autonomy and knowledge

A further feature of being human is that the internalised moral sense (namely, the ideals towards which they strive, the duties to which they submit and the virtues which they acquire) requires personal thought and effort. In the sense that people, upon continual reflection and deliberation in the light of difficulties raised, accept them because they see them (namely, the ideals, duties, and virtues) to be desirable, so they are developing as autonomous persons – having the capacities and thoughtfulness to engage in this moral life. They are doing so, not for external rewards or from mere obedience or from what is fashionable or from an immediate desire, but from reflection, deliberation, seeing the possible consequences of one's purported actions in the wider context of a life worth living. Hence, the development of such autonomy is central to moral development.

Much thinking is needed in many situations which confront one, and greater autonomy is attained where one has a grasp of the relevant kinds of knowledge and understanding. Such knowledge and understanding arise from many sources – from what Oakeshott refers to as the different 'voices in the conversation of mankind' within the arts, humanities, and sciences that we have inherited. But having such knowledge without the moral sense leads to the very horrors which made

116 Key issues emerging: The need for philosophy

the principal 'suspicious of education'. Beware the common claim that 'autonomy' *in itself* is the aim of education (freedom to pursue one's own path informed by knowledge, howsoever sophisticated) when it is exercised without a developed 'moral sense'.

Relationships with others

A further feature of the principal's understanding of 'becoming more human' would be, as indicated, the recognition of the wider community of which one is necessarily part. Indeed, as the much-neglected philosopher, John MacMurray, argued in a public lecture to Moray House College of Education, Edinburgh, entitled 'Learning to be Human',

> The first principle of human nature is mutuality ... This principle, that we live by entering into relation with one another, provides the basic structure within which all human experience and activity falls, whether individual or social. For this reason, the first priority in education - if by education we mean learning to be human - is learning to live in personal relation to other people. Let us call it learning to live in community. Inhumanity is precisely the perversion of human relations.
>
> *(MacMurray, 1958)*

Or, indeed, as the editor's introduction to Durkheim's *Moral Education,* puts it:

> The duty imposed by the group, the affection generated by one's fellows, the use of reason with which the group endows us, and the group's social mechanism (education) through which duty, affection, and reason are generated – these constitute the social seedbed of morality.
>
> *(Durkheim, 1961, p.xxvi)*

The school is, or should be, where such consciousness is broadened and where the recognition of others as persons is realised, not only through the wider relationships which it provides, but also through the transmission of an inherited culture of ideals and social understanding – indeed, what Charles Taylor refers to as the 'horizons of significance' which one draws upon in explaining and justifying what one believes and does (Taylor, 1992, pp.33–35). Thus, the importance attached by Durkheim (as we shall see) to the school, as a social system, and to the teacher as the agent of moral education within it.

Spiritual dimension

This term is used loosely here, in anticipation of a more detailed account below. But it points to the presence in the deliberations referred to of the constraints arising from a view of human destiny which transcend the material world and which are captured within different religious traditions. It arises where theological thinking enters into the 'human anthropology' referred to, namely, 'the study of the human in all its complexity' (Lane, op. cit., p.13) – their aspirations, the sense of hope and of despair, the perceived poverty of a purely secular vision, the awareness of mystery. Such theological contributions to that 'making sense of what it is to be human' are captured in the religious traditions, as those are referred to below. But in their respective articulations there is much in common between them.

Interim conclusion

The prevalent public and secular culture is not morally neutral regarding what it means to be human or to live a distinctively human life. But if it proclaims liberal values, it must thereby respect the telling of different stories of what it means to be human and to live distinctively human lives, so long as they are in their different ways contributing to the common good (to be developed further in Chapter 11). As Rowan Williams (2012) says of the Christian community within the wider civic society:

> In the face of the narrative of modernity, the Church declares that its account of human nature and calling and possibility is constituted by a set of highly specific events, figured forth in sacramental action. And the community that gathers around these actions is one in which human beings are deliberately shaped in the likeness of one particular form of life, the form that is defined in the story, the identity, of Jesus Christ.

The undermining of 'moral sense'

Many of the 'horizons of significance', which in previous generations have been points of reference in moral deliberation (in particular, though not exclusively, incorporated in religious traditions) have waned or disappeared in much of contemporary culture, as argued in Chapter 5 – unacknowledged by many but regretted by others. In their place, what Taylor refers to as 'modernity' is characterised by three interrelated features.

The first lies in the 'dark side of individualism ... a centring on the self' (Taylor, 1992, p.4ff.). It is an 'autonomy' without a moral reference. To act autonomously becomes the moral imperative. Great importance is attached to individual 'self-fulfilment'. Indeed, autonomy becomes an end in itself, with emphasis on choosing the sort of life which is to grant that self-fulfilment. Significance, therefore, is attached to personal freedom to do what one wants, limited (perhaps) so long as the exercise of that freedom does not do too much harm to others also pursuing their personal desires and wishes. Such pursuit of freedom, reflected (for example) in what is referred to as the 'permissive society', and 'being true to oneself', leads to a degree of moral relativism. 'These are my values', and, unless they impinge upon another's freedom, then no one can dispute them or take them from me. Thereby,

118 Key issues emerging: The need for philosophy

certain restraints (assumed within previous cultures) disappear, reflected, for example, in the unbridled pursuit of profit and the depersonalisation of relationships in much of everyday life.

The second feature of 'modernity', as outlined by Taylor, is the primacy of instrumental reasoning, and the undermining of what it means to be a 'person'. 'Technical rationality' permeates both public and private services, in which what is valued is reduced to what can be measured (for example, what is learnt in schools through the rigid testing regime). Public life is shaped by the 'management-speak' of targets, performance indicators, audits, efficiency gains, and 'the science of deliverology'. 'Persons' become atomised into objects and thereby part of the metrics. School appraisals by the inspectorate, with their lengthy tick-lists, are subject to this terminology as much as is the factory production and producers of consumer goods. Even universities have succumbed to precise measurement of 'impact' in research publications that feature in the 'social science research index', and now to Teaching Quality Assessment. There is little questioning of the appropriateness of this 'bureaucratic rationalism' in the running and reporting of schools, hospitals, universities, and care services. There has emerged, in other words, a new language in which otherwise personal and public services are accounted for. Contractual relations take the place of personal and caring relations within this increasingly 'bureaucratic rationality' shaped by the 'invisible (and impersonal) hand of the market' in what are still referred to as 'public services'.

However, schools, though the victims of this 'bureaucratic rationality', can, and often do, resist it as far as possible, preserving, through an ethos of caring, the dignity of each person and the growth of that through the interpersonal communication with others. However, that is not easy where schools are 'audited' against 'performance criteria' which determine where they will be placed in the public league tables, as is reflected in the recent and well publicised case of the London grammar school which excluded those students who got 'only' grade B in Year 12 assessments, thereby jeopardising the school's chance of topping the league table in the following year.

However, as the philosopher John Macmurray argued in *Self as Agent*:

> Against the assumption that the Self is an isolated individual, I have set the view that the self is a *person*, and that personal experience is *constituted* by the relation of persons.
>
> *(Macmurray, 1957, p.12)*

It is in the development of those inter*personal* relationships within the spirit of caring communities and relations that a 'moral sense' is maintained, resisting the very impersonal culture which now shapes modern life. The pursuit of autonomy as an educational aim can be much exaggerated, being one element in the individualism which is characteristic of modernity. It has its limits through the necessary interrelations within the different communities of which one is part.

The third feature in the 'undermining of moral sense' lies in the diminished teleological understanding of what it means to be human – that is, a recognition of 'the bigger picture or horizon against which human life is lived' (see Whittle, 2015, p.12) and which helps define the ends or purposes worth pursuing. This bigger picture or horizon might well be identified with a religious way of understanding and interpreting experience. Such a religious account arises from a questioning of the purpose of life, from articulating a spiritual ideal to which life should be directed, and thus from a broader anthropological understanding of what it means to be a person.

However, it may also be the case that one can discern that 'bigger picture', those ideals, in an articulated account of 'secular ethics'.

The rise of secular ethics

There are two interrelated aspects of ethics.

On the one hand, there are the foundational and overarching justifications and beliefs for what one does or prescribes, which permeate a community or organisation or profession, and which are the reference points for moral discourse. In philosophical discourse, for example, one might point to a utilitarian theory of morals in which the ultimate justification of actions lies in the quantity of pleasure brought about.

On the other hand, 'ethics' refers to the more specific duties, motivations, and dispositions of individuals, influenced by the foundational ethical account illustrated earlier.

Clearly, the former so easily influences the latter. For example, the influential philosophical work of A.J. Ayer argued that for any proposition to be meaningful it must logically be open in principle to verification by reference to observation. Moral propositions clearly failed that test, and so were declared to be meaningless. They were but the expressions of emotion – hence, what came to be called 'the emotive theory of ethics' (Ayer, 1936, ch.6). Such a theory (to be dealt with at greater length in Chapter 10) severs the connection between moral life and rationality, and leaves a vacuum, so easily filled with the pursuit of pleasure as an end in itself, and also, within prevailing economic thinking, the pursuit of profit without reference to wider social consequences.

Religious traditions, aware of the influence of prevailing ethical background on the moral disposition and behaviour within a more secular society, seek to enforce different modes of thinking, feeling, and behaving. They attach importance to Faith schools for that reason, providing what is often referred to as a different 'ethos', infiltrating the ways in which the pupils acquire a distinctive morality. In particular, such schools would seek to counteract the 'secular tradition' referred to in Chapter 5.

It is important first, however, to be reminded of the different senses of 'secular' already referred to in Chapter 5 – first, that of indifference to religion in one's account of the world and of responsibilities within it; second, that of an alternative account to that of religious traditions (materialist and often, though not necessarily, tinged with hostility to religion); third, that of the 'dark side of individualism ... a centring on the self'; fourth, that of the primacy of instrumental reasoning which undermines the intrinsic dignity of being a person.

120 Key issues emerging: The need for philosophy

It is the second meaning with which I am concerned here and with which many humanists and secularists would want to be associated. Hence, the significance and the important influence of Emile Durkheim's book *Moral Education.*

As described in Chapter 4, post-revolutionary France created a thoroughly secular society, meaning one which, in public policies and institutions, the influence of religion would be removed. That necessarily included schools. But removing religious influence from public life, particularly that of the Catholic Church, could so easily be seen to produce a moral vacuum, since morality (duties and virtues) were embodied within religious beliefs, narratives, and practices. It was the aim of Emile Durkheim, therefore, to show how there could be a strictly secular morality (that is, one based purely on rational principles). In doing so, however, he did not seek simply to dismiss the content of the morality which prevailed, even though dressed in religious clothing, for he saw Christianity as an essentially human religion,

> since its God dies for the salvation of humanity, Christianity teaches that the principal duty of man toward God is to love his neighbour.
>
> *(Durkheim, 1961, p. 6)*

But, so Durkheim argued, the dignity given to moral rules by religious justification can be preserved without such a justification. Furthermore, it creates new ideals to which moral development reaches out. The ethical basis therefore of moral living, as argued by Durkheim, might be described as follows.

First, moral behaviour means, at its most basic level, establishing and consistently following rules – abiding by certain norms. Morally good persons have developed the disposition (the virtues) to follow such rules even if they do not suit their immediate purposes. One is not free to change the rules simply to suit one's taste. Those rules have authority, they provide a 'sense of duty' to which one appeals in relevant situations. By contrast, the immoral person feels free of such constraints, has little sense of duty, and feels able and willing to do what he or she pleases, irrespective of the consequences.

Second, in being part of communities (for example, the family or the civic society), one has inherited such rules which, generally speaking, are constitutive of that community living. One comes to recognise the social attachments and relationships intrinsic to being human, and thus the distinctive rules of, and constraints on, behaviour arising from this living in communities and associations. In living thoughtfully, that conception of 'community' expands – from family, to local associations, to the civic and national communities, and indeed to humanity itself, namely,

> the goal of realising among its own people the general interests of humanity – that is to say, committing itself to an access of justice, to a higher morality, to organising itself in such a way that there is always a closer correspondence between the merits of its citizens and their conditions of life with the end of reducing or preventing individual suffering.
>
> *(Durkheim, op. cit., p. 77)*

Third, however, such rules cannot anticipate all conceivable situations, and there is constant need for deliberation over the applicability of the relevant rule and indeed of the ends or purposes which they serve. Moral education, therefore, needs, from an early age, to get the child to see (and feel) the importance of disciplined rule-following behaviour, and later to appreciate the ability to deliberate over the application of such rules to novel situations, the essence of moral thinking thereby being a form of rational discourse. In order to consistently follow such rule-governed behaviour, there is need to develop the *habits* of so doing and thereby the dispositions or *virtues* which dispose one so to follow, even where that might be personally difficult or uncomfortable. A central virtue is that of justice, ensuring that each person within the community is treated with equal respect and dignity, and thus differently only when relevant aspects of the situation justify such differences. The onus of proof lies on the shoulders of those who promote differences of treatment.

In so saying, Durkheim would argue that morality is independent of religion, although religious belief and practice may well incorporate and reinforce the moral prescriptions.

Thus, in pursuit of this ideal, it is the intention of the French public schools to provide a moral education in 'Republican values' in place of that of the Catholic Church. Such an education (as shown in Chapter 4) emphasises the equality of all, irrespective of social background, gender, ethnicity, and indeed religion. Hence, all French public-school pupils now take a course in '*laique* ethics', emphasising a culture of sensitivity, democracy, rule of law. This is accompanied by a long list of texts from philosophers supporting 'a culture of engagement'. In all this, the teacher is 'the Republic incarnate', bringing the ideal to life. Thus, the Minister of Education asks the question (and answers it):

> For this is the question that we are all faced with, with new intensity: How can we share the values of the Republic with everyone? How can we construct a republican and *laique* culture without negating our differences? The most important response comes from the field, the teachers themselves, those who facilitate the famous practical application of the republic ideal. It is they, the teachers, who have always held in their heart the mission of bringing the ideal to life. And they are the ones whom I am addressing here.
>
> *(Valland-Belkacem, 2015, in Duclert, V., ged, p.ii)*

Therefore, such a secular morality has its own distinctive foundation, namely, 'the Republic ideal', explicated through a philosophical tradition in which the future citizens are to be nurtured.

The liberal ideal

Closely associated with such a view of 'secular ethics', has been the ideal of personal freedom – no longer being subject to authority in terms of the sort of life one might or should choose to live. Such an ideal, as argued by John Stuart Mill

122 Key issues emerging: The need for philosophy

in his *Essay on Liberty*, holds that the only constraint to be imposed by civic society upon such freedom of choice and action is where such choice and action are harmful to others. Thus, emerging from the spirit of the 'Enlightenment' has been this 'liberal ideal' through which personal freedom, compatible with the freedom of others within the community, is of paramount importance. It is in keeping with such an ideal that, central to development as a person through education (helping the children, in the words of the principal, 'to become more human') is that of 'autonomy'. To be autonomous is to make up one's own mind – no longer dependent on external authorities (especially religious ones) in deciding what one should believe or do. Moreover, acting autonomously, it is argued, is enhanced by the development of reason in its different modes. Hence, the title of the influential paper by Professor Hirst, 'Liberal education and the nature of knowledge', and the paper by Robert Dearden, in the same volume, entitled 'Autonomy' (Dearden, Hirst, and Peters, 1972).

It is important to distinguish here, however, quite different ethical traditions which underpin practical, and therefore moral reasoning, and the pursuit of freedom. Reference was made earlier to A.J. Ayer's 'emotive theory of ethics', according to which moral statements (not open to verification) are therefore neither true nor false, but are merely expressions of emotion. One might see such a position as in keeping with what Alasdair Macintyre refers to as 'some notorious aspects' of the philosopher David Hume's 'original expressivism'.

> On Hume's view our passions, and consequently our preferences, can be neither rational nor irrational, neither according with reason nor violating its canons, so that 'tis not contrary to reason to prefer the destruction of the whole world to the scratching of my finger'.
>
> *(MacIntyre, 2017, p.46)*

In what MacIntyre refers to as 'expressivism', the motive for action lies in the fulfilment of what is desired, and thinking practically lies in deliberating how such desires might be met or how they need to be adapted in order to be fulfilled, or even rejected when their pursuit leads to undesirable consequences (that is, their desires are not fulfilled). In a way, morality becomes privatised, without reference to external standards which constrain what is desirable.

An alternative ethical framework

An alternative ethical framework lies in the constraints arising from what it means to be human and from acting accordingly, even when those constraints go against what one desires. Such constraints arise from deliberations over what counts as human flourishing both in oneself and in those with whom one is inter-related (for example, in the family and in civic society) – harking back to John Macmurray's first principle of human nature being mutuality, the principle that we live by, through entering into relation with one another.

In such deliberation one inherits a tradition – philosophical, humanistic, and theological – concerning what it means to be human and thereby to flourish. There is a concept of 'the good life', which constrains what is desirable and which is reflected, say, in the virtues and in social obligations. Practical moral reasoning in this case would be more than thinking about the most effective way of getting what is desired. Rather it would be directed at what is *desirable*, where 'desirable' may well not be equatable with whatever desires are presently motivating one. Furthermore, such deliberation concerning what is good – what counts as human flourishing – has a history which needs to be taken seriously in the deliberations. We are thus back once again to 'traditions' and to 'horizons of significance' – ways of understanding human flourishing, which have been inherited and developed through constant reflection on what constitutes 'the life worth living', and which therefore become reference points in moral deliberation and practical reasoning into which the next generation is to be initiated.

The danger of dismissing this alternative ethical framework in the name of liberalism lies in the unconstrained pursuit of desire, as witnessed, for example, in the massive accumulation of wealth in an increasingly unequal society, and in the destructive dominance of market forces in the provision of education and health. It is only by thoughtful reference to such traditions through the habit of deliberation that one can come to question and constrain the selfish pursuit of liberty. There is a dark side to the advocacy of autonomy where that consists in making up one's own mind without reference to moral limitations based on what is meant by human flourishing – or indeed in taking seriously D.H. Lawrence's injunction: 'Find your deepest impulse and follow that' (quoted in MacIntyre, op. cit., p.68).

Faith-based ethics

Thus, if education is concerned with the development of the human person, then there is a need to foster within the educational system different understandings of what it means to be a person – and to be one more fully. Parents, who are concerned about what they see to be the 'secular culture' (in the different senses as explained in Chapter 5), which permeates society and hence schools, may well wish for a school which embodies values, reflected in a religious tradition, which sets its sights and formulates its ideals beyond the general welfare and coherence of society as described by Durkheim. Indeed, the responsibility for them to do so is reflected powerfully in the Chief Rabbi's reference in *The Politics of Hope* to Jacob Neusmer (Sacks, 1997, p.x):

> Civilization hangs suspended, from generation to generation, by the gossamer strand of memory. If only one cohort of mothers and fathers fails to convey to its children what it has learnt from its parents, then the great chain of learning and wisdom snaps. If the guardians of human knowledge

124 Key issues emerging: The need for philosophy

stumble only one time, in their fall collapses the whole edifice of knowledge and understanding.

Such traditions re-conceive the concept of 'person' and of what therefore it means to be human. In the three monotheistic world religions, which are referred to in this book and which seek their own schools within the state system, the concept of the person is transformed by the relationship with the 'Divine Person', as that is revealed through the prophets of the Old Testament, through the Gospels and the history of the Early Church in the New Testament, and through the Qu'ran's and Hadith's accounts of the Prophet's life and teaching. And in the light of that relationship, so the dignity of each person, howsoever poor or unattractive or undeserving he or she may seem, is preserved and enhanced. 'Man (sic) is made in the image of God', from which follows the identical dignity of all who thereby deserve unconditional respect.

However, such unconditional respect is in practice difficult to maintain, increasingly so, due to the undermining of mutuality and reciprocity in a market-driven approach to (and a privatisation of) public services in education, health, social care, and economic relations. Human beings become 'metrics' within the emerging economic model of society. Therefore, one can understand the importance which parents may attach to the resistance provided by a religious perspective in an increasingly secular environment, since religion reproduces a distinctive view of what it means to be human. This is put thus in the conversation between the humanist philosopher Joseph Habermas and the future Pope, Joseph Ratzinger.

> [W]e find in sacred scriptures and religious traditions intuitions about the salvific exodus from a life that is experienced as empty of salvation; these have been elaborated in a subtle manner over the course of millennia and have been kept alive through a process of interpretation … kept alive in the communal life of religious fellowship.
>
> *(Habermas and Ratzinger, 2006, p. 43)*

That 'salvific exodus' includes 'sensitivities to lives that have gone astray, failures of individuals' plans for their lives', and 'sense of personal unworthiness'.

This is exemplified by the three monotheistic religions referred to in this book and referred to particularly in Tradition III as explained in Chapter 5.

Christianity

Central to the Christian tradition, therefore, is the recognition both of 'sin' (failure in different ways to live up to what it means to be human) and of 'redemption' (the invitation and the opportunity to overcome those sinful ways). Such redemption is made possible through contrition, resolution, prayer, and perseverance. Whatever one's failings, there is reason for hope and for mercy. And these are 'kept alive in the communal life of religious fellowship', where one learns, too, to embrace all others in such a mode of thinking and living. Such a tradition, therefore, because of the distinctive relationship it gives between individual persons and the redeeming God, is seen to portray a deeper sense of the human dignity of each and every person than is achieved by a purely secular account.

Furthermore, such a tradition is embedded within particular practices (for example, the liturgical and sacramental life of the Church), within the powerful narratives of the Old and New Testaments, and within the path to holiness as embedded in the 'beatitudes' of St Matthew's Gospel and in the request to love our neighbours as we love ourselves, which is achieved through the constant struggle to love God with all our mind and actions, but guided by the Ten Commandments and the life of Christ.

It would include, too, the deep respect for the environment, as argued strongly in *Populorum Progressio,* namely, that the world is, as it were, loaned to all people, and not divided up into fiefdoms for the few. The struggling and suffering of the majority of the world trump all attachments to property and power.

Within schools, which claim to embody such a tradition of thinking, the deliberations referred to as a crucial element in 'moral seriousness', would be informed by the life of Christ as narrated in the scriptures, clearly stated in the instruction 'Come, follow me'. This self-formation is likened to a vocation, therefore, to pursue a particular way of life, as argued by Paddy Walsh in his unpublished paper, presented at Heythrop Conference, 2017, 'Philosophy, Theology and the Christian School'.

Judaism

Similarly, within the Jewish tradition is the idea and the experience of 'holiness', namely, seeing people, places, and experiences of different kinds somehow leading to 'Tawhit', or oneness with God. It is embedded in the *Tora*, received by Moses, becoming the written and oral tradition, which was been handed down through the Elders and the Prophets, though subject to constant deliberation and development. It is intrinsic to the teaching of the next generation through its distinctive pedagogy and practices. This is put eloquently by the Chief Rabbi, Jonathan Sacks, as quoted in Chapter 1:

> It is embedded in and reinforced by a total way of life, articulated in texts, transmitted across the generations, enacted in rituals, exemplified by members of the community, and underwritten by revelation and tradition. It has not pretensions to universality. It represents what a Jew must do.
>
> *(Sacks, 1997, p.89)*

Thus, there is a rich textual tradition, developed over 3,000 years, and a living spoken tradition of oral Torah intertwined with every aspect of living, and encompassing every aspect of human experience.

126 Key issues emerging: The need for philosophy

Islam

In Islam, education is seen as a 'formation' within a particular faith tradition, reaching 'Tawhid', that is, oneness with God. That is achieved through understanding and following the life of 'the Prophet', as reflected in the Qu'ran and Hadith. The importance of this led to the development of the madrasas in the 10th-century higher institutions of learning, which showed the way to a reflective and fulfilled religious life – a 'tawhidic vision' of reality. Muhammad personifies the human potential of ascent to the divine through living this reality, knowing the meaning of obedience and service to God.

In pursuit of such an ideal, the madrasa systems universally taught the Qu'ran, Arabic, Hadith, law, theology, historic aspects of Islam, logic, and philosophy. Two different emphases are worth noting: on the one hand, the mystical life reflected in Sufism; on the other hand, the emphasis on reason, as reflected (as in scholastic philosophy) in the influence of Plato and Aristotle.

The more mystical, inspirational and spiritual aspect is well illustrated in this statement by Eberhardt:

> Oh, to lie upon the rugs of some silent mosque, far from the mindless noise of city life, and, eyes closed, the soul's gaze turned heavenwards, listen to Islam's song for ever.
>
> *(Eberhardt, 2002, quoted in Winter, p.29)*

But that mystical element was accompanied by the on-going attempt to understand the Qu'ranic revelations via rational strategies gained from the Greek philosophical inheritance – an iteration between objective reasoning and the inner spiritual experience.

In sum

What is shared by all three traditions is that the moral standpoint is embedded in the respective rituals and practices, and as such open constantly to 'elucidation', that is, as described by Phillips, 1970, p.17, *'unpacking* the significance of values, ideals, different conceptions of worship and love, and the roles they play in peoples' lives'.

Part of that 'unpacking' over the millennia has been the mutual compenetration of Christianity [and one might add Judaism and Islam] and Greek metaphysics not only producing the intellectual form of theological dogmatics and hellenisation of Christianity, but also the assimilation by philosophy of genuinely Christian ideas (Habermas and Ratzinger, op. cit. p.x).

Indeed, the non-statutory guidance on religious education in English schools in 2010 put the matter clearly:

Religious education provokes challenging questions about the ultimate meaning and purpose of life, beliefs about God, the self and nature of reality, issues of right and wrong, and what it means to be human.

(DCSF, 2010, pp.6/7)

Conclusion

If education is essentially an ethical undertaking, concerned with enabling young people to recognise their humanity, the potential of that humanity to be developed, and the dispositions to lead their lives accordingly (autonomy in that sense), then it needs to recognise the different traditions in which, over time, such recognition and development have been articulated. This is particularly important where those traditions are increasingly obscured by the secular world (and, as explained, there are different senses of 'secular') which increasingly obtains. As the 'horizons of significance', as explained by Charles Taylor (which once were the reference points for moral deliberation and decisions) are obscured by the secular indifference to religion or by its active dismissal of religion or by a way of life which, ignoring the religious dimension, emphasises personal pleasure and self-fulfilment, then there is understandably seen to be a need quite consciously and explicitly to provide alternative voices, rooted in long-standing traditions, practices and argument.

Such traditions would not be seen in contradiction to the careful articulation of the 'secular morality', as explained by Durkheim. Indeed, there is much in common. There is, for example, the shared agreement about the link between education and nurture – the importance of the communal environment, the embodiment of values within shared practices, the centrality of equal respect and the virtue of justice. But there are differences in the deeper grounding of such values. Differences particularly emerge where, as an element in the post-modern tradition as described by Taylor, there are powerful voices which say of 'the self', 'there is nothing deep down inside except what we have put there ourselves'.

Many believe that a deeper, religious framework is essential to counter that 'undermining of moral sense' as described earlier. Hence, the teaching of the faiths (the religious understandings as embodied in explicit beliefs, virtues, practices and worship) of the distinctive religions.

The objection, however, will inevitably be that an educational defence of such a framework demands a rational foundation, objective and evidence-based reasoning. And that has not yet been given. Are there not problems in faith-based education, and thereby in the promotion of Faith schools, in that, however worthy and effective the religious dimension, it is outside those forms of knowledge, those rational defences, which public education demands?

To this philosophical difficulty we turn in the following chapter.

128 Key issues emerging: The need for philosophy

References

Ayer, A.J., 1936, *Language, Truth and Logic*, London: Penguin.

DCSF, 2010, *Non-Statutory Guidance on RE in Schools*.

Dearden, R.F., Hirst, P.H., and Peters, R.S., eds, *Education and the Development of Reason*, London: Routledge and Kegan Paul.

Durkheim, E., 1961 edition, *Moral Education*, New York: The Free Press.

Habermas, J. and Ratzinger, J., 2006, *The Dialectics of Secularism on Reason and Relations*, San Francisco: Ignation Press.

Lane, D., 2015, *Catholic Education in the Light of Vatican II and Laudato Si'*, Dublin: Veritas.

MacIntyre, A., 2017, *Ethics in the Conflicts of Modernity*, Cambridge: Cambridge University Press.

MacMurray, J., 1957, *Self as Agent*, London: Faber and Faber.

MacMurray, J., 1958, 'Learning to be human', *Oxford Review of Education*, 2011/2012, 38(6) 661–674.

Phillips, D., 1970, 'Philosophy and religious education', in *British Journal of Educational Studies*, 18.

Populorum Progressio, Vatican City: LEV.

Rahner, K., 1972, 'Anthropology and Theology', in *Theological Investigations*, vol.9.

Sacks, J., 1997, *The Politics of Hope*, London: Jonathan Cape.

Strom, 1981, 'Facing history and ourselves: integrating a holocaust unit into the curriculum', *Moral Education Forum* (Summer).

Taylor, C., 1992, *The Ethics of Authenticity*, Cambridge: Harvard University Press.

Valland-Belkacen, N., 2015, in Duclert, V., ed., *La Republique: ses valeurs, son ecole*, Paris: Folio.

Whittle, S., 2015, *A Theory of Catholic Education*, London: Bloomsbury.

Williams, Rowan, 2012, *Faith in the Public Square*, London: Bloomsbury.

Winter, T., 2016, 'Education as drawing out', in Memon, N. and Zaman, M., eds, *Philosophy of Islamic Education*, London: Routledge.

10

EPISTEMOLOGY

Knowledge, truth, and reason in religious education

Introduction

The position we have so far reached is that, at the basis of educational practice, where that is identified with 'development of persons' or (as said by the college principal) with 'making our children more human', are foundational premises expressing what it means to be human – whether they are embodied, for example, in the liberal ideal of autonomy, or in a purely naturalistic account of, say, the molecular biologist, or in religious understandings of what it means to be human and to become more so. A problem, however, lies in the justification for such foundational premises. If they are without rational justification, does not their assumption in subsequent educational practice and teaching constitute indoctrination – which would seem to be the one 'mortal sin' in the secular ethics?

In addressing this problem, it is useful to rehearse some of the philosophical problems in defining what it means to '*know* that something is the case', and to distinguish between good and bad reasons.

Knowledge, truth, and reason

It is necessary first to distinguish between propositional and practical knowledge, although the links between the two are important for our purposes, as will be indicated later.

Propositional knowledge consists of statements of what is the case. Traditional philosophical analyses of 'knowing that something is the case' go as follows. 'X knows that P (where P stands for any statement) if, and only if, (i) X believes that P, (ii) P is true, and (iii) X is justified in believing that P is true (see, for example, Woozley, 1949; Scheffler, 1965; Ayer, 1956). Truth lies in the correspondence between, on the one hand, the proposition and, on the other, what is the case

130 Key issues emerging: The need for philosophy

independently of the 'knower'. Justification, therefore, refers to the evidence which demonstrates this correspondence between proposition and what is actually happening in the world. Experience verifies (or fails to verify) what has been asserted.

The development of science, for example, lies in the accumulation of such verified propositions, increasingly organised into theoretical frameworks which enable one to predict what will be experienced if certain actions or experiments are conducted. When the predictions fail to predict correctly, then the theory needs to be modified or rejected. Thus, scientific knowledge grows through constant adaptation as a result of criticism and further experimentation. Such knowledge, therefore, cannot be identified with certainty – there is always the possibility of the predictions being falsified by further experience. But, no matter – as Karl Popper (1972, p.34) argued – knowledge grows through criticism. That growth or accumulation of knowledge is passed on and developed further, generation after generation, and it is the job of education to initiate the learners into what has been inherited, having survived critical appraisal.

There is another sort of proposition which can be verified but not by reference to experience, namely, purely logical propositions which include mathematical ones. They are ultimately verified by reference to the principle of contradiction. 'All trees have leaves' is true, not by reference to experience but by reference to what we mean by 'tree'.

Therefore, as was stated in Chapter 8, the writings of A.J. Ayer (1936), in his seminal book *Language Truth and Logic*, argued that, since all propositions claimed to proclaim the truth, and since only two types of proposition are verifiable (namely, empirical which appeal to experience, and logical which appeal to the principle of contradiction), all other propositions which fail this test are thereby meaningless. Those clearly include all theological and religious claims. Along, however, with religious propositions must also go moral and aesthetic claims. What one 'believes' in these cases cannot be verified; such judgments are therefore but an expression of taste or feeling ('the emotive theory of ethics').

On the analysis just given, everything, including human action, can be explained in purely scientific terms – which here and elsewhere is referred to as 'naturalism'. There is no 'ghost in the machine'. We have seen the consequence of such a philosophical view in educational theory and practice when behaviourism was fashionable, namely, the science of behaviour in which one could relate the observable and measurable behaviour of the pupil to physical causes, thereby developing general causal laws which can be verified or falsified. We have seen its growing influence, too, in the 'science of teaching' in which 'input' is related to 'output', that is, to very specific and measurable outcomes.

But is there not a logical flaw in this account of knowledge according to which only those propositions are meaningful which are either empirically verifiable or true by reference to the principle of contradiction (given the meaning of the terms used), and according to which therefore the assertion of religious beliefs must be meaningless? The logical flaw is that the truth of the assertion itself must be meaningless. The 'principle of verification' as the criterion of meaningfulness is neither true by definition nor falsifiable by reference to experience.

However, what Ayer (and those within what might be referred to as the 'positivist tradition') were correct about was that there is a logical connection between 'knowledge' (and thereby the search for 'understanding'), 'truth', and 'relevant evidence'. For any claim being made, it is always possible to ask for the relevant evidence for making that claim. Such evidence may be far from proof, and indeed further evidence and criticism may well undermine the claim. Knowledge based on evidence does not entail 'certainty'. But, whether shown to be true by the evidence or shown to be false, the claims being made are intelligible precisely because, in that particular form of discourse, there are recognised bases for agreement or disagreement (not necessarily proof) with the claims being made and consequently the beliefs held.

Therefore, we see in the major religious traditions the development of arguments through which beliefs are clarified, evidence put forward and questioned, and conclusions tentatively reached. There is what Newman (1890) referred to as the 'development of doctrine' over time through historical scholarship, theological dialogue, and philosophical reflection. Central to such appeal to reasons and evidence are, and have been over the centuries, philosophical analysis and argument – often with roots in the Greek writings of Aristotle and Plato. We see this in theological work of the 4th century St Augustine, in the scholastic tradition exemplified in the 13th century work of St Thomas Aquinas, in the work of such Arabic philosophers as the 11th century Avicenna and the 12th century Averroes who shaped the philosophical thinking of Islam, and indeed in the philosophical writings of the medieval Jewish philosopher, Maimonedes. Hence, also the 'naturalism' of many within the scientific tradition (which also has its roots in the Greek and Roman philosophers, for example, the atomism of Democritus, the evolutionary theory of Epicurus, the *De Rerum Natura* of Lucretius) has always been challenged within philosophical discourse.

Belief and rationality

The Christian declaration of faith, however, begins with 'We believe ...', not 'We know ...'. The distinction between the two is reflected in the definition of knowledge given earlier. Knowledge entails belief, but not vice-versa. The traditional analysis of 'knowing that something is the case' requires the beliefs to be verified, ultimately by reference to empirical experience. However, much of our lives are based on beliefs which cannot be verified in that strict sense, but for which reasons are given and where those reasons have been examined and refined as people have sought to make sense of experience. Such beliefs are embodied in ways of life, in long-standing traditions of thought and criticism, and in shared religious practices and worship. They are part, in Oakeshott's words, of 'the conversation between the generations of mankind'.

Beliefs can be strong or weak, clearly articulated or vaguely felt, based on evidence or based on authority, conscientiously thought about or taken from popular culture. They constitute a frame of mind on specific matters. Even though many

132 Key issues emerging: The need for philosophy

beliefs are not reflected upon, questioned or evidence-based, they can be so, and thereby made explicit and open to further examination and critique, even where such evidence may by no means lead to certainty. There is evidence, for example, that John loves Joan (the smile, the gracious words, the care given) but none of these bits of evidence add up to what we mean by loving. Indeed, John may be deceiving her. They are evidence, but do not prove, that he loves her. Similarly, people may believe in God in the light of experiences which they and others believe constitutes evidence. Bishop Ian Ramsey (1964), formerly Professor of Religion at Oxford University, thus likened the relation between evidence and religious belief and theological theorising to the 'fitting of a boot or a shoe'.

> We have a particular doctrine which, like a preferred and selected shoe, starts by appearing to meet our needs. But on closer fitting to the phenomena the shoe may pinch. When tested against future slush and rain it may be proven to be not altogether water-tight or it may be comfortable – yet must not be too comfortable. In this way, the test of a shoe is measured by its ability to match a wide range of phenomena, by its overall success in meeting a variety of needs.
>
> *(Quoted in Astley, 1994, p.53)*

Such a doctrine, 'matching a wide range of phenomena', may be communicated to others in conversation, or through the example of their lives, or in what they write. In this way, there arise traditions of shared experiences, articulated in oral and written form, embodied in forms of life, passed on to the following generations, and constantly subjected to rational analysis and criticism. Philosophical, including epistemological critiques, have to take seriously those experiences and those ways of life in which the experiences are embodied. As Habermas stated in his 'conversations with Ratzinger', later to be Pope Benedict XIV:

> I do not wish to speak of the phenomenon of the continued existence of religion in a largely secularised environment simply as a societal fact: philosophy must take this phenomenon seriously from within, so to speak, as a cognitive challenge.
>
> *(Habermas and Ratzinger, 2015, p.38)*

It is this taking of the phenomenon of religious thought seriously as a 'cognitive challenge' which has given rise to theological argument and discourse.

Post-modern challenge to knowledge, truth, and reason

The 'Enlightenment' was the growing belief in the development of knowledge through systematic and empirical investigation, the clear formulation of 'what is the case' independent of the enquirer, and the subjection of it to testing and to criticism. Knowledge, having survived critical investigation, accumulates, thereby

Epistemology **133**

suggesting further lines of enquiry. Science presupposes an objective reality which sets limits on what can be validly believed.

There has, however, been an assault on the very notion of knowledge, truth, and justified belief (highlighted by President Trump's constant reference to 'fake news' and 'alternative facts'), in what has been referred to as the 'post-truth era'. What is claimed to be true is really the re-construction of events to suit the interests of the claimant. 'Truth' lies in the thoughts and subjective ways of seeing the world of those who disagree. Such constructions enable them to re-conceive what is happening, and thus create 'alternative facts' to support their view of the world. Hence, what you read in the newspaper depends on what the writers of the paper want you to believe. 'Alternative facts' can always be provided to challenge the received account.

However, this is not just a matter of cheap journalism or the 'fake news' of politicians. The 'post-modern challenge' to the hopes and aspirations of the 'enlightenment project' does itself have its backers in such philosophers (much referred to) as Lyotard, Derrida, and Foucault. Educational theory and research, for example, has been widely influenced by (amongst others) Guba and Lincoln (1989). Their book sharply distinguishes between different generations of research – the first being the adoption of what they claim to be a quite inappropriate scientific (or 'naturalist') model, such as described earlier. However, so they argue, the poverty of the scientific model did, over time, become clearer, and so there was gradual progression to a paradigm which Guba and Lincoln espouse. The contrast between the two paradigms is explained as

> outcomes of [enquiry] are not descriptions of the 'way things really are' or 'really work', or of some 'true' state of affairs, but instead represent meaningful constructions that individual actors or groups of actors form to 'make sense' of the situations in which they find themselves. The findings are not 'facts' in some ultimate sense but are, instead, literally *created* through an interactive process that *includes* the evaluator as well as the many stakeholders … What emerges from this process is one or more *constructions* that *are* the realities of the case.
>
> *(p. 8)*

Thus, it no longer makes sense to talk of the 'true' state of affairs. Rather is it the case that we each try to 'make sense' of the situation we find ourselves in. We do this through 'constructing' connections, meanings, frameworks through which experience is sieved and made intelligible. 'Facts' are not discovered, but created. 'Knowledge' is a 'social construct' – a view propagated by sociologist of knowledge in the 1970s (for example, Young, 1971), and still influential in some university departments of education.

There are inevitably dangers to those of religious belief (and therefore the advocates of Faith schools) in such post-modern philosophising. Are not religious beliefs, so it would be argued, anything other than the shared conceptions of the world and of human destiny by particular religious associations (their 'social constructions')

134 Key issues emerging: The need for philosophy

through which reality is created? There is no reality independent of their conceptions of it which would verify their truth. Due to the many different ways in which societies have come to account for experience, one can only conclude that there are 'multiple realities', each making sense of experience in its different manifestations to the holders of them. Therefore, one cannot teach a religious belief as if it were the true one; rather is any religious belief a particular 'social construction' of one, out of many possible, 'multiple realities'.

But there are equally problems for those who would exclude religious beliefs on the grounds of the naturalism of the Enlightenment, for they too have conceptualised experience in a particular way, and made assumptions about what alone is real. Indeed, it was against the 'pre-dominance of the Enlightenment Project' that the post-modern alternative arose, questioning the very nature of 'objective reality'. As Nietzsche argued, there are no facts, only interpretations – the reason of the strongest is always the best. In such a climate, the 'holocaust deniers' flourish.

There is a need, therefore, to seek a compromise between the modernist and postmodernist positions. It is true that how we see the world, how we experience what happens, depends on the concepts through which we make sense of it. To acquire scientific knowledge, for example, requires coming to understand the key ideas and theories which, over time, scientists have developed in understanding the world and our experience of it. Part of that development lies not only in 'new facts' but also in new ways of conceptualising those facts. Equally, our social and moral lives require particular 'social constructions', which are embodied in the language we have inherited. But all those 'social constructions' are constantly reformulated because of the further experiences which they are supposed to make sense of, or because there is an interaction with other people's ideas which provide a more effective and defensible account of the world, or because they have been subjected to critical appraisal. There are objects and events in the world independent of our thinking of them (including *human* beings), but there are different ways in which these objects might be conceived. However, not any conception is acceptable – there are limits to how we might conceive things, imposed by reality independent of the 'knower'. It makes no sense to deny the objective reality of a world external to ourselves, although at the same time it does make sense to recognise the different subjective ways in which we try to make sense of it. What might be referred to as 'critical realism' was expressed thus by Aquinas as '*objective quoad id quod concipitur, non autem quoad modum quo concipitur*' ('objective as far as that which is conceived, not however as far as the way in which it is conceived'). And that 'constant trying to make sense' arises from the failure of existing conceptions to anticipate what will happen or from the inconsistency arising from other and more fruitful ways in which we claim to know.

This constant dialogue over time and between traditions of thinking is what has characterised not only scientific thinking, but religious thinking, too. Therefore, religious education, as opposed to teaching about religion, is to introduce the next generation into a particular tradition of thinking about the world, of appreciating the significance of certain experiences, of directing one's life towards certain goals, and of responding to what might be seen as a rather limited secular awareness.

The limits of naturalism

As already pointed out, the logical flaw in the assertion that only those propositions are meaningful, which are either empirically verifiable or true by definition of the terms, is that the truth of that assertion itself must be meaningless. The 'principle of verification' as the criterion of meaningfulness is neither true by definition nor falsifiable by reference to experience. A similar point, relevant to our concerns in this book, is made by Habermas in his conversations with Joseph Ratzinger, prior to Ratzinger being elected as Pope Benedict XIV.

> Does the free, secularised state exist on the basis of normative presuppositions that it itself cannot guarantee? Secular rationality comes up against its limitations when it attempts to demonstrate itself.
>
> *(Habermas and Ratzinger, p.21)*

Certainly, in everyday conversations reasons are given which are not limited by Ayer's principle of meaningful statements. There are different forms of discourse – what Philip Phenix (1964) referred to as different 'realms of meaning', within which we make sense of experience, each with its distinctive conceptual framework and criteria of judgement, including aesthetic, moral, personal and religious. In particular, that 'personal realm of discourse' recognises other people as having thoughts, intentions, and motives. Answers to the question 'Why did it happen?' may well not be satisfied by reference to physical causes. For example, how might one explain someone raising his arm? Was it a purely muscular reaction or was it a signal to someone else? If the latter, then one needs to refer, in explaining this physical event, to the intentions and the understandings of the signaller. What makes the physically observed behaviour *intelligible* is the purpose which lies behind it.

Thus, there are limits to scientific explanation, namely, where reference needs to be made to the intentions, motives, and understandings of the other person. Even where physical explanations can be given why something works (for example, a motor car), a full explanation would need to refer to the design of the mechanism, and thus to the intelligence and intentions of the designer. A full explanation of the car's successful journey requires reference to its intelligent design by someone who understood the relevant laws of mechanics.

Moral propositions and discourse (the 'moral realm of meaning') similarly appeal to very different sorts of reason than is captured in the explanatory discourse of naturalism (for example, the appeal to justice, the sense of duty, the conception of a worthwhile life, the importance of truthfulness) all of which may have arisen from much deliberation and practical reasoning, as demonstrated so clearly in the work of Aristotle and subsequent philosophers, or in the accounts given by advocates of 'secular education' such as Durkheim, as shown in the previous chapter.

Therefore, the unavoidable failure of science to satisfy the search for understanding of why things are as they are, or why one should pursue a particular course of action, gives rise to logically different kind of explanatory discourses, ones which

136 Key issues emerging: The need for philosophy

pursues the question 'why?' when dissatisfied with the purely empirical answer. There is more to be explained than fits in to the scientific story. How does one understand the *intelligibility* of what science reveals? Such a question might be pursued following the wonder felt at how the universe began, or in how (from what once would have been a purely random collection of matter) there has emerged an intelligible world – that is, one which displayed all the symptoms of intelligent design.

But such a dissatisfaction with purely naturalistic explanations is reflected, too, in the sense of mystery which inspires much art, music, and poetry. There is frequently a struggle to give a deeper appreciation and understanding of the world, which we perceive, through images and rituals which point to, but do not fully grasp, a deeper sense of reality. Such creations and practices are an embodiment or an exploration of understanding – a sense of wonderment, which can lead to religious expression and awareness. To refer once again to the conversation between Habermas and Ratzinger,

> without initially having any theological intention, the reason becomes aware of its limitations, thus transcends itself in the direction of something else.
>
> *(op. cit., p.40)*

Thus, the question 'Why?', as we address the 'cognitive challenge', and as we search for explanations of events, may not be logically satisfied by a purely empirical or scientific answer. It is quite intelligible to pursue such questioning in the light of the obvious intelligibility of what is happening, such intelligibility suggesting the design and thus a designer. It would not be 'nonsense', therefore, to pursue such questions, because there is no contradiction between scientific explanations of causality, on the one hand, and, on the other, intelligibility in terms of intention and design. Indeed, it is because of this underlying sense of purpose and design in our understanding of the universe that people over the ages have pursued such questions, entering into the mystery of how the universe came to be and how it is intelligible in terms of the very laws which science has discovered. John Lennox (2009), in his response to Richard Dawkins, points to 'the towering figures of science' (Kepler, Pascal, Boyle, Newton, Faraday, Babbage, Mendel, Pasteur, and Clerk Maxwell), for whom this reconciliation between scientific and religious understandings is seen, not just to make sense, but to be in harmonious agreement – indeed, scientific success leading to religious understanding and wonder. Lennox (p.8) quotes Johannes Kepler thus:

> The chief aim of all investigations of the external world should be to discover the rational order which has been imposed on it by God, and which he revealed to us in the language of mathematics.

Even more forceful is the assertion of Sir John Houghton FRS, quoted by Lennox (p.19):

> Our science is God's science. He holds the responsibility for the whole scientific story ... The remarkable order, consistency, reliability and fascinating

complexity found in the scientific description of the universe are reflections of the order, consistency, reliability and complexity of God's activity.

Hence, we might link such profound conclusions of scientists, regarding divine agency in the very intelligibility of the universe, with what might be seen as the simple (often seen as naïve) questions of the child. Lennox (p.31) quotes Sir Peter Medawar:

> The existence of a limit to science is, however, made clear by its inability to answer child-like elementary questions having to do with the first and last things – questions such as 'How did everything begin?', 'What are we here for?', 'What is the point of living?'

Religious beliefs and practices, therefore, are the product of questions and explanations concerning the intelligibility of the physical world which are not satisfied by the 'naturalism' of scientific enquiry. Furthermore, they are the product of critical exploration and rational discourse through philosophical and theological dialogue and enquiry. They constitute a rational tradition, in the same way that scientific enquiry constitutes a fundamental and evolving tradition of enquiry. They cannot be rejected on the grounds that such a perspective is either meaningless or without rational justification – views which underpin much of the secularist critique of religion and thereby of religious education and Faith schools.

Nonetheless, there would seem to be limits to a purely rational grasp of the religious quest. That philosophical reasoning, which leads to the reasonableness of believing in God and in the divine source of life and human fulfilment, needs to be enriched through practices and rituals, which go beyond the purely philosophical reflection and argument. There is the *personal experience* of that divine life through initiation into traditions of prayer, contemplation, communal worship, and feelings of mystery.

Personal experience

One mathematician and philosopher in the 17th century, influenced by the enlightenment ideal and therefore suspicious of the rational account of God's existence as argued by Aquinas, wrote in *Pensees* (Pascal, 1660):

> The metaphysical proofs for the existence of God are so remote from human reasoning, and so complex, that they have little impact … We know the truth, not only through our reason but through our heart.
>
> *(quoted in McGrath, 2006, p.104/105)*

Therefore:

> If we subject everything to reason our religion will lose its mystery and its supernatural character. If one offends the principles of reason [however] our

138 Key issues emerging: The need for philosophy

religion will be absurd and ridiculous … There are two equally dangerous extremes, to shut reason out and to let nothing else in.

For Pascal, 'personal experience' mattered.

It is the case, as has been indicated, that the 'naturalism', which has rejected the rationality of religious belief, has indeed, if not 'shut reason out' completely, at least restricted its nature to that which can be empirically verified, and has done so on the basis of premises which themselves have not a rational basis. In so doing, it has 'let nothing else in', and therefore has failed, in Habermas' words (quoted earlier), to take this phenomenon of religion 'seriously from within, so to speak, as a cognitive challenge'.

There are words through which that sense of the divine personal presence is expressed – for example, recognition of the 'sacred' and the 'holy'. What they make possible is a form of knowing which arises as much through engagement in practices as it does in the contemplation of propositions. 'Practical knowledge' – the knowledge which is embodied in a way of life but not made explicit – is too often ignored. But, as such, and in a religious form of life, it embodies a belief in the Divine Person – tentative maybe, and using by analogy terms which apply to the rational and feeling lives of finite persons.

Therefore, in *The Idea of the Holy,* Rudolph Otto (1923) sees the words 'holy' and 'sacred' to be a 'category of interpretation and valuation peculiar to the sphere of religion', which has its reflection in the language of religious traditions from their onset – in Hebrew, 'qadosh', in Greek 'ayios', in Latin 'sacer'. These words refer to a distinctive experience, far removed from everyday experience and better described as the 'numinous', which in turn has a long history in the human attempt to make sense of the feeling of mystery, and of there being a greater power behind the world as we experience it. Difficult to define maybe, but manifest in liturgy and expressed vividly in poetry as it aims to make sense of something which is beyond the normal world of experience – as illustrated in the words of Ruskin, quoted by Otto (along with Blake, Coleridge, Wordsworth, and others).

> Lastly, although there was no definite religious sentiment mingled with it, there was continual perception of Sanctity in the whole of nature, from the slightest thing to the vastest; an instinctive awe, mixed with delight; an indefinable thrill, such as we sometimes imagine to indicate the presence of a disembodied spirit. I could only feel this perfectly when I was alone; and then it would often make me shiver from head to foot with the joy and fear of it.
>
> *(op. cit., p.215)*

Religious beliefs are developed, both personally and communally, through continuous critical reflection upon such personal encounters, enabling a tradition of thinking and practising to be developed over the ages, into which it makes sense to initiate each generation. Such beliefs will be embodied in spiritual exercises, artistic artefacts, musical expressions and liturgical practices, all of which endeavour to

Epistemology **139**

reflect that which reason points to but can never completely capture. Intrinsic to that tradition is the constant attempt to make greater sense of it through theological speculation and philosophical criticism.

Consequences for religious education

Religious education is the place in the school for the pursuit, in an open-minded way, of this enquiry into questions concerning the intelligibility of the world, and into the rational traditions which have transcended the purely empirical account, and which open up both a moral perspective concerning the good life to be pursued and an explanation of the physical world, but probing beyond the purely naturalistic answer. It would recognise the urge to express in poetry and the arts a sense of there being something more to explain, which is manifest in the rituals and practices within religious traditions.

But is this possible, it is asked, where there are no agreed criteria as to what counts as appropriate evidence or verification of conclusions reached? Unlike other modes of discourse which are the basis of the school curriculum, there are no agreed criteria for what might be true or false. And to teach such beliefs without such agreement, so it is argued, would be to indoctrinate.

Put a little more philosophically, the argument is that schools should teach those curriculum subjects where the judgments made are based on agreed public criteria for what counts a valid evidence or tests of truth. And such conditions are claimed not to apply to religious beliefs.

However, the argument of this chapter has been that, to the contrary, to think religiously and to have religious beliefs is to participate in a tradition of thinking which has evolved over time with its philosophical basis as to what counts as good and valid reasons, and evidence for the claims made. Such reasoning would be seen to arise from what are seen to be the limited explanations given by the naturalism of empirical enquiry. To have religious beliefs, arising from thoughtful reflection on the intelligibility of the world as experienced, is a rational process with its own criteria of good and bad reasoning and relevant evidence.

Those who would want to abolish 'religious thinking' from the curriculum (as opposed to the secular teaching about religions from a purely sociological or historical point of view) would point to the absence of agreed criteria of good or bad reasoning, or of agreed tests for verification. However, it is not clear that the teaching of historical understanding, or indeed literary and artistic appreciation, are based on universally agreed criteria of truth, or indeed of literary and artistic appreciation. Deliberation and argument about the relevance of claimed evidence are part and parcel of these other disciplines or subjects. But in these, just as in religious studies, there is an inheritance of thinking and scholarship through which beliefs are refined and developed.

There is between the three monotheistic traditions much in common with respect to their understanding of the rational basis for beliefs and practices. The differences between them (and within them) are rooted in different historical

140 Key issues emerging: The need for philosophy

narratives but also in different appeals to relevant evidence. Hence, it is seen to be important both to initiate the next generation into the way of thinking and behaving which has been achieved in their respective histories, but also into the development through criticism within (and through critical conversation across) different religions and humanist accounts. There is a need to respect the religious narratives of the particular faith, but also the enduring philosophical arguments, the personal experiences of the learners, and an openness to the world's needs.

There is need, therefore, in religious education for a personal response, first, to the prevailing culture within a particular religious framework, second, to the wider secular culture which is dominant within society, third, to the interaction or conflict between the two. There are hidden assumptions behind the prevailing religious and secular cultures (in whichever of the four understandings of 'secular' is considered) which need to be exposed and opened to criticism. At the same time, those personal responses need to be made within an understanding of the religious and secular frameworks – the fundamental ideas which underpin them.

Indoctrination?

It is often assumed that to initiate young people into a religious tradition of belief and practice is an instance of indoctrination. That, as was shown in Chapters 1 and 5, would seem to be the assumption by the Humanist Associations and more generally within a secular culture. However, the accusation is usually made without evidence or justification. It is as though the accusers of indoctrination have themselves been indoctrinated into so believing.

Nonetheless, it was forcefully expressed by Professor Dawkins when he said that Faith schools were

> the most obvious and serious case of government-imposed religion [which] don't so much teach about religion as indoctrinate in the particular religion that runs the school.
>
> (New Statesman, *19.12.11*)

What then does it mean to have been indoctrinated? In answering this question, we need to revert to the account of knowledge made earlier. 'To indoctrinate' would indicate that a person has been taught certain beliefs, first, without there being appropriate evidence for those beliefs, and, second, in such a way that the believer has no doubts about their truth despite their lack of evidence. Indeed, such believers would have been so taught that they would be unable to dispense with such beliefs – they become basic and unquestioned.

Religious education, where that is intended to lead, not simply to knowledge about religion, but to religious belief, is seen as a matter of indoctrination by its very definition. And that is because there is no such thing as religious knowledge as 'knowledge' is explicated above. Since there are no agreed truth criteria whereby religious propositions can be demonstrably shown to be true or false, they must join the group of meaningless propositions.

In response, however, it is again necessary, first, to distinguish 'knowledge' from 'certainty' (as indeed, as was argued, is also the case of science), and, second, to distinguish verification in the strict sense from appropriate evidence, as explained earlier. More important in all claims to justified belief is whether there is a rational form of discourse, which is philosophically defensible, which has survived philosophical criticism, and which is critical of the narrow (and thereby untenable) criteria of rational explanation argued by those who espouse an exclusively positivist account of the universe.

In this respect, religious beliefs are similar to aesthetic, moral, and political beliefs. The teacher of literature, drawing upon a tradition of literary criticism, helps the student to appreciate poetry or the novel by introducing what are regarded as the classics and by pointing to features which show why they are classics. Similarly, political argument, coolly conducted, also draws on evidence and subjects the opponents' commitments and arguments to critical scrutiny. The possibility of so doing enables politics to be a subject of study at the university. Again, reasons are given for moral decisions, and the foundations of those decisions are the focus of philosophical reasoning. In so helping students so to gain understanding and appreciation of aesthetic, political, and moral beliefs, the teacher would not be accused of indoctrination.

Furthermore, such coming to appreciate and to understand may require some initiation into the practices (and rituals) which encapsulate the significances and understandings. Such was the argument of McLaughlin who saw such initiation into religious practice as a route into the autonomous acceptance of religious understanding (McLaughlin, 1984). But would not such initiation in the case of religious understanding be a case of indoctrination?

However, as Callan (2009) wrote with regard to McLaughlin's defence of 'initiation':

> The initiation of children into religious practice could secure an understanding of religion unavailable or at least less readily available, in the absence of initiation, and that the relevant understanding enables or enhances in some way an autonomous choice regarding religion.

With the massive decline in Sunday schools and of church attendance, most children will have little contact with the practice of religion and with an intelligent grasp of what it means or signifies. They will, however, have received 'an initiation' into the beliefs and practices which constitute the secularism (in its different senses described in Chapter 5), which characterises much of the society which they experience. If 'initiation' implies indoctrination, then those too, living in a secular culture, must be indoctrinated who have never been exposed to a different and religious understanding of what it means to be human

142 Key issues emerging: The need for philosophy

Conclusion

As was argued in the last chapter, education is concerned with the development of those qualities, moral purposes, knowledge, and autonomy which constitutes what it means to be human and to become yet more so. For many people, and within long-standing traditions, religious belief and practice have been seen as central both to an understanding of what this means and to the way such development is to be achieved. But in a much more secular society, that contribution of religion is threatened. It is seen to fail the test of genuine knowledge, and thus, if promoted through the schools, to undermine the autonomy of the pupils – where being autonomous is seen as a primary aim of educational provision.

In response, it has been argued that, to the contrary, religious beliefs similarly arise from long traditions of philosophical thinking in relation to evidence and reflection. Perhaps this does not lead to absolute certainty, but to judgement in the light of evidence and reasons which are made explicit and open to argument.

It is the argument, therefore, of those who are committed to Faith schools that there are such rationally held beliefs and that it is educationally important, therefore, that such beliefs should be introduced and understood within their traditional narratives (as indeed are the sciences), but subject to appraisal within the tradition of scholarship and criticism – philosophical, theological and historical.

However, in so arguing, the advocates of Faith schools need to note the 'evangelical secularism' of National Secular Society, founded by Charles Bradlaugh in 1866. As reported by Copley (2005, p.34), their campaigning expressed the strong belief that religion is a private matter (despite its public face in philosophical and theological argument, in its advocacy of community life and values, and in its significance for the lives of many). Therefore, it argued that taxation privileges for religious bodies should be removed, that Faith schools should be abolished and even that there should be a fixed date for Easter (without reference presumably to the Christian Churches). Such dogmatism, strongly held despite contrary evidence, would seem much better evidence of indoctrination than the holding of long-standing theological and philosophical traditions of religious beliefs and modes of life.

References

Ayer, A.J., 1936, *Language, Truth and Logic*, London: Penguin.
Ayer, A.J., 1956, *The Problem of Knowledge*, Harmondsworth: Penguin Books.
Astley, J., 1994, *The Philosophy of Christian Education*, Alabama: Religious Education Press.
Callan, E., 2009, 'Why bring the kids into this?' in Haydon, G., *Faith in Education: A Tribute to Terry McLoughlin*, London: IoE.
Gearon, L., 2014, *On Holy Ground: The Theory and Practice of Religious Education*, London: Routledge.
Guba, E.G. and Lincoln, V.S., 1989, *Fourth Generation Evaluation*, London: Sage.
Habermas, J. and Ratzinger, J., *The Dialectics of Secularism on Reason and Relations*, San Francisco: Ignatius Press.
Lennox, J., 2009, *God's Undertaker: Has Science Buried God?* Oxford: Lion Hudson.

McGrath, A.E., 2006 (2nd ed.), *Christianity: An Introduction*, Oxford: Blackwells.

McLaughlin, T., 1984, 'Parental rights and the religious upbringing of children', *Journal of Philosophy of Education*, 18(1).

Newman, J.H., 1890, *An Essay in the Development of Christian Doctrine*, London: Longmans Green.

Otto, R., 1923, *The Idea of the Holy*, London: Oxford University Press.

Paschal, B., 1660, *Pensee*, Grand Rapids: Christian Classics Ethereal Library.

Phenix, P., 1964, *The Realms of Meaning*, New York: McGraw-Hill Book Company.

Popper, K., 1972, *Objective Knowledge: An Evolutionary Approach*, Oxford: Clarendon Press.

Ramsey, R., 1964, *Models and Mystery*, London: OUP, quoted in Astley, J., 1994, *The Philosophy of Religious Education*, Alabama: Religious Education Press

Scheffler, I., 1965, *Conditions of Knowledge*, Chicago: Scott Foresman.

Woozley, 1949, *Theory of Knowledge*, London: Hutchinson.

Young, M.F.D., 1971, *Knowledge and Control*, London: Methuen.

11

CIVIC SOCIETY

Common good and social pluralism

The central issue

A major argument *against* Faith schools, as we have already seen, is that a central aim of publicly funded education, (namely, the pursuit of the '*common* good' through the creation of a *socially cohesive* society) is under threat partly, it is claimed, because of educational discrimination and segregation on religious grounds. Such an accusation is exacerbated by the further accusation that such discrimination leads to ethnic and social class selection, though this is strongly denied by the religious bodies, as indicated in Chapter 3. The Butler-Sloss Report (2015) on *Religion in Public Life* (referred to in Chapters 2 and 3) had argued that it would be community schools, through their non-discriminatory intake and curriculum (thereby recognising the significance of diversity) which fostered 'the common good'. Thus, Andrew Copson, chief executive of the British Humanist Society, in supporting that report, argued that 'vital to the future of Britain as a cohesive society will be the ability of people of all religions and non-religious beliefs and identities to act together for the common good'.

However, paradoxically, Faith schools, too, justify their distinctiveness partly in their pursuit of the *common* good, not simply 'the good' of their religious followers, as was pointed out in Chapter 8. A main educational purpose of the Church of England's voluntary controlled schools, as expressed in two major reports referred to in Chapter 5 (Dearing, 2001, and Chadwick, 2012), was to foster, within the Christian spirit, service to others, especially those in social and economic need. The Chadwick Report, in marking the bicentenary of the National Society, argued for the importance of the Christian ethos in fostering caring relationships, service to the community, and responsiveness to the needs of the local communities. Chapter 8 showed the increasing emphasis given by religious traditions to promoting the shared 'common good'.

Indeed, Catholic Faith schools (which comprise the vast majority of the voluntary aided schools) claim that their purposes, which are relevant to the pursuit of the 'common good', are clearly expressed in the 'foundation charter' published by the CCE, 1977, *The Catholic School,* referred to in Chapter 8, namely, commitment to the service of the common good in education, a commitment to solidarity and community in educational practice and a commitment to the service of the poor. Such belief and recommendations are emphasised in many documents (for example, from the Catholic Bishops' Conference of England and Wales in 1995, *The Common Good in Education,* and, in 1996, *The Common Good and the Catholic Church's Social Teaching*). It would seem an obligation on the schools under their diocesan trusteeship to pursue these recommendations as essential to their raison d'etre.

In assessing these rival claims between those who, in pursuit of the 'common good', justify religiously separate schools, and those who insist on the 'common school', it is necessary, first, to think carefully about what it *means* to promote 'the common good', and, in the light of that, to see how far its attainment does, or does not, requires 'the *common* school'.

The common good and civic society

It is difficult, if not impossible, to avoid some notion of 'the common good' in an account of any political body or civic society which claims legitimacy over a given territory and people. Such an aim, actively pursued, would provide the legitimacy for civic society to exercise legislative control over members of the community. But, although such an aim would seem essential, it is less clear what such 'common good' would contain (that is, both the general well-being of all members of the civic society, despite their diversity, and the conditions necessary for promoting such well-being). One might agree with the general aim, but not necessarily with the descriptive content of it. That raises four issues:

(i)   *Basic requirements of individuals*: what might be the basic requirements for each individual in civic society, irrespective of social background, ethnicity, religious affiliation, etc.?

(ii) *Respect for constitutive communities*: since civic society is constituted not simply of individuals but also of associations of individuals (including faith communities), how might respect for their *distinctive* values be part of the *common good*?

(iii) *Procedures for reconciling differences*: what might be the *procedures* for reconciling disagreements between individuals and between associations over what is considered to be for the *common good*?

(iv) *Illumination of the common good from the perspective of constituent associations*: how might distinctive understandings and values by such associations illuminate, and thereby contribute to, an understanding of the *common good* within civic society?

The following attempts to answer these crucial questions.

146 Key issues emerging: The need for philosophy

Basic requirements for each individual

What basic requirements would one insist upon if one had no idea 'from behind the cloak of ignorance' of the material and social advantages one was to have? (John Rawls, 1972, p.136ff.). No doubt they would include decent housing, adequate health-giving food, opportunities to gain knowledge through education, efficient road and communication systems, adequate supply of water and drainage, access to health service, and thus the need for an overarching authority to ensure the provision of such basic needs for all.

Respect for constituent associations

However, the political community or civic society is made up, not just of individuals linked by social contract, but also of smaller associations, namely, the 'rich mosaic' of families, friendships, voluntary associations, charities, congregations, and moral traditions, which Sacks (1997) refers to. Each association, though sharing much in common with others, would have its own, aims, values, and moral rules. Such must be the case within a pluralist society. The state, therefore, needs to respect the legitimate rights and activities of these constituent associations, to which the individuals belong, with their histories and traditions, but must at the same time ensure that the distinctive values and beliefs of each association are not imposed on all others. For example, a faith community's beliefs and practice about the nature of marriage need to be respected but could not legitimately be imposed on those who strongly hold different views (for example, on same sex marriage).

There is no inherent inconsistency, for example, between the Muslims loyalty to the Umma (the sense of identity with the international Muslim tradition and community) and loyalty to the civic society in which they have their home – as indeed is the case with the Jewish and the different Christian communities. Indeed, through education within their distinctive traditions, these different communities might draw strength and commitment to contribute creatively to the wider civic society if they are given the opportunity to do so. This could mean (as argued by Archbishop Rowan Williams, 2004, referring to a paper by Maleiha Malik entitled 'Muslims and participatory democracy'):

> Since the interests of minority groups are not adequately safeguarded by the classical liberal principles of individual entitlement and non-discrimination, we need a more sophisticated model of the relation between the State and its minorities, which in turn requires some rethinking of the original picture of the State contracting with a mass of atomised individuals.

For instance, in the state's 'acknowledgement of communal identities' through processes of consultation. Failure so to acknowledge may well result in members of that (or other) religious communities developing a hostile approach to the wider society. As Williams continues, it requires the State to think clearly about what it understands by religious belonging and not to reduce it to the level of a private voluntary association of the like-minded.

Procedures for reconciling differences – a 'fair society'

However, significant disagreements between associations or individuals might be seen to subvert legitimate interests of the community at large or of particular communities within it. Therefore, an essential element of the 'common good' is agreed procedures within a political community for reconciling differences between individuals or between the claims of the particular associations and the wider society. Serving 'the common good'

> means deciding impartially between all claims, and trying to satisfy those for which the best case can be made out. The common good is not therefore a goal, but a procedure for making moral judgments ... with due consideration to the claims of everyone.
>
> *(Benn and Peters, 1959, p.328)*

Central to 'the common good', therefore, is the principle of justice – of public reasoning whereby a case for different treatment is presented in terms that others can understand, and whereby each is treated with respect and differences are reconciled. The 'common good' thereby becomes compatible with pluralism. There will, of course, be limits to such pluralism. Rousseau, within his *Social Contract* (1762), was deeply suspicious of there being different associations within the wider political community, believing that they would inevitably undermine 'the general will'. Indeed, certain associations may do so. A criticism of religiously segregated schools, arising particularly in the 'Trojan Horse affair' (see Chapter 1), was that some religious schools were in danger of doing that. A High Court ruled in October 2017 that the mixed-sex Al-Hijrah school in Birmingham, which segregated male and female pupils from age nine in lessons and breaks, amounted to discrimination. (It may seem inconsistent that, despite such a ruling, single sex girls' schools should not be seen equally guilty of discriminatory behaviour.) How far, then, can different interests and beliefs be protected before the 'common good' is seen to be diminished? That requires the conditions for wide deliberation of all relevant interests in order to reach possible consensus – and the political and judicial frameworks for such deliberation.

Illumination of 'common good' from the perspective of particular associations

However, it may be the case that a religious association has a distinctive view about the 'common good' which is at variance with that which prevails in practice and yet which could make a positive contribution from its philosophical position to an

148 Key issues emerging: The need for philosophy

understanding of what general well-being of its members within society entails. Thus, the document *The Common Good and the Catholic Church's Social Teaching* strongly questions the neo-liberal beliefs which underpin much of public life and social arrangements, including education. In maintaining its caution towards free market economics, for example, it seeks to re-emphasise in our society the concept of the 'common good', in particular that education is not a commodity to be offered for sale.

> Education is a service provided by society for the benefit of all its young people, in particular for the benefit of the most vulnerable and the most disadvantaged – those whom we have a sacred duty to serve. Education is about the service of others rather than the service of self … it is a noble and ennobling vocation which is diminished both by the constraints and by the language of the market place.
>
> *(CBC, 1997, quoted in Grace, 2016, p.185)*

It has been generally accepted over the decades, since the English and Welsh government in 1833 first invested money in elementary education, that universal education (and later secondary education) was a general good which should be available for all – something possible only if supported out of public funds even though the providers were, in the main, the different religious associations. Such associations (in particular those of the Church of England, Non-conformists, and later the Catholic Church) would therefore seek to provide, first, the general education desired by all (and indeed by the economic and social needs of the state), but, second, their distinctive understandings of personal development – so long as they were compatible with the good of all. In other words, the contribution which the different religious bodies claim to be making to the 'common good' is their respective understandings of what constitutes a good and distinctively human life – important to be acknowledged, one might think, in the different cultures which make up a pluralist society.

A particular association (a religious community, for example) might practise and promote particular values, and would have the right to argue for them within the wider society. However, it would not be compatible with the pluralistic nature of society to force those values as a *universal practice* on others who do not share the underlying moral argument. For example, a prolonged account of this in relation to the right for abortion is given by Stiltner, 1996, in his 'case study of the abortion debate'.

The common school

Nonetheless, criticism of schools segregated on religious grounds is that, however much they proclaim the pursuit of the 'common good' as a central educational aim, and indeed that their distinctive traditions might enrich the understanding of the 'common good', their very separateness undermines the mutual respect and shared understandings necessary for developing and preserving 'the general will'. Such can only be achieved through learning to live with differences and indeed to benefit from them – social, religious, ethnic, and cultural.

Problems arise either where the values promoted by the religiously affiliated schools are seen to undermine the good of society as that is generally conceived or because, despite the respective promotions of the general good of society, separating young people into different schools impedes understanding between different communities, which would seem essential for harmonious living. The separate schools in Northern Ireland are seen by many to be a case in point. Better, it has been argued, to have a 'Common School' (or an 'integrated school', as described in Chapter 4) where the conditions for separate associations with the different aims, values, and practices can come to understand each other and have respect for differences of belief.

Hence, the importance, so it is argued, for 'the common school'.

An argument for the 'Common School' could no doubt refer with profit to what the former Chief Rabbi, Jonathan Sacks (2002), argued in *The Dignity of Difference,* namely, that it is not enough to learn how to tolerate differences. Rather is it essential, in the kind of society we live in, to respect and to learn from those differences – to realise thereby that no one has the complete monopoly of the truth and that there is always room for greater understanding of one's own faith and moral tradition through the recognition of what is true in other traditions.

Thus, it might be argued (although Sacks did not draw this conclusion) that one aim of education should be the pursuit of the common good facilitated by a common schooling, arising from the interaction of differences, rather than in spite of them. Perhaps the best advocate of such a conclusion would be the American philosopher, John Dewey, who addressed similar problems in the need to create a common understanding as a basis for civic society within a very diverse population. Indeed, it was through facing differences that one was stimulated into deeper thinking about the issues and a better understanding of one's beliefs. To quote Dewey (1916, p.326), 'thinking is occasioned by an unsettlement and it aims at overcoming a disturbance'. For Dewey, diversity was a source of educational health, not a barrier to it.

To understand how Dewey saw the transformation of diversity into a life-enhancing force, one needs to think of Chicago, to whose university he went in 1894, and then of New York where (at Columbia University) he taught for 26 years after his appointment in 1904. Both cities were growing exponentially, as poor people moved into the cities from rural areas and as so many immigrants came from all over the world – people of different languages, religions and ethnicities, and with different experiences of persecution and poverty. It was within this highly diverse, culturally mixed and rapidly expanding New York that Dewey wrote *Democracy and Education.* It was in such an environment that Dewey came to see the school as having a central role in promoting unity out of diversity, mutual respect out of adversity, and a sense of community out of different economic activities. The political community required this respect for, and learning from, diversity, and indeed would be enriched by such diversity where received views could be challenged.

150 Key issues emerging: The need for philosophy

Helping young people to develop this respect and this openness to alternative views was seen as a central requirement of the future citizen. In the introductory pages of *Democracy and Education,* Dewey states:

> Men live in a community in virtue of the things which they have in common. What they must have in common in order to form a community or society are aims beliefs, aspirations, knowledge – a common understanding, as the sociologists say.
>
> *(p. 4)*

One need not go to the United States and John Dewey for such sentiments. It was Tawney, influential on the British Labour Party and on the development of a system of secondary education made up of comprehensive schools, who wrote:

> [I]n spite of their varying character and capacities, men possess in their common humanity a quality which is worth cultivating and … a community is most likely to make the most of that quality if it takes into account in planning its economic organisation and social institutions – if it stresses lightly differences of wealth and birth and social position, and establishes on firm foundations institutions which meet common needs, and are a source of common enlightenment and common enjoyment.
>
> *(Tawney, 1938, pp. 55–56)*

Therefore, the most important of such foundations, providing a 'source of common enlightenment and common enjoyment', would be the 'Common School', where through intercommunication, shared experience, and guidance from the teacher, the pupils would develop into true citizens of an integrated community through a shared culture. Such a 'Common School', therefore, would have no selection on the grounds of social class, ethnicity, religion, or academic achievement. A principal aim of education was to prepare young people, not only how to live together in society (rich and poor, black and white, religious and non-religious, Jews, Muslims, and Christians, highly intelligent and those with learning difficulties), but also to be enriched by participation in a society which was characterised by these very differences. Differences, if rightly regarded, were essential to the common good, not barriers to its attainment.

In achieving that, schools should aim to provide the tools whereby pupils are able to enter into the ethical and social discourses about the life worth living through the humanities, arts, and sciences. Having acquired the appropriate concepts and ways of testing the truth of claims made, then they would be better able to decide on the kinds of belief and the form of life to be followed.

Indeed, it was partly under Dewey's influence that the American high school would be seen by many as much more than a place for what Dewey referred to as the transmission of 'traditional learning'. Peshkin's case study of a small-town school in the Midwest portrayed the importance attached to 'community' within the school in preparation for the wider community outside the school (Peshkin, 1978). There has indeed been a history of community schools in Britain – for example, Cambridge Village Colleges established by Henry Morris in the 1930s, which brought together schools, youth service, and adult education within one establishment under local control. But this emphasis on the creation of community never became universally established. Indeed, the changing economic climate of schooling, with emphasis on competition and market forces, rather than cooperation, militates against that sense of cooperation and community.

As we saw in Chapter 1, the importance of this for Britain was emphasised by Lord Ouseley (2001) in his report following the Oldham riots of 1998, namely, that there were signs that communities were fragmenting along racial, cultural, and faith lines. Schools, it was argued, have a key role in preventing this fragmentation.

The problem might be seen as exacerbated by the growth of Muslim schools, especially with so many (when not voluntary controlled or aided) remaining outside the accountability which prevails within the national system. It may seem that a system increasingly fragmented on religious (and thereby ethnic) grounds needs to recall the proclaimed virtues of a truly common 'Common School', promoting (in Tawney's words) a common culture – one which, as with Henry Morris' community colleges, embraces youth service (which has suffered from closures) and service to parents and local community as part of their educational mission to heal divisions, foster mutual understanding, and see 'dignity in difference'.

Counter argument

There are many different kinds of exceptions to the 'Common School' in society.

First, of considerable significance in Britain is the survival of an independent sector of 'public schools' with (generally speaking) high fees and socially skewed entry. The products of such independent schools gain disproportionate number of places at the prestigious universities of Oxford and Cambridge, and thence key jobs in the legal world, government, civil service, and industry. Second, grammar schools remain in several local areas, where children are divided at the age of 11 for progress into different schools on the basis of tests, the validity of which for detecting innate intelligence has not survived rigorous research. Success depends very much on prior coaching, accessible to those who can afford it. Third, areas served by the neighbourhood school are themselves very often identified by social class, or indeed ethnic, segregation from mainstream society.

In comparison with the exclusiveness of private education, of selective grammar schools, and of concentrated disadvantage of some neighbourhood schools, the development of Faith schools would be of minor significance in the undermining of the advantages of the 'Common School', as portrayed above. Indeed, they in many cases create more ethnically mixed intake, as shown in Chapter 3, and, as the catchment area of the Faith schools is in all probability much larger than the neighbourhood in which the schools are situated, they are more likely to be more socially mixed. Nonetheless, the argument of those who oppose Faith

152 Key issues emerging: The need for philosophy

schools on the basis of undermining the 'common good' must be that the values of the 'common good', as stated earlier, are undermined solely on the grounds that pupils of different faiths and none are not benefitting from interaction between themselves.

In certain cases, this is claimed (as shown in the several reports referred to in Chapter 2, namely, those by Ouseley, Cantle, and Butler-Sloss) where self-segregated ethnic and immigrant communities fail to integrate with the wider population and where, therefore, the neighbourhood school may reinforce a religiously based separation. But these are exceptional circumstances from which it would be invalid to draw conclusions about religiously affiliated schools in general. The many voluntary controlled schools, mainly Church of England, are not religiously exclusive and indeed, as shown in Chapter 5, have maintained their original 19th century mission to provide education for all, especially the poor, though inspired by values derived from the Christian inheritance. The voluntary aided schools (mainly Catholic), make religious affiliation the main, but by no means exclusive, condition for acceptance – over 30% of pupils in Catholic schools are not Catholic.

However, the argument for such schools being compatible with promotion of the 'common good' (given that they are not socially or ethnically exclusive, although no doubt there are exceptions) lies in the value to society of preserving the richness of distinct traditions with regard to what constitutes 'being and becoming more human' as a central aim of education (as argued in Chapters 5 and 9). Within those traditions and their promotion of the 'common good' is a philosophy of social values, arising from a religious vision, which society should take seriously.

A philosophy of social values

Running through the intricacies of the debate over the common good is the concern for the advancement of social values, which underpin the pluralist societies in which people live. These social values might be summarised under the following headings:

(i)   Social solidarity
(ii) Subsidiarity of responsibility
(iii) Respect for individual rights within the social whole.

It is necessary to examine each of these in turn.

Social solidarity

Individuals necessarily live in communities. Their growth, welfare, and indeed sense of their own worth, depend on this wider social and cultural life. Being social, they are not totally autonomous, drawing on the values, habits, and understandings which they have inherited from their respective communities, whether secular or religious. Civic Society, therefore, is formed to provide the protection and the support for such individuals to live fully human lives. That requires agreed procedures for ensuring this happens – through a legal framework, through provision of necessary infrastructures, through educational opportunities for all, and through help for the sick, vulnerable, and needy. '*Solidarity*', recognising the humanity of each and every one and recognising too the need for mutual support, would be fundamental to the message promoted by a religious tradition (and hence by its educational institutions).

As such, the pursuit of solidarity would be strongly critical of those forces within society which, underpinned by economic theories, make the pursuit of profit the dominant social aim, irrespective of the means (affecting the quality of life of many people) by which such aims are to be realised. Faith schools necessarily stand for such a strong message.

Subsidiarity

Compatible with the pursuit of 'solidarity' is the importance attached to 'subsidiarity', that is, recognition of the different associations which constitute society, each with its different ideas of personal fulfilment – including the different religious associations and family units. Society is constituted of such associations which contribute to the rich mix of society. The rights of such associations need to be protected and enhanced so long as they are compatible with the welfare of all. In particular, therefore, it would be wrong for the 'higher authority' of the Civic Society to take away from the constituent associations (for example, religious association and families) those responsibilities which are rightly theirs, unless the exercise of them brings harm to others or undermines civic society.

Indeed, as expressed in *Quadragessimo Anno*, (subtitled 'on constructing the social order'):

> It is an injustice, a grave evil and a disturbance of the right order for a higher association to arrogate to itself functions which can be performed efficiently by lower and smaller societies.
>
> *(Pius XI, 1931)*

This is particularly the case with the family (or 'domestic household'), which may have distinctive ideas concerning the humanising function of the schools, to which they send their children, in continuing the social education which has been taking place in the family. On this matter, the European Convention on Human Rights (2000, article 4) is clear:

> The freedom to found educational establishments with due respect for democratic principles and the right of parents to ensure the education and teaching of their children in conformity with their religious, philosophical and pedagogical convictions and these rights shall be respected.

154 Key issues emerging: The need for philosophy

Respect for individual rights within the social whole

Within such a 'commonwealth', therefore, are different associations (especially the family) with rights to possessions which are essential for a life of human dignity (a home, clothes, food, warmth) arising from the produce of their labour. Large scale acquisitions of property or capital whereby those rights of labour are denied would be unacceptable. In the light of such human rights, there are dangers in untrammelled economic freedom – the isolation created by rampant individualism, leading to impoverishment of households which were the basic units of civil society. There are limits to freedom where that impinges on the rights of others and upon human dignity. There are limits to how far wages should be determined by market forces. Therefore, the freedom to be pursued is much more than 'free from restraint' (a 'negative sense of freedom'), and much more to do with being empowered to live a life consonant with the dignity of a human being. This might be seen as an implicit critique of Hobbes' basis of society in a 'social contract', because the contract so entered into, though free in a negative sense, may not be so in a positive sense – that is, made in the absence of knowledge, power, and economic conditions required for entry into this contract.

In sum (and paradoxically) a 'religious association' with a well-argued understanding of the 'common good' (which may challenge dominant aspects of the prevailing secular society) would seek to preserve that understanding within its own faith institutions – thereby (but under certain conditions) making a significant contribution to the 'common good'.

In particular, reference is made to the family (or 'domestic household'), which has rights and duties prior to those of the overall civic society. One such right and duty would be that of raising their children within their distinctive religious tradition which has contributed to our understanding of human nature and values.

Problems encountered

First, Dewey's common school, as a contribution to the creation of a common culture for the future citizens, seemed appropriate enough in the socially mixed but self-contained communities such as that described by Peshkin or in the ethnically mixed community of an inner-city environment like that of Chicago and New York, where it was the neighbourhood school serving this diversity. However, as societies develop, so neighbourhoods themselves become less diverse. The middle classes move into the suburbs, leaving the inner cities with a greater concentration of the poor and disadvantaged. Immigrant populations form their own self-segregated communities – as the Jewish and Irish immigrants did in the 19th century, and as the Muslim population is doing today in certain major cities. The neighbourhood school (the common school), in recruiting from the locality, would in many cases be neither socially nor ethnically mixed.

One solution would be to bring children from the suburbs into the inner cities, but that would not politically be an acceptable solution. Very often such 'bussing in' is for children of a faith (Jewish, Christian, or Muslim) who seek the nearest Faith school which often, for historical reasons, is situated in the more disadvantaged areas. Ideally solutions lie, not in a bussing policy (the enforced moving of school populations), but in the creation, through local housing policies and the restoration of social housing, of mixed neighbourhoods. In some respects, Faith schools contribute to a solution. Many Catholic schools, for example, were established in neighbourhoods where there was a concentration of Catholic immigrants, mainly Irish, but now very often from other countries. It is not necessarily by design that Catholic schools are more ethnically mixed than community schools or voluntary controlled schools (see the data in Chapter 3). Rather it may be the case that they were (and are) the first choice of immigrant families coming from countries with predominantly Catholic populations. It would be argued, too, that, when established, such schools were in the very cities where they needed to serve the poor and disadvantaged.

Second, in 2015, the Social Integration Commission criticised the drive to open religiously affiliated (especially Muslim) free schools, which could lead to an increased number of children being educated in socially and ethnically similar groups, making wider social integration more difficult. Where that is the case, such schools would be failing, under the excuse of the faith, to fulfil the missions enjoined by the teaching of the respective faiths, as shown in Chapter 8. Faith schools should be serving the common good in respect of admitting pupils from the range of ethnic and social diversity – such indeed is their express mission. There are no doubt exceptions. It must be tempting for schools to be socially selective under the guise of faith (as explained in Chapter 3) when under pressure from the inspectorate to 'raise standards' and to ascend the league tables. But it would be the duty of the trustees to ensure this part of the mission was enforced.

Third, the claimed right of parents to have their children educated exclusively in a religious-affiliated school is challenged, though paradoxically such a claim is made within the language of a secular liberal political philosophy (see McLaughlin, 1984). To the objection that this would be indoctrinatory, thereby limiting the eventual autonomy of the child, reference was made in the previous chapter to the benefit of such initiation in pupils' improved ability to look critically at the otherwise purely secular influences which otherwise might obtain.

Fourth, the objection would seem to remain, namely, that one aspect of the common school (whereby a common culture, befitting the future citizens, is developed) is missing the intermixture of different religious voices and traditions. This objection will be picked up in the concluding chapter.

Openness to the modern world

There is a temptation, in nurturing the faith within a particular tradition, to erect barriers to outside influences, thereby failing to see the benefits which arise from greater openness, first, to others' ways of understanding (especially those of other religious traditions), and, second, to the social and economic problems which affect

156 Key issues emerging: The need for philosophy

the common good. It is felt necessary, first, to strengthen the understanding and commitment within tradition, whether that of Islam, Judaism, or Christianity. From such a base one is more able to engage with others in a deeper and more informed way – hence, an argument for Faith schools.

But there is danger in such 'self-segregation' of religious communities – whether Jewish, Muslim, or Christian. How, for example, to ameliorate the 'ghetto' approach, as described by Helen Miller (2013) within Jewish schools, based historically on self-defence, whilst at the same time protecting and enhancing a particular way of life – a distinctive culture for which one feels responsible? Similarly, within Muslim communities, how might the sense of community, described in Chapter 7, be preserved without investment in their distinctive schools and madrasas? Might Christian communities, due to the decline of Sunday schools, see the source of their preservation in Faith schools? In 1953, 83% of adults had attended Sunday schools as children; by 2000, that figure reduced to 14%. But, as Geoffrey Walford (2001) pointed out, there was a considerable growth of Evangelical Christian schools as parents reacted to what they perceived to be the increase of secularism in the state-maintained schools.

How might one reconcile such 'self-segregation' with the pursuit of openness? Preservation of distinctive religious traditions, concerning what it means to be human and to live within community, would seem to undermine their avowed determination to contribute to a more open and cohesive society. Are the two reconcilable – ensuring the continuity of the Jewish, Islamic, or Christian faiths, yet being open to the beliefs and values of others in dialogue?

As Novak (1992, p.78) argued in his book *Jewish Social Ethics*:

> Jews and Christians must first be able to talk to each other before they can talk to the secular world, which is further removed from both of them. Discourse must begin with those whose traditions overlap the most.

Helen Miller, 2013, having demonstrated the importance for Jews on the growth of Jewish schools, subsequently argues that there should be more dialogue between Catholic and Jewish educators, and collaboration on shared problems. Furthermore, as Dr Taj Hargey, Director of the Muslim Educational Centre in Oxford, argued, Muslims must

> cast off the variants of imported religious dogma – the 'warped Wahabi/ Salafi and Deobandi/Tablighi indoctrination which is not derived from the Holy Qur'an

> *(Oxford Times, 30.5.16)*

yet which emphasises their alienation from the wider society. Rather should Islamic schools demonstrate authentic Qu'ranic principles of 'cosmopolitan pluralism and peaceful co-existence'. Equally important, such understanding must be shared and explored with non-Muslims who have not been exposed to true Islam. Such a sharing would expose the similarities between major religious traditions – the sense of the sacred, the disciplined pursuit of holiness through development of the virtues, respect for life, the importance of prayer and ritual, and showing how all have a stake in the common good.

An excellent example of this sharing between Christian and Muslim which enhances not just understanding of each other but also a deeper spirituality was shown in the weekend of Muslim-Christian friendship which took place in Taizé in May 2017 – 'a matter of spending time together in order to share a spiritual experience around the theme: the taste of God'.

Therefore, one sees an increasing commitment between different faiths to work together for what they have in common, thereby learning from each other's traditions, establishing the conditions for social harmony in the more pluralist society, and preserving together a strong, if generalised, religious tradition in an often aggressively secular world. After all, development of understanding (as indeed development of doctrine over centuries) has arisen through participation in traditions of philosophical, theological, and social thinking shared between the religious traditions. The scholastic tradition of the Middle Ages drew upon the scholarship of the Islamic philosophers Avicenna and Averroes; it was shared, too, with Jewish philosophers such as Maimonides.

The urgency of thinking and working together is apparent as the Brexit referendum has unleashed a xenophobic streak in elements of British society. Both here and in the United States there is concern about the isolation of the Muslim communities within the common society. Islam, in many peoples' minds becomes associated with ISIS and terrorism. Thus, the banning by President Trump of all entrants to the United States from seven mainly Muslim countries recreates the claim by Bernard Lewis in his book *The Muslims Discover Europe* (1957) and re-iterated by Samuel Huntington (1996) of the 'clash of civilisations' – never the twain shall meet.

But the so-called 'clash' is created by ignorance, and ignorance requires an educational response from the religious traditions *in collaboration* to show what is common between them and the possibility of learning from each other. As the celebrated Jewish philosopher, Moses Mendelssohn (1983, p.135), pleaded in his book *Jerusalem: Or, On Religious Power and Judaism,*

> Regard us, if not as brothers and fellow citizens, at least as fellow men and fellow inhabitants of the land. Show us ways and provide us with means of becoming better men and better fellow inhabitants, and permit us to be partners in enjoying the rights of humanity as far as time and circumstances permit.

In the recommendation of post-Vatican II Council's 1965 Encyclical, *Gaudium et Spes*, there must be in the Church

> openness to the modern world – a call for dialogue, a new awareness of anthropology as central to the proclamation of the Gospel, new ways

158 Key issues emerging: The need for philosophy

of thinking about human beings, life, society, and our relations with nature' – and, indeed, a new appreciation of the existence of elements of truth and grace as well as the presence of seeds of the word in other religions.

Hence, the plea within the faith communities for openness to others' contribution to understanding – growth through dialogue. From within the Christian position, one might promote the social philosophy, described above, and pose the Gospel question 'But who is my neighbour?'

Conclusion

The pursuit of the 'common good' is the basis for civic government having authority within society, first, to ensure the common good in terms of basic needs for a fulfilled life, second, respect for the diverse associations (including religious communities and families) which make up society, and, third, requirements for harmonious settlement of differences.

That, however, requires a careful account of what is meant by the 'common good', various aspects of which have been described in this chapter:

- meeting basic needs for human development and flourishing – healthy food, clothing, housing, warmth, opportunities for education, interpersonal respect irrespective of race, religion or social class;
- protection of, and support for, the constitutive associations and communities of civil society with their respective beliefs and values, so long as they are compatible with the good of the total society;
- opportunity and means for the respective associations (in recognition of the importance of 'subsidiarity') to protect their distinctive values and responsibilities which would include the rights of parents to have their children educated according to their wishes, so long as that education is compatible with the good of the whole;
- contribution to be encouraged which the distinctive moral and social values (espoused by particular associations such as faith communities) might make to an understanding of the 'common good'; and
- procedures, reflecting the virtues of justice and fairness, which would be acceptable to all for reconciling disagreements and for ensuring the minimum content for all.

With regard to the contributions which religious associations, and thereby their Faith schools, might make to the 'common good', special reference was made to the social philosophy and teaching which has evolved within a religious tradition – social solidarity, subsidiarity, and individual rights to be treated with dignity.

However, the danger needs to be faced that such values might be negated if the Faith schools do not remain 'open to all' whilst at the same time preserving their distinctive beliefs, narrative and ethos.

References

Benn, S. and Peters, R.S., 1959, *Social Principles and the Democratic State*, London: George, Allen and Unwin.

Butler-Sloss Report, 2015, Living with Difference, Report of the Commission on Religion and Public Life, Cambridge: Woolf Institute.

CBC (Catholic Bishops Conference), 1997, *The Common Good in Education*, London: Catholic Education Service.

CCE (Congregation for Catholic Education), 1977, *The Catholic School*, Vatican City: Libraria Evidrice.

Chadwick Report, 2012, *Going for Growth: Transformation for Children, Young Person and the Church*, London: SPCK.

Dearing Report, 2001, *Way Ahead: Church of England Schools in this New Millennium*, London: Church House Publishing.

Dewey, J., 1916, *Democracy and Education*, New York: The Free Press.

Grace, G., 2016, *Faith, Mission and Challenge in Catholic Education*, London: Routledge.

Huntington, S.P., 1993, 'Clash of civilisations?', Foreign Affairs, 72(3).

McLaughlin, T., 1984, 'Parental rights and the religious upbringing of children', *Journal of Philosophy of Education*, 18(1).

Mendelssohn, M. and Arkrush, A., 1983, *Jerusalem: Or, on Religious Power and Judaism*, Hanover: Brandeis University Press.

Miller, H., editor, 2013, *International Handbook of Jewish Education*, New York: Springer.

Novak, D., 1992, *Jewish Social Ethics*, New York: Oxford university Press.

Ouseley Report, 2001, *Community Pride, Not Prejudice*, Bradford Vision.

Peshkin, 1978, *Growing Up American*, University of Chicago Press.

Pius, XI, 1931, *Quadragesimo Anno: On Constructing the Social Order*, Vatican City: LEV.

Rawls, 1972, *A Theory of Justice*, Oxford University Press.

Sacks, J., 1997, *The Politics of Hope*, London: Jonathan Cape.

Sacks, J., 2002, *The Dignity of Difference*, London: Continuum.

Stiltner, B., 1996, *Religion and the Common Good*, Maryland: Rowman and Littlefield Publishers, Inc.

Tawney, 1938 (3rd edition), *Equality*, London: George, Allen and Unwin.

Walford, G., 2001, 'Evangelical Christian Schools in England and the Netherlands', *Oxford Review of Education*, 27(4).

Williams, R., 2004, 'Convictions, Loyalties and the Secular State', The Chatham Lecture, Trinity College, Oxford.

PART IV

Drawing conclusions

12

FOR OR AGAINST FAITH SCHOOLS?

Finding an answer

Introduction

This book addresses the questions concerning the continued support for Faith schools within a public system of education paid for by the taxpayer. Although it is focused on the public system within England and Wales (and thus *in some aspects* unique to the historical development of such schools in those countries), the issues raised are by no means confined to those countries. This particular historical phenomenon, and its evolution over 200 years through critical questioning and through the development of a more secular society, raises issues of international significance.

The historically evolving context of the development of Faith schools was explained in Chapter 2, namely, the origins of elementary education through the provisions of the National Society of the Church of England, of the British and Foreign Schools Society of the Non-Conformists, and, after 1850, of Catholic schools under their diocesan authorities. There remained, as a result and until recently, a threefold national system of locally maintained schools, namely, voluntary aided, voluntary controlled and community schools. To be counted now amongst such schools are the increasing number of Jewish and Muslim schools (and indeed those of other religions), having sought successfully for voluntary aided status. In recent decades, the establishment and growth of academies and free schools have created a more complicated background to the role of Faith schools within the overall system.

This arrangement has always had its critics even in its very early stages, as we saw in Chapter 2. Thus, in 1907, the newly formed Secular Education League insisted that the teaching of religion was not the responsibility of the state, particularly after the 1902 Education Act had confirmed that Church schools, supported on the rates, would include the growing number of Roman Catholic schools. 'No Rome on the Rates'!

164 Drawing conclusions

Yet Faith schools, until comparatively recently and despite some opposition, have been generally accepted as an integral part of the publicly funded education system. However, as explained in Chapter 1, the social context of education has changed: a more 'secular age', a more multi-cultural society, and concerns about 'social cohesion'. Such changes have led to a more systematic challenge to, and criticism of, an educational system divided on religious lines.

There have been political responses to these challenges, in particular the requirement that Faith schools, when (as often is the case) they are over-subscribed, should admit a certain percentage not of that faith, especially those children who suffer from different forms of disadvantage – for example, those with special learning needs or in material poverty and for whom the Faith school would be their neighbourhood school. Admissions arrangements need to be re-examined to ensure the schools reflect the social and ethnic mix of their neighbourhoods. Furthermore, there has been political pressure to 'put a cap' of 50% on the members of that faith admitted to any new Faith schools.

There is also a problem where there is a concentration of a single ethnic and religious affiliation within a neighbourhood and where also there is a concentration of poverty and social disadvantage (as illustrated in 'the Trojan Horse affair' described in Chapter 1). The children of such neighbourhoods need particular support to be prepared to enter more fully into the wider society. Such children, though not of that religious persuasion, should not be denied entry to nearby Faith schools.

Therefore, in what follows:

First, the different sorts of *criticism against Faith Schools*, as they have emerged in preceding chapters, are summarised, together with an appraisal of such criticisms – in particular the extent to which Faith schools, if to continue, need to adapt their practices.

Second, *arguments for retaining Faith Schools* within the state system, as have emerged in preceding chapters, are summarised, albeit influenced by the responses given to the criticisms.

Finally, in the light of the arguments for and against, conclusions are reached about the actions to be taken. Matters cannot remain as they are.

Arguments against Faith schools

There have emerged roughly four kinds of argument against current arrangements:

(i)   opposition to there being any public and financial support for schools which proclaim a religious mission: *secular objection*.

(ii) the claimed failure to provide a 'common school' in response to an ever more divided society: *social cohesion objection*.

(iii) the claimed use of religious affiliation as a basis for hidden selection in a non-selective system: *social selection objection*;

(iv) corruption of official admissions rules through 'games schools play' in response to competition between schools: *abuse of admissions criteria objection*.

Each of these will now be examined in turn, together with a response based on the arguments and evidence produced in the respective chapters.

Secular objection

The secular objection had two main arguments.

The *first* argument (referred to in Chapters 1and 5) was that religious ethos and beliefs no longer provide the background (or 'horizon of significance') to our society – thereby to institutional or individuals' values. The decline in religious attendance and belief signals a very different social landscape from the time when Britain was essentially a Christian country, when religious symbolism permeated public life and when the school system emerged under the patronage and control of the Christian churches. As Dawkins argued, modern society requires a 'truly secular state', from which followed that there should be state neutrality, and 'in all matters pertaining to religion, the recognition that faith is personal and no business of the state' (Chapter 5). Therefore, it is argued that it would be unacceptable for those who have no religious beliefs (and this might well be the majority) to be required (often against their wishes) to contribute through their taxes to the support of religious foundations and the nurturing of religious beliefs.

> *In response*, the supporters of Faith Schools question the characterisation of Civic Society as universally secular. Rather is it, as argued by Rabbi Jonathan Sacks, 'a confusing mixture of reasons and associations, which emerge, like a great river from its countless streams and tributaries, out of a vast range of histories and traditions' (Chapter 5). That 'vast range of histories and traditions' is constituted of religious beliefs and practices, the product of many generations of thought and enquiry. As such, it was argued, such beliefs and practices within a pluralist society should be respected in so important a matter as the education of the next generations, so long as they contribute to the common good as that is explained in Chapters 8 and 11. The 'truly secular state' does itself embody a particular view of the world, of human fulfilment and of the values to be pursued (a 'tradition', as explained in Chapter 5), which is as controversial to the non-secular mind as the religious view of the world is to the secular mind. Indeed, it is a matter of concern to many that, unchallenged, the 'truly secular state', as it permeates the institutional modes of thinking of our schools, could itself be a form of indoctrination which needs to be challenged.

The *second,* and more significant, 'secular argument' was that, emerging from the 'Enlightenment' (referred to in Chapters 5 and 9), education is concerned with the enhancement of rationality in its different forms and that, since religious beliefs are not open to rational justification, they should not, therefore, be taught in publicly funded schools. To teach what is non-rational as though it were rational is to indoctrinate and to undermine personal autonomy. This was emphatically expressed by

166 Drawing conclusions

Paul Hirst, as quoted in Chapter 5, namely, that 'there has already emerged in our society a view of education, a concept of education, which makes the whole idea of Christian education a kind of nonsense and the search for a Christian approach to, or philosophy of, education a huge mistake'. Indeed, there was the assumption that religious forms of discourse did not survive the rationalist critique in the post-enlightenment era.

> *In response,* it was argued in Chapter 10 that a major difficulty with the arguments for personal autonomy based on a particular view of rationality, which excluded religious forms of discourse, is that the defence of so limiting what is to be rational would itself fail the test of rationality – just as A.J. Ayer's argument for the meaning of a proposition to lie in its mode of verification must itself be meaningless because it does itself fail the verification test. We engage in reason in many different ways – when we appreciate a painting, when we assess the value of a person's life, when we deliberate on the morally correct action, or when we speculate about the origins of the universe. The history of religious belief over the ages arises from a continuing debate between philosophers (for example, between the Platonism of St Augustine and the Aristotelianism of St Thomas Aquinas), and such philosophical arguments continue and develop in relationship to new phenomena and experiences which need to be made sense of.

The case for Faith schools cannot be defeated by the appeal to a narrow conception of rationality. But it must take seriously a respect for rational appraisal both of the faith and of how that faith is constantly evolving through deliberation, rational engagement, and response to criticism. That surely must be part of religious education.

Social cohesion objection

As explained in Chapter 1, a major change in society over the last few decades is its multi-cultural and multi-ethnic nature. Where there have not been political and social initiatives required to create social cohesion, there have been serious cases of public disruption. Reports, which followed those disruptions (Cantle, Casey, Ouseley – referred to in Chapter 1 and elsewhere), have referred to the contribution that schools can and should make to ensuring 'social cohesion'. As then argued in Chapter 11, the common school, bringing pupils of different social, ethnic, and cultural backgrounds together, would be seen by many as the most appropriate preparation for citizenship in a democracy, which serves all its citizens irrespective of background. Usually, but not exclusively, that lack of social cohesion is seen to be due to the failure to integrate immigrant populations, thereby resulting in racial disharmony. The Cantle Report into community cohesion warned of British society being increasingly divided along ethnic lines, with segregation in neighbourhoods (and consequently schools). Such segregation was shown to lead to mistrust and alienation from within the minority communities, but also to prejudices and misunderstandings amongst the 'majority population'. Therefore, it recommended that all schools should consider ways in which they might ensure that their intake is representative of the range of cultures and ethnicity in their local communities, and that at least 25% of pupils came from each community. The Ouseley Report saw an increasingly segregated school system with society becoming less cohesive, less a community. The Casey Report argued that Britain is more divided than ever, especially where communities, in the northern towns referred to, are segregated on religious or ethnic lines, each living 'parallel lives'.

There are limits, of course, to what schools can do in so far as the 'parallel lives', of which the Casey and Cantle Reports speak, are for a large part created by the geographical segregation of communities, whose local schools reflect the geographical isolation from mainstream society. An example of that would be the problems raised by the so-called 'Trojan Horse affair' in Birmingham, referred to in Chapter 1 and elsewhere, where local community schools (not designated Faith schools) were predominantly Muslim, and whose governing bodies (it was claimed) had come to be dominated by particular interest groups. But, so the argument goes, this is by no means the whole truth and a better effort generally can be made to ensure greater integration within the 'Common School' – made more difficult (so it is argued) as a result of school segregation along religious lines.

In response, however, the pursuit of social cohesion must not be seen simply in terms of ethnic integration. The 'August riots', which took place in London in 2011, though occasioned by the shooting of a black man by police, reflected the disillusionment of people from a poor and deprived community. There were 700 young people aged 10 to 17 prosecuted – 117 were acquitted. The rioters came from the range of ethnic groups within the multi-ethnic communities; teenagers were being drawn into the criminal justice system for the first time. From the youth cohort aged 10 to 17, 45% were or had been in the bottom 10% of school achievement, 45% had special educational needs, 40% were on free school meals, 30% showed persistent absenteeism from school. The pursuit of social cohesion as the essential basis of a healthy society requires a fairer distribution of the disadvantaged, and of those with special needs, amongst all schools.

Furthermore, Faith schools as a whole would dispute the *general* account of failing to do its fair share of pursuing social cohesion, as witness the figure given in Chapter 3. Catholic schools (providing the bulk of the voluntary aided schools) claim to have a greater ethnic mix than all other schools. Furthermore, the government measure of poverty in the 10th decile of low income (Income Deprivation Affecting Children Index – IDACI), would indicate that Catholic primary schools cater for a greater proportion of children from the very disadvantaged areas than do the non-Faith schools in those very same areas. However, as indicated in Chapter 3, there are cautionary comments to be made on the figures given. First, special mention is made of *primary* schools. It may be the case that, as Catholic secondary schools serve a wider Catholic population than do smaller primary schools, they embrace a wider population and thereby would be more selective in their

168 Drawing conclusions

intake. Second, if, as a result of being more selective in some cases, they are not playing their full part in promoting social cohesion, then that is a case for enforcing a fair admissions arrangement in those particular cases – first, by the governing body or the diocesan authority in its mission to serve the poor, second (where that fails) by the Office of Schools Adjudicator, whose powers in this respect were described in Chapter 2. It is quite clear from the various Faith authorities, quoted in Chapters 8 and 11, that a major aim of their schools is indeed to serve the poor and the disadvantaged.

Nonetheless, more needs to be said about this in the concluding section of this chapter.

Social selection objection

As stated in Chapter 1, the 2016 Sutton Foundation Report claims that most socially selective primary schools are likely to be Faith schools using the oversubscription criteria to select disproportionately well-off pupils, though this is at odds with the report of IDACI and others, referred to in Chapter 3. According to the Sutton Report, over 1,500 primary schools in England are 'highly socially selective' (especially Catholic schools), particularly in London and other urban areas.

> *In response,* the lengthy report by the think-tank Theos (referred to in Chapter 3) concluded otherwise, namely, that the evidence reviewed suggests there is little reason to think that Faith Schools are socially divisive. Therefore, the figures suggesting social selection are disputed, as argued in Chapter 3. But no doubt there is evidence of some such social selection as documented in the BHS Report 2016, *An Unholy Mess,* despite one rationale for Voluntary Aided and Voluntary Controlled schools being 'service to the poor', irrespective of religious affiliation. This is emphasised in several Church of England reports referred to in Chapter 5, and, since the 'aggiornamento' of the Vatican II Council, the many documents referred to in Chapters 8 and 11, which offered a new paradigm for Catholic education including a 'fundamental option for the poor'.

Given the proclaimed aim for Faith schools to give priority to those who are poor or in need, it is incumbent on Faith schools to demonstrate that they are doing so and especially that no such disadvantaged children in the locality of the school are deprived of a place should their parents wish them to be admitted. Especially is this the case where pupils, though not of that faith, seek to find a local school which would admit them. The accusations of the BHS Report must be examined and addressed.

Abuse of admissions criteria objection

As was relayed in Chapter 3, the Fair Admissions Campaign in April 2014 published what it referred to as a 'comprehensive summary' of all the complaints made to the Office of Schools Adjudicator about Faith schools since the introduction of the 2012 schools Admissions Code. According to the research, 75 such malpractices were identified within the two-year period – for example, children receiving preferential recognition whose parents contributed to the church by voluntary activities such as flower arranging and church maintenance, or the use of interview which would not be permissible in non-Faith schools. Furthermore, the BHA 2015, Report for the Fair Admissions Campaign states 'how virtually all religiously selective state schools in England are breaking the law' through failing to prioritise looked-after or previously looked-after children, and through parents telling lies about their religious practice, claiming that 'when a system makes criminals out of schools, liars out of parents and, in the midst of it all, an awful lot of children get left behind, it is time to reform'.

> *In response,* it is difficult to assess how serious the problem is, given the many thousands of voluntary aided and voluntary controlled schools (approximately two-thirds of schools within the national system, and being of different kinds). It is also difficult to assess, whether such schools (of whatever kind) are more guilty than non-Faith Schools of adjusting their admission arrangements to suit the ambitions of the school as they try to improve their respective positions in the national league tables. But that of course would be no excuse where it occurs. Reference was made in Chapter 1 to 'the games people play' in order to get their children into 'a good school', and steps have been taken generally, as explained there, to ensure that admissions criteria are explicit, clear, and fairly applied. It is not sufficient, for example, for admission to depend on the say-so of the parish priest without an appeals procedure being possible based on public and approved criteria.

There is no clear evidence of wide-scale social discrimination in school selection. But that does not mean that there are no such discriminatory practices, requiring vigilance on the part of the admissions authorities to ensure that the schools are promoting the welfare of the most disadvantaged pupils in their neighbourhoods, and, as far as Catholic voluntary aided schools are concerned, following the requirements promulgated by the Church authorities, as made clear in Chapters 5, 8, and 11. Such accusations when they occur, need to be thoroughly investigated.

Summary

From what has been summarised , there are two major categories of reasons why Faith schools should not be supported within a publicly funded system.

First, their existence is said to militate against 'the Common School', that is, the school which embraces all children irrespective of ethnicity, social class, special needs, or material prosperity, in which the school becomes an environment which supports social cohesion and a common citizenship. Social and ethnic differences should be seen not as a barrier to learning but as the context in which different views are challenged and new understandings opened up. Such an argument relies much on

170 Drawing conclusions

claimed empirical evidence – the claim that Faith schools do *in fact* discriminate against pupils on the basis of ethnicity, social class, or ability. They are thereby said to fail to contribute, as they should, to the creation of a more cohesive society.

However, such general claims are disputed. Evidence is produced to indicate that voluntary aided schools in particular have a good record in ensuring greater ethnic mixing (see especially Chapter 3) and also in pursuing its 'service to the poor and to those in need'. But there are clearly exceptions to the latter, *partly* explained by the wider embrace of Catholic secondary schools to a Catholic population beyond the immediate locality, which is its neighbourhood. Nonetheless, the claims need to be examined. All such schools should be held to account formally to their governing bodies and diocesan trustees as to their admissions arrangements for those within their broader catchment areas who, despite social, material or learning needs, are denied admission. Are, for example, *all* Catholic schools pursuing the 'fundamental option for the poor' – the paradigm outlined for Catholic schools by the Second Vatican Council?

Second, reasons given why Faith schools should not be supported concern the more philosophical questions regarding:

- first, *ethical* considerations (see Chapter 9) about the aims of education within a public-school system in a predominantly secular society, where those within a secular tradition would seek to have excluded the formation of young people's lives within a religious tradition – thereby raising questions in ethics concerning what is worth learning and what counts as an educated person;
- second, *epistemological* considerations (see Chapter 10) about the nature of religious beliefs and therefore the rational basis for promoting them in the curriculum – and hence the philosophical questioning about the place of religious studies in the curriculum;
- third, *political and social* considerations (see Chapter 11), especially regarding respect for differences in a pluralist society whilst pursuing the common good, and the superior rights of parents over the rights of the state in having their children educated within a religious tradition.

Hence, we need, in providing the alternative picture, to refer back to those more positive chapters, particularly the philosophical accounts in Chapters 9, 10, and 11.

Arguments for retaining Faith schools

The arguments for retaining Faith schools, as they have been developed through the book, are now summarised, albeit with regard to, and tempered by, the criticisms summarised above.

Ethical basis

At the centre of justification for Faith schools is an understanding of the aims of education – the view, shared by the different religious communities, that they have a distinctive voice in articulating (in the words of the college principal quoted in Chapter 9) what it means to be human and indeed to become more so. The defenders of Faith schools challenge the background 'horizons of significance', which characterise the prevailing secular society. Although, as indicated in Chapter 2, there has long been a secular critique of the religious foundations of school, that secular critique has in recent years become more strident, its view of what it means to be human more pervasive, and its consequent understanding of Civic Society more exclusive. But, so it was argued in Chapter 5, the secular tradition of understanding the human and civic worlds is but one tradition amongst several. Civic Society is made up of different communities, histories, and traditions, and these understandably are translated into different conceptions of education and its aims. The concerns, therefore, of those who felt strongly the importance of preserving a faith tradition in defining the spiritual dimension to the aims of education, was put clearly by Cardinal Basil Hume in response to the Parliamentary Bill, leading to the 1988 Education Act:

> I come reluctantly to the conclusion that, in its obsession with technology and economic prosperity, society is in danger of losing its vision and its soul. Certainly, this Bill as it stands offers us an educational system and curriculum at the heart of which is spiritual emptiness.
>
> (The Times, 13.1.88)

Similarly, the former Chief Rabbi, Jonathan Sacks, sees there to be in the Faith school

> the deepening and preservation of their beliefs with all their depths of understanding the human story they portray through inherited practice.

Epistemological basis

A powerful argument against publicly funded Faith schools, as we have seen in Chapter 10, is that the central aim of education is to 'develop autonomy'. That is what makes us distinctively human. Autonomy lies in the development of reason in its different forms. Therefore, the teaching and forming of religious beliefs, because said not to be based on reason, have no place in 'education', and, therefore, cannot provide the grounds for establishing Faith schools paid for out of public funds. Indeed, as we saw, those who think otherwise are accused of indoctrination, namely, the teaching, as true, beliefs which cannot be verified or justified – as encapsulated in Richard Dawkins' statement, quoted earlier in Chapter 9, with reference to Faith schools, namely, 'the most obvious and serious case of government-imposed religion [which] don't so much teach about religion as indoctrinate in the particular religion that runs the school'.

However, the major response to such a claim was, first, that the basis of so narrowing rationality could not itself be rational in that the foundation of what counts as rational could not itself be based on reason (the problem which the philosopher

172 Drawing conclusions

A.J. Ayer failed to solve). But second, there are different forms and traditions of reasoning or 'realms of meaning', of which Phillip Phenix (referred to in Chapter 10) wrote, within which we engage in argument, address problems of different logical kinds, refer to relevant evidence, open up to critical enquiry our claims to knowledge, and explore issues of a philosophical and theological kind about the origin of life, about intelligent design, about the moral life worth living, about what it means to develop one's humanity. The pursuit of these questions has a history; the thinking and believing have developed over the millennia through philosophical and theological critique and speculation. They constitute a tradition manifest in different, but deep-down interrelated ways of living. It is this mode of thinking and living, with its distinctive 'horizons of significance', to which religiously affiliated schools seek to introduce the pupils. Moreover, such an initiation cannot be reduced to a purely didactic account, for, as argued in Chapter 10, our understanding and appreciation are partly attained and developed through the practices and rituals of the religious tradition, which express 'the sense of the sacred'. Theoretical understanding is embedded in practice. The defenders of Faith schools would argue that, for their particular traditions to be understood, there has to be an understanding 'from the inside', as it were − a sharing in a set of practices with their own inbuilt ways of seeing and understanding the world. They would accuse the ways in which young people are taught about other religions − a quick 'Cook's Tour' through the belief systems of the world − as too superficial to warrant being called education. Only those who have been initiated into a religious form of life are able to engage in the perennial 'conversation' between religions on what they see to be the most important questions to be asked.

In short, a religious education introduces the neophytes to a mode of understanding the world and society, which is itself the product of much ongoing thought and deliberation, philosophical argument and analysis. It regards with suspicion a secular world in the senses, earlier explained, of (i) indifference to religion, or (ii) antagonism towards religion, or (iii) an impoverished view of what it means to be a person, or (iv) in consequence, what are seen to be diminished 'moral horizons' of reference.

Political basis

Such religious and moral traditions are constitutive of different communities which make up civic and pluralist society, each contributing to the sort of society it is.

The values underpinning education in such a pluralist society should not themselves be homogeneous in *every* respect but should (if that is so wished) reflect the beliefs and values of the respective communities. Members of such communities, therefore, feel entitled to an education which respects and deepens their religious understanding and moral values. Hence, there is suspicion of an educational system which demands a secular uniformity, ignoring the strongly held views and values of a large portion of the constituent members of that society. Therefore, parents might invoke the European Human Rights Act (1998, Article 9.1):

> In the exercise of any functions which it assumes in relation to education, and to teaching, the state shall respect the rights of the parents to ensure such education and teaching in conformity with their own religious and philosophical convictions.

Parents, in being responsible for the upbringing of their children, believe they have a right not to have their values negated by a set of educational values to which they do not subscribe. The issue lies, therefore, in the compatibility of preserving, on the one hand, the distinctive ethos of the separate Faith school wanted by parents, with, on the other hand, the wider needs of society to create a culture which integrates people of diverse social, ethnic and religious backgrounds.

Historically, in England and Wales, the churches (especially the Anglican Church) preceded the state in the provision of education. To this day, the land on which so many primary schools are located is owned by the Church. The entry of the state into educational provision after 1870 (apart from the subsidies from the Privy Council from 1833 onwards) was essentially to fill the gaps, arising from the growth of towns as people migrated from the countryside. The state's responsibility for education (that is, for content and pedagogy) is a comparatively recent phenomenon. The state instead was to make sure that there are the appropriate conditions for universal education – and therefore to plug the gaps where those conditions did not prevail.

At the heart of the education are values, reflected in the aims of the education on offer. In a society, which is to a great degree pluralist in belief, there will be different values and different aims. Not to respect the historic roots of the diversity of educational provision, arising in many cases from considerable sacrifice and dedication on the part of those who paid for the building of those schools, would be to presuppose a unity of aims and thus of values which in fact does not prevail. Diversity of aim should be reflected in diversity of provision, essential if individuals and families are to be protected from the Leviathan of the state – and, indeed, from a purely secular ethos which increasingly prevails.

Lessons to be learned and conclusions to be drawn

Those who support Faith schools must be aware of many of the legitimate concerns, raised by opponents, which have been referred to throughout and summarised briefly in this chapter. The tradition of having Faith schools, as that has developed, needs to adapt (as all traditions do, and as argued in Chapter 5) and to grow through the criticisms which have been levelled against them and through recognition of the changing social conditions.

Therefore, although the force of the argument in this book is that of preserving the long tradition of Faith schools within the public system of education, such preservation must adapt to conditions arising from

- the very different social and ethnic context in which schools are established, and
- the important criticisms which have been explicitly or implicitly levelled against them, especially in terms of social cohesion.

174 Drawing conclusions

There are nine lessons to be learnt and therefore changes, where appropriate, to be made. These might be summarised as follows.

Sorting out the facts and figures

There are many, and seemingly conflicting, statistics on the ethnic and social composition of Faith schools of different kinds – and conclusions to be drawn from them, as in the significance attached to IDACI, as argued in Chapter 3. There is a need, therefore, for systematic examination of those figures and of the conclusions drawn from them, with a view to reconciling differences, and with special reference to the extent to which Faith schools, through their admissions, fail to accommodate a fair proportion of pupils from less advantaged and from minority backgrounds.

Respecting those who seek to resist the secularisation of education

From a secular point of view, Faith schools should not be publicly funded because they inevitably seek to indoctrinate the pupils in religious beliefs and values. But the conclusion of this book (see especially Chapter 10 and elsewhere) is that secular understanding and values (of the different kinds explained in Chapter 5) so permeate society and thereby the ethos of the Common Schools, that many understandably seek an education which resists such wholesale secularisation (in the different forms explained in Chapter 5). As Copley asked, 'Why is it that we are on constant alert against religious indoctrination whilst at the same time almost completely unprepared for secular indoctrination?'

Providing for the poor, special needs, and marginalised

Faith schools should recognise their obligation, given the required preference for the poor and for those in need, not to turn away such pupils on the grounds of not sharing the faith. No-one, especially the less well off, should be forced to travel away from their local school because they are not of the same faith. As Thomas Groome argues in his book, *Education for Life* (referred to in Chapter 11), such a concern both for those of the faith and for those not of the faith is part and parcel of a Catholic philosophy of education. Such is clearly the case with the schools sponsored by the Church of England – as was argued in the Dearing and Chadwick reports (see Chapter 5). Therefore, as concluded in Chapter 3, all Faith schools should consider the impact of their oversubscription criteria on pupil-premium children and those with special needs, and prioritise them in their admissions (irrespective of religious affiliation or none).

Provision for those not of the faith

Given that over 30% of pupils in Catholic schools are of another faith, arrangements should be made for such pupils to have their own religious worship and instruction,

For or against Faith schools? **175**

and to celebrate their own religious festivals, albeit as much as possible within a shared spiritual ethos. This is particularly important for the considerable number of Muslim pupils in Church schools (over 25,000 in Catholic schools). Their presence is to be encouraged, for, as the Report of the Social Integration Commission (2015) stated, 'the small number of Muslim Faith schools in the United Kingdom are experiencing particular difficulties in ensuring their pupils are able to meet and mix with children from different backgrounds'. It would help if they were able to attend a local Faith school which provided opportunities for them, not only to share religious understandings with pupils of different faith, but also to pursue their own religious prayers and practices.

Admission policies

Admission policies should, therefore, embody the following principles.

- All Faith schools should consider the impact of their oversubscription criteria on pupil-premium children and those with special needs, and prioritise them in their admissions (irrespective of religious affiliation or none).
- Where Faith school is the only local one (such that failure to admit entails pupils travelling to distant schools), pupils should be admitted irrespective of their faith or none.
- Trustees of the Faith schools should be vigilant about the ways in which parents, take steps to gain admission to popular Faith schools – for example, through late baptisms.
- Each Faith school's admissions code (bearing in mind service to the respective faith communities which they were established to serve) should be clear, properly enforced, with complaints procedures transparent to the local community.
- Voluntary aided schools admitting a cohort of students not reflecting the social disadvantages of their areas should heed the word of the first synod of the Province of Westminster in 1850: 'the first necessity … is a sufficient provision of education adequate to the wants of our poor'.

Strong accountability

Given the obligation not only from Civic Society but also, in the case of Church authorities, to provide a service to the poor and disadvantaged, there needs to be a thorough accountability of the admissions to Faith schools to ensure that this service is being provided – an accountability provided by both the Office of the Schools Adjudicator and by the respective religious authorities, based on evidence of the social composition of the neighbourhood. There needs to be, furthermore, a transparent system of appeal against decisions which debar applicants from admission (for example, where they would otherwise be separated from their neighbourhood and their friends). In particular, the trustees of the Faith schools should be vigilant about the ways in which some parents take steps to gain admission to

176 Drawing conclusions

popular Catholic schools – for example, through late baptisms. Each Faith school's admissions code (bearing in mind service to the respective faith communities which they were established to serve) should be clear, properly enforced, with complaints procedures transparent to the local community.

Openness to different beliefs

It would be positive step for Faith schools to link with voluntary Schools of a different faith, since what the different monotheistic religions have in common in a secular world is more significant than what separates them, as reflected in the account of Christian/Muslim spiritual convention given in Chapter 11. And as Novak (also referred to in Chapter 11) argued:

> Jews and Christians must first be able to talk to each other before they can talk to the secular world, which is further removed from both of them. Discourse must begin with those whose traditions overlap the most.

Once mooted by the then Bishop of Oxford was a multi-faith school where different religious traditions would join in addressing, from their distinctive perspectives, those issues of moral, social, and political nature which affected what human flourishing means. The Integrated schools in Northern Ireland (see Chapter 4) provide an example of how different Christian denominations work together to their mutual advantage, and could be a model for inter-faith education elsewhere.

Community schools welcoming different faiths

Community schools, too, should seek to accommodate the different faiths, enabling, under the umbrella of religious education, pupils to receive instruction and formation in their respective traditions, and in the light of which to make better informed contributions (in the shared curriculum) to a critical and historical understanding of religion and secularism within society.

Place of philosophy in Faith schools

As stated in Chapter 6, religious education provides the opportunity to engage with philosophical studies and reasoning. The Faith schools, as the beneficiaries of a long tradition of philosophical reasoning, should ensure a systematic introduction to that tradition, especially in the areas of ethics, epistemology, political philosophy and metaphysics.

AUTHOR INDEX

Alexander, H. 30, 36
Allen, R. 18, 20, 38, 41, 44, 47
Andrews, J. 42, 47
Aquinas, Thomas 131, 134, 137, 166
Aristotle 94, 98, 126, 131
Armstrong, D. 50, 59
Arthur, J. 74, 79
Astley, J. 103,109, 132, 142
Augustine, St 131, 166
Averroes 131, 157
Avicenna 131
Ayer, A. J. 119, 122, 128, 129, 130, 131, 142, 166

Barnes, L. P. 11, 20, 67, 79
Bell, D. 81
Benn, S. 147, 159
Boeve, L. 10, 20
Bradlaugh, C. 142
Brown, A. 9, 20
Bruton, R. 53
Bullivant, S. 9, 20, 43, 47
Butler, R. A. B. 28

Cairns, J. M. 32, 36
Callan, E. 91, 141, 142
Calvert, I. 100, 101
Cameron, David 13
Carmody, B. 54, 59
Chadwick, O. 72, 79
Chadwick, P. 24, 27, 36, 68, 79, 90, 91
Clarke, C. 20, 21, 38, 47, 81, 87, 88, 91
Conway, Prof. Paul 52

Cooling, T. 79
Copley, T. 41, 42, 72, 79, 85, 91, 142
Copson, A. 14, 144
Cremin, L. A. 56, 59
Cullinane, C. 42, 47

Dawkins, R. 73, 136, 140, 157, 171
Dearden, R. 122, 128
Dewey, J. 56, 72, 79, 149–50, 154, 159
Durkheim, E. 20, 23, 55, 59, 71, 73, 75, 79, 91, 80, 95, 101, 102, 109, 115, 116, 120, 121, 127, 128, 135
Durodie, D. 13, 20

Felsenstein, D. 30, 37

Gallagher, T. 49
Gearon, L. 71, 79, 84, 86, 92, 93, 101
Grace, G. 25, 37, 39, 44, 47, 75, 79, 95, 98, 101,102, 109, 148, 159
Greer, G. R. 50, 59
Groome, T. 70, 79
Guba, E. G. 133, 142
Guizot, Francois 23, 55

Habermas, J. 73, 80, 124, 125, 126, 128, 132, 135, 136, 138
Hargey, T. 156
Harman, J. 14
Harris, J. 39, 43, 47
Henson, Bishop 27, 68
Hewer, C. 96, 101
Hirst, P. 71, 73, 80, 122, 128

178 Author index

Hobbes, Thomas 44, 47, 154
Houghton, J. 136
Hume, Basil, Cardinal 171
Hume, David 122
Hume, Walter 51, 59
Huntingdon, S. P. 84, 92, 157, 159
Husserl, Edmund 85

Jacovobits, Chief Rabbi 30
Janmohamed, S. 77, 80
Johnes, R. 42, 47
Jones, P. 52, 59
Judge, H. 26, 27, 28, 37, 56, 59

Kant, Immanuel 71, 80
Kuhn, T. 64, 80

Lane, D. 10, 20, 80, 104, 107, 108, 109, 114,
    117, 128
Lawrence, D. H. 123
Lennox, J. 136, 137, 143
Lewis, B. 157
Lincoln, V. S. 133, 142
Loach, K. 72

McGrath, A. E. 137, 143
MacIntyre, A. 122, 123, 128
MacKenzie, M. L. 51, 59
McKinney, S. 50, 52
McLaughlin, T. 91, 141, 143, 155, 159
Macmurray, J. 116, 118, 122, 128
Maimonedes 131, 157
Maitland, Lady Olga 65
Malik, Maleiha 146
Mann, Horace 56, 72
Manning, Cardinal 25
May, Theresa, Prime Minister 35
Medawar, P. 137
Mendelssohn, Moses 157, 159
Mill, J. S. 121–2
Miller, H. 29, 37, 100, 101, 156, 159
Mishnah 100
Moffat, C. 12, 20, 49, 59
Morris, Henry 151

Nash, Lord 17
Nelson, J. 49, 59
Neusmer, J. 76, 123
Newman, J. H. 5, 75, 131, 143
Nicholson–Ward 99
Nietzsche, Friedrich 134
Novak, D. 156, 176, 156, 159

Oakeshott, M. 64, 65, 80, 115, 131
Oldfield, E. 43, 47
Otto, R. 94, 101, 138, 143

Parameshwaren, M. 18, 20, 38, 41, 47
Pascal, Blaise 136, 137, 138
Peshkin, T. 150, 154, 159
Peters, R. S. 122, 128, 147, 159
Peterson, A. D. C. 22, 23, 37, 55, 59
Phenix, P. 135, 143
Phillips, D. 126, 128
Pius, XI, Pope 77, 80, 153, 159
Plato 94, 126, 131
Polkinghorne, J. 89, 92
Popper, K. 130

Rahner, K. 87, 98, 114, 128
Ramsey, Ian 132, 143
Ratzinger, J. (Pope Benedict) 7, 3, 80, 124,
    125, 126, 128, 132, 135, 136
Rawls, J. 146, 159
Ravitch, D. 57, 59
Romaine, J. 15, 20
Rousseau, Jean-Jacques 147
Runcie, Archbishop 69
Ruskin, J. 138

Sacks, J. 18, 30, 68, 75, 76, 80, 86, 92, 95,
    96, 97, 101, 123, 125, 128, 146, 149, 159,
    165, 171
Sahotah, P. 43, 47
Scheffler, I. 129, 143
Sennett , R. 64, 80
Shah, Saeed 78, 80, 89, 92, 96, 101
Simon, B. 28, 37
Smart, N. 85, 92, 93
Spellman, Cardinal 57
Steinberg, Milton 100, 101
Stenhouse, L. 86, 92
Stiltner, B. 148, 159
Strom, M. S. 114, 128

Tawney, R. H. 26, 37,150, 151,159
Taylor, C. 63, 64, 70, 74, 80, 86, 92, 102,
    109, 116, 117, 118, 127, 128
Temple, W., Archbishop 27, 37
Tierney, S. 99
Trump, Donald, President 133

Ullathorne, Archbishops 24

Valland-Belkacen, N. 55, 59, 121, 128
Vignoles, A. 44, 47

Walford, G. 156, 159
Walsh, P. 125
Webb, Sidney 26
Welby, Archbishop 8
West, A. 44, 47
White, J. 73, 80, 98

Whittle, S. 1, 87, 92, 101, 119, 128
Williams, R., Archbishop 117, 128, 146–7, 159
Winter, T. 126, 128
Wiseman, Cardinal 25

Woodhead, L. 9, 20, 21, 38, 47, 81, 87, 88, 91
Woozley, A. 129, 143
Wright, A. 81, 92

Young, M. F. D. 133, 143

SUBJECT INDEX

academies: Academies Enterprise Trusts
16, 20; Church of England 18; faith 17;
Multi–Academy Trust 18; schools 34, 35,
36, 48
Accord Coalition 15, 17, 38, 44
accountability 13, 175
Acts of Parliament: Balfour Act 1902 8, 23,
25, 26, 28, 35, 71, 163; Butler Act 1944
7, 24, 25, 27, 28, 29, 32, 33, 35, 66, 67,
71, 75, 81, 83; Education Act 1923 49;
Education Act 1936 26; Education Act
1988 33, 69, 81; Education (Schools) Act
33; Fisher Act 1918 26; Forster Act 1870
8, 23, 25, 28, 29, 35, 66
admissions arrangements 8, 14, 16–20,
41, 44, 45, 46, 175; Office for School
Admissions 44
agreed syllabus 28, 67, 81, 83, 93
anthropological (turn) 65, 98, 108, 114, 117
assemblies 28, 81
autonomy 72, 73, 79, 95, 115–16

BHS/BHA 2, 15, 18, 38, 41, 42, 46, 144
Birmingham Local Agreement 33
British and Foreign Schools Society 8,
22, 25
Bryce Commission 26
Bullivant Report 43
Butler–Sloss Report 8, 11, 14, 15, 34, 38, 88

Cantle Report 11, 14
cap (50%) 16, 17, 19, 34, 42
Casey Review 12, 39

Castle Street Board School 28
Catholic Education Service 40, 98
Catholic Faith Schools 8, 16, 24–7, 32, 34,
35, 43, 74, 75–8, 98–100
Chadwick Report 82
Christian narrative 68
Christianity 124–5
Church of England 22, 23, 35, 69
church schools 163
citizenship 72
civic society 66, 117, 144–58
Clarke Report 11, 31
common good 14, 20, 35, 38, 93, 106,
109, 145–8
common school 43, 59, 70, 72, 81, 83,
148–52, 169
Comprehensive Future Conference 14
confessional 66, 71, 74, 83, 89, 93
conscience clause 22, 24, 28
controversial issues 85–7
Co-operative Union 28
Cowper–Temple clause 23, 67

Dearing Report 68, 82, 103, 108
disadvantaged 14, 15, 38, 45, 46, 47, 103
discrimination 19
dual system 24, 25, 27, 28, 29, 36, 49
Durham Report 68

education: aims of 73, 75, 77, 113–14;
liberal 19
Education Policy Institute 42
Enlightenment, age of 71, 72 73

Subject index 181

environment 103, 107–8
ethnic diversity/selection/segregation 15, 34, 38, 39, 40
ethnic minority pupils 43, 44, 45, 85
ethics 108, 113–28, 170; faith-based 123–4
extremism 12, 13
ethos: church 19; Christian 22, 27, 36, 69; general 40; Islamic 31; religious 35

Fabian Society 26
family 76, 77, 106–7, 109
France 15, 21, 23, 54–5, 66, 71, 72, 77
Fair Admissions Campaign 2, 14, 18, 38
Free Church Federal Council 32
free school meals (FRM) 41, 43, 44, 47

game playing 44, 45, 46

Hadow Report 1926 26
Hindu schools 75
HMI 25, 28
human, to be (development) 74, 76, 77, 95, 96, 114–17, 123, 127, 129
humanism 14, 71, 73
Humanist Philosophy Group 73
Humanities Curriculum Project 86

IDACI 42, 43, 45
immigrant population 45, 74–7
indoctrination 1, 71, 72, 73, 95, 140–2
integrated schools 12, 49, 59
Ireland 12, 13, 21, 52–4
Islam 126
Islamic curriculum 11; perspective 89

Jewish: covenant 75; Faith Schools 29–30, 36, 75, 76, 77, 100–101; Free State 16; leaders 18; Manchester Jewish School 29; supplementary education 30; tradition 75, 76
Judaism 125

knowledge, truth and reason 129–43, 170; rationality 131–2

Lagan College 49
liberal ideal 121–2
Liberal Party Spring Conference 16
liturgy 99
local education authorities 3, 7, 16, 20, 26, 28, 33, 36, 67

management, language of 72, 74, 86, 93
market-based approach 72, 74, 76
marriage, sanctity of 12

materialism 65, 71, 72
modernism 71, 117–18
moral: climate/ethos/horizon 12–13, 74, 78, 90; codes/values 65, 76, 96, 117–19; seriousness 114–15
Muslim: community 11; faith 81; leaders 18; schools 13, 15, 29, 30–1, 34, 36, 75, 77, 96–8; voluntary aided 31
multicultural community 43, 77, 84
mystery 88

National Association of Teachers of Religion Report 36
National Curriculum Council 90
National (Schools) Society 7, 22, 24, 25, 27, 66, 68, 163
National Union of Teachers 28
naturalism 135–7
non–conformists 22, 23, 24, 66
Northern Ireland 12, 21, 39, 49, 50, 73

Ofsted 16, 33, 87
OSCE 84
Ouseley Report 11
oversubscription 38, 41, 46

Pakistan 70
parents/parental rights 19, 20, 66, 71, 76
personal experience 137–9
persons, development of 65, 72, 76, 95, 113–14, 124
Pew Research Centre 84
phenomenological 85, 93
philosophy, in schools 86, 176
political: basis 172–3; challenges 13, 14; system 76
poor, service to 20, 34, 40, 45, 46, 47, 48, 67, 68, 103–4, 174
Positivist Society (London) 73
post–modern 74, 76, 132–4
Presbyterian Church 50
Protestant 35, 49
public life 14, 15, 34, 65
pupil premium 18

rationality 94
rationalist education 71, 73
reason 71, 73, 79, 89
REforREal 82, 85
relationships with others 116
religious: discrimination 15, 16; education/ teaching 71, 81–9, 93–101, 139–40; ethos 12, 13; literacy 88–9; practice 1; segregation 35; worship 14

182 Subject index

Religious Education Council of England and Wales 82
Rerum Novarum 105
ROSLA 27
Royal Commission 1818 23, 66

SACRE 33, 81, 83, 85
sacred 68, 75, 90, 95
School Boards 7, 23, 24, 25
school leaving age 26
schools: board 8, 29, 67, 71; Christian 14; Church of England 8, 14, 15, 24, 66, 67; community 8, 16, 28, 66, 71, 176; elementary 8, 21, 22, 24, 26, 27, 28; free 17, 20, 34, 35; non-conformist 8; secondary 8, 26, 27, 28, 71, 85
Schools Council 87
Scotland 21, 50–2; Board Schools 51; Burgh Schools 50; Catholic Schools Society 51; Curriculum for Excellence 52; denomination/non-denomination schools 52, 163; 1872 Education (Scotland Act) 51; Glasgow 50, 51, 52; 1918 Education (Scotland) act 51; Scottish Education Department 1947 51
secular: Defence League 14; education 71, 73; Education League 23, 71; morality/values 10, 19, 59, 69, 75, 117, 119–21; National Secular Society 19, 36; society/age 2, 8, 10, 11, 15, 19, 21, 23, 24, 27, 32, 36, 59, 65, 68, 70, 81, 95, 127, 165–6, 174
segregation, language of 39
sexual relations 12
Sikh 36, 75
social changes 8–10; cohesion 14, 19, 20, 38, 43, 49, 59, 166–8; diversity 34; mobility 42; segregation 12, 14, 38, 42, 43, 46;

selection 18, 41, 16, 89; teaching/education 77, 102–7; values (solidarity, subsidiarity, respect) 152–4, 170
Socialist Democratic Federation 13, 14
society: liberal 95; multicultural 1, 10–12, 14; service to society 102–9
special educational needs 38, 44, 46, 174
Spens Report 1938 26, 27
spiritual ethos/dimension 46, 59, 65, 66, 68, 69, 70, 75, 82, 89–91, 99, 116–17
state/government responsibility 20, 21, 27, 33, 48, 59, 65, 66, 71, 74, 76, 86
statistics, use of 39, 43, 47
Surrey syllabus 67
Sutton Foundation 18, 38, 41
Swan Report 85
Synod of Westminster 25

Theos Report 43
tradition, concept of 2, 63–5; Christian 82; Jewish 75; religious 65–70, 93, 94–101, 102; political 66; secular 70–4
Trojan Horse Affair 11
TUC 28

United Nations 84
USA 21, 56–8, 66

Vatican II 46
voluntary schools 26, 27, 46; aided 8, 11, 16–18, 28, 31, 33, 38, 66, 74–8; controlled 8, 16, 18, 28, 66, 68, 74

Wales 3
Westminster, Diocese of 35
worship, act of 33, 67, 81, 82, 93